El Puchero

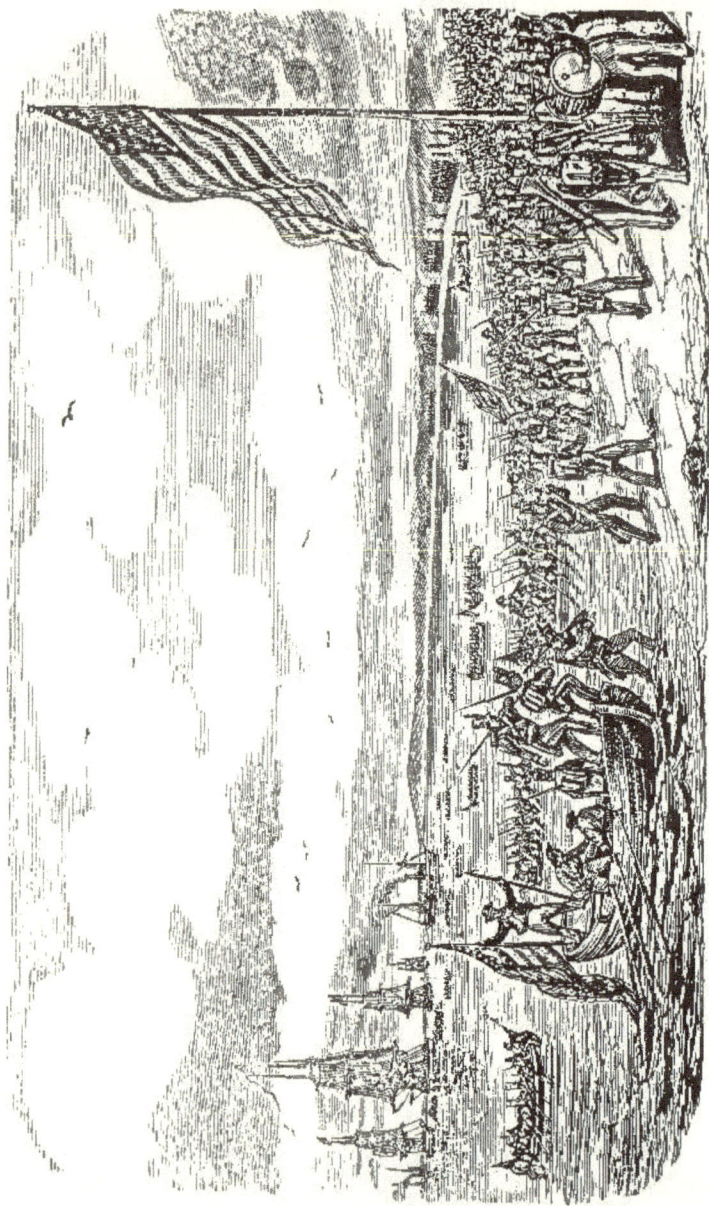

LANDING OF THE AMERICAN TROOPS NEAR VERA CRUZ.

El Puchero

The Letters of a Surgeon of Volunteers
During Scott's Campaign of the
American-Mexican War 1847–1848

Richard McSherry

LEONAUR

El Puchero: The Letters of a Surgeon of Volunteers During Scott's Campaign
of the American-Mexican War 1847-1848
by Richard McSherry

First published in 1850 under the title
El Puchero or a Mixed Dish from Mexico Embracing General Scott's Campaign,
with Sketches of Military Life, in Field and Camp, of the Character
of the Country, Manners and Ways of the People, etc.

Published by Leonaur Ltd

ISBN: 978-1-84677-500-0 (hardcover)
ISBN: 978-1-84677-499-7 (softcover)

http://www.leonaur.com

Contents

Preface

When the author of the following letters was taking his rough and hurried notes in the confusion of the march, and sometimes during the din of battle, he had little thought of giving them to the world. The friend,[1] however, to whom the letters were addressed, a distinguished lawyer and a man of eminent literary taste, recommended their publication, to which the author assented on condition of that gentleman's making the campaign complete by giving, from official documents, the battles of Vera Cruz and Cerro Gordo. This he was kind enough to undertake, and from his pen came the spirited sketches at the end of this volume. He did more; he wrote a highly finished essay on the political history of the war, which, however, he withdrew, because it was supposed to give the book itself a political bias foreign to its general design.

The name, El Puchero, was assumed on account of the discursive and mixed character of the work, which is composed, without much regard to order, of various elements of war and peace, and of such general considerations as present themselves to the observation of a stranger in a foreign land. May, 1849.

P. S. When the letters were preparing for publication it was not the intention of the author to give his name to the world with them. In compliance, however, with the desire of the publishers, it appears on the title-page. He has to regret now that he

---

1. David Holmes Conrad, Esq., of Virginia.

has not done justice to many of his friends and brother officers, by associating acts of personal gallantry with their names, which he could not have done in carrying out his first intentions without throwing off his incognito.

El Puchero

We reached this great metropolis some days ago, after an unsuccessful attempt to get to Vera Cruz. We sailed from Norfolk the latter part of March, expecting to be present at the gathering of laurels anticipated on the fall of the stout Castle of San Juan de Uloa.

Our little cruise, however, brought but barren perils instead of honours, for when off Cape Hatteras, in the middle of the night and the storm, we found our little craft was filling fast.

She was a steamer, an iron steamer, so deep laden that every old salt that saw her predicted she would never go to sea in such condition, or that if she did, she would never return. Their predictions were not verified, she did go to sea, and she did return, though they spoke knowingly. She went out in the midst of evil bodings.

A friend in bidding you farewell would look upon you with a sort of melancholy, as if he felt something he could not express; the sea gulls were skimming about in the harbour, as is their custom when the storm rages fierce at sea; the sky was black and lowering, and the March wind blew fitfully, as it does, now sighing and moaning, now howling and threatening.

Still we stood on; the Ripraps and Old Point Comfort were behind us, when a crash was heard amid the roar of the elements, causing all hands to rush rapidly on deck. The cause was soon discovered. Our stern boat was so near the water that she was struck by a sea, stove in, fairly crushed, and one of the davits by which she swung was carried away. This was a bad beginning—a boat gone before we got to the Capes. But this was not all, for it soon appeared that there was a considerable leak somewhere; the officers' rooms on the starboard side were taking in torrents of water. The pilot was very unwilling to take her out to sea; and the captain, upon reflection, determined to run back under the lee of a friendly bit of *terra firma*, where some investigation could be made.

We accordingly took shelter under Sewell's Point for the night. The leak was found, as supposed, and stopped, and the next morning we stood out again for the broad Atlantic. A little after noon we were well out on its heaving bosom. The pilot took leave of us, saying as he went, he would rather go in the most miserable little sloop than in all the d——d steamers that were ever built—but we stood on. The wind had abated, though the sea was running high, and favouring us. There was no threatening danger apparently, but I had begun to feel we might never return. This, perhaps, was owing in part to the sense of loneliness and dreariness that the great dark, boundless, and fathomless sea throws over every man, when he has been enjoying for a time the peaceful happiness of the homestead. Towards evening the wind freshened; at midnight it blew a gale.

I had not slept—I was in no frame of mind for sleeping, but if I had been, numerous little streams of salt water were falling on my bed from the deck above, and I was devising expedients to keep dry. At length, wearied out, I was sinking into a sleep in spite of my untimely shower-bath, when a general disturbance, and a rush of men into the ward-room, woke me, warning me at the same time that there was danger. A moment sufficed to explain. I jumped from my berth to pull on my boots, but found them swimming in water; the men were tearing up the hatch letting into the spirit-room and hold, which were full of water and overflowing. The steamer was divided into three compartments, and the after one was filling rapidly; so much so, that the active baling of the whole crew made no impression on the accumulating waters. Where were your pumps? you may ask. They were where we could get no good of them, that is, in the middle compartment, separated from the after one by heavy iron bulkheads. It's true there was a valve making communication between the two, but it was deep under water and choked by the washings from the store-rooms.

Now, what was to be done? Baling by buckets was hopeless, and our pumps useless. That she was settling by the stern was evident, and we began to think more of seeing Davy Jones than Santa Anna. But in fact it was no time for thinking—the captain was giving orders on deck, heaving over an extra supply of coal that was weighing her down; the first lieutenant, a man that "had a heart for every fate," was urging on the work with an admirable serenity; the second was backing him and indeed each and every officer and man seemed to feel himself called on to summon his energies and bend himself, might and main, to his duty. Fortunately, though the sea was still running high, the wind was falling, otherwise, floating as she was, bows rising and stern sinking, we were in a fair way for shipping a sea, and going down stern foremost. But this was not our destiny.

The engineer, after great labour with his party, had succeeded in breaking off some rivet-heads, and, driving the rivets through the bulkhead, the water found its way into the engine-room. Now came a mighty power to help the weary crew. When the engineers manned the pumps, the work began to tell; in a little while, between pumping and baling, the valve was found and cleared, and then the work went rapidly on. Not a man on board but breathed freer; though throughout none had shown unmanly fear.

The whole scene passed in about two hours of a dark and stormy night, from six bells in the mid watch to two in the morning watch, that is, from three to five o'clock a.m. The crew had become nearly exhausted, and but for the expedient that brought the engines to relieve their labours, we must all have perished. Now, however, that the pressing danger had passed, the captain determined to stand for Charleston, have his craft overhauled, and the leaks stopped effectually. But a new difficulty presented itself—our trusty engines well-nigh ceased to serve us. We had been supplied with a bad quality of coal, that ran in glazed cakes of clinker, or refuse, over the bars, and thus the fires failed.

We were still upon a stormy sea, no land in sight, in a leaky ship that had nothing to trust to but her engines to keep her free. Our engineer and his assistants, however, were not men to stand with their hands in their pockets when there was work to be done—they almost lived in the fires; keeping one engine going with light wood, while raking the clinker out of the other; and thus raking out and firing up did they live, like salamanders, until we reached, with great difficulty, Ocrecoke Inlet, on the "rock-bound coast" of Carolina.

Here we obtained an indifferent supply of wood fuel waited for a smooth sea, and coasted back to Norfolk as best we could, thence to Washington, where we lightened our hapless craft of everything that could be removed from her, when we took her finally to New York, where she will probably rest for years, or, it may be, for ever! When perfectly empty, her own weight sinks her as deep in the water as she ought to be full freighted; and it was thence in part that she was so leaky, for seams in her sides that were intended to be always above water, were always under, and not being water-tight, they were a source of perpetual annoyance and danger.

We reached this city in time to witness the brilliant illumination commemorating the anniversary of General Taylor's great victories in Mexico. On the same day came news of General Scott's success at Cerro Gordo, which added additional zest to the rejoicings. I met with friends from Virginia and Baltimore, and with them struggled through the mass of human beings that filled the streets, countless as the "sands on the sea-shore." Wearied at length of the glare, the glitter, and the immensity of this modern Babel, I sought my bed at the Astor, where I dreamed all night of fire works and firearms, honour and glory, and sieges and shipwrecks.

When rid of the steamer, I fancied myself rid of the war, and being very little inclined to seek renown upon the battlefield, I gave myself up to sweet delusions of a happy period to be enjoyed with "wife, children, and friends" My enjoyment, alas! was as short-lived as the insects that come into life with the rising sun to die with its setting. Scarcely had I crossed the threshold of my mountain home, when a yellow-coated document was handed me directing my immediate return to New York for a tour of most arduous duty. No time was allowed for preparation; the call was imperative. I was to go, and to go at once; there was nothing to be done but to obey. A few days found me quartered at Fort Hamilton, below New York, where the regiment was forming with which I was to serve; in a few more we were beating to the southward against a strong southerly wind.

When a man first ventures on salt water, if at all imaginative, he can make a very good story of a very common cruise. The novelty of all surrounding objects strikes him forcibly; the solemn grandeur of the ocean, the sailing qualities of the ship, her tall spars and ample canvass, the queer ways of the old sea-dogs, their immense appetites, while the very idea of eating nauseates the landsman, their ignorance of the most common-place knowledge on shore, and their intelligence in the mysteries of their craft, their songs and practical jokes, &c., &c.,— all combined, make the landsman feel himself in a new, if not a better, world, and he has only to portray vividly to make his story interesting. First impressions are here, as elsewhere, strongest; a little experience makes a man so much at home at sea, that he cannot fancy any account of his life there would be entertaining.

On board of our ship, fife and drum superseded the boatswain's whistle; we hear more of "right face" and "left face" than of "starboard" and "larboard," for most of the men are recruits, and many of the officers are young men who have just girded on their swords for the first time. A gallant captain, whose head had grown gray in the service, feeling an honest pride in the discipline and drill of his corps, spent all his spare time giving "first lessons," now to the young gentlemen, and now to the recruits. This gives occupation to those concerned, and amusement to those who are not, but the idlers had at times to run ingloriously, like Mr. Pickwick and his party, not to be caught in a charge of "bristling bayonet."

So far our voyage has been uninteresting. We came by the "Hole in the Wall," a natural sea-traversed tunnel, and the Bahama Banks, where we were detained by calms and head winds; we had the gratification of seeing a dozen other ships baffled like our selves, some of them troop ships. A steamer hove in sight as if to tantalize us, showed herself and was off, leaving, in a little while, nothing but a streak of black smoke on the horizon to show where she had been. We had to content ourselves examining the clear coral bottom over which we were lying, or fishing for groupers, &c., that we never caught.

The captain of the ship one night took it into his head to tell us his history, which was somewhat as follows. He was born of humble parentage at Marblehead; his first recollections are, that he was sent out with the fishermen, and that it was his business to hawk his fish through the streets on his return. He thus commenced a sea-life before he was seven years of age. All the proceeds of his industry were appropriated by his parents; he never knew an article of luxury, not even comfort, and never was allowed a cent to spend. He led a life of absolute slavery from seven to seventeen years of age; he knew his parents as exacting task-masters, but not as guardians and friends.

At the age of seventeen, he became master of half a dollar, and supplicated his mother to let him go forth to try his fortune, to which she gave a very reluctant consent. His highest ambition was to go to sea be fore the mast. Accordingly he started for Boston, and was soon gratified. Having suffered many privations, he returned at the end of a year with money enough to buy himself a suit of clothes, with a hundred dollars to spare. His mother, after censuring his extravagance (he had spent fifteen or twenty dollars in twelve months), appropri-

GENERAL SCOTT.

ated the remaining money to herself. She looked upon him as a bondsman bringing home his hire. He pursued his career, improved his opportunities, and at twenty-one was mate of a ship. In time he was advanced to the command of a vessel, and though emancipated, he left half of his pay for the support of his parents as long as they lived. This man is as rough as a bear; coarse in his manners and hard-favoured in his features, but his virtues as a son, in my eyes, redeem him. He told us that what he said of himself was the common history of the greater part of his native community.

Calms and squalls. So it is ever in the tropics when out of trade-winds, or sea and land breezes. We were brought by "cat's-paws" from Bahama Banks to Cuba. Now our sails spread to the refreshing sea-breeze. I cannot imagine a more perfect destitution of comfort than to be becalmed at sea under a tropical sun. The thermometer ranges from 84 to 90 in the shade; it's hot on deck, sweltering below—your provisions are dry and salty, and you be come parched and feverish, and then when you want to relieve your thirst, to be offered warm, perhaps slimy water, enlivened by animalcules—is it not enough to make a Christian man forswear the sea and its abominations? Yet the love of adventure or the love of gold, or mere restlessness, or some wicked genius, that delights in human misery, sends endless thousands to live and die on the unfriendly element. And so it will ever be—why? Let echo answer.

We are now off Havana in a snarl with the authorities. Some of our officers went in to obtain fresh supplies, but they entered in formally, without regular permission, although they believed it was granted them by an officer as they passed the Moro Castle. It seems his permission was of no avail; they landed without examination by the health officer, and are not allowed to return without paying each a fine of two hundred dollars. This they consider as unjust as it is inconvenient. Our consul is doing his best to get them released, but his only success is that of keeping them out of the *calabosa*. Meantime we on shipboard have to be content with gazing on the gay-looking town, and the bright green hills which surround it; the ample harbour which we dare not enter, and the frowning castles that protect it. There is a beautiful contrast of long low houses, dazzling white, with the green cocoas overtopping them, in all the rich verdure of the tropics, in the background. The scenery is highly picturesque. As we stand off and on, numerous dolphins are playing around us; their varying hues surpass the richest plumage of the feathered tribe.

Some of our party have returned to the ship, after paying their fines others remained to contend with the authorities about their injustice. We wait no longer, but bidding *adieu* to the shores of Cuba, direct our course at once to those of Mexico.

CAMP VERGARA (NEAR VERA CRUZ), JULY

After leaving Havana, we passed near enough to see the action of a water-spout, but not to feel its influence, fortunately. One of the officers who had been victimized at that city, told me he saw a pilot working in a chain-gang, pointed out to him by our Consul, whose only crime had consisted in taking some passengers from an American man-of-war to the city, when the ship was passing by the harbour and too much pressed for time to go in herself. He attributes the unjust treatment which himself and companions received, to the greediness of the port captain, who had winked at their landing that he might pocket their fines.

As we neared this coast, we kept a bright look out for volcanoes, Tuxtla and Orizaba: the fires of the former are occasionally to be seen at night, according to Blunt's "Coast Pilot," but we failed to discover them. Favourable winds brought us rapidly towards Vera Cruz, and on the evening of the 29th *ultimo*, we made the light, and took a pilot on board. His accounts were highly encouraging—General Scott was dead, had just died at Puebla of dysentery—the army was hemmed in at that city without supplies or resources; every train that started for the interior was cut off; yellow fever was annihilating our troops in the *tierras calientes*; *guerrilla* war fare was effecting the same on the highways, &c., &c., all of which this worthy Mexican seemed to believe without reservation.

We soon found, indeed, that except as to the death of the distinguished chief of the army, there was some foundation for all the rumours he had given us, though monstrously exaggerated. Landing at Vera Cruz, we found that scarce an American had failed to have an attack of the fever, and that it was fearfully fatal. Without our lines, the *guerrilla* war is in full blast; every motion of our troops is watched and noted, and no individual nor small party can go out of reach of the sentry's fire, without a strong probability of being lassoed and murdered.

Our command was not landed at the city, but on the beach about three miles off, at a camp where some two thousand men are now collected under Brigadier-General Pierce. We came ashore in surf-boats, each of which is capable of transporting from sixty to eighty men. They are very strong vessels, built to stem the breakers; being too large to get up to the beach, we had to follow the example of Caesar's army invading Britain; we jumped over, all standing, and waded to the camp-ground. We landed on the 3rd of July, and had a most inhospitable reception.

During the night, a tremendous norther set in, a rare occurrence at this season, accompanied by torrents of rain. The camp is on a sand-beach, between a low range of sand-hills and the sea, in a space from one to two hundred yards wide. The exposure is to the northward and east ward—so we were planted to receive the full benefit of the gale. Somewhere about midnight, or later, we were roused by shouts and yells from all quarters, blended with the confused roar of wind, sea, and rain. Our rest was broken most effectually. The scant bedding we had prepared for the field, was becoming saturated with water; the tent was leaking from above; the sand below was absorbing the water from the eaves like a sponge. Two of us occupied one tent, and putting our wits together, we noticed that no water dropped in over the ridge-pole, so we gathered up what was yet dry of the bedding, and sat bolt upright, amidships. Now we were so snug that we laughed at the afflictions of our less protected neighbours, for we could hear by their exclamations that they were drenched and were running about, helter-skelter, to look for quarters. "Captain ——'s tent is down," "There goes the Major's," "None standing in Company B.," and so forth, were the cries all around us, and we were getting very funny at the expense of people who "built their houses on the sand the wind and the waves came," &c., but our glorification was very short.

"Who lives here?" says a familiar voice; "let me in; my tent is gone and my overcoat is soaking."

Before any answer could be given, the strings of the tent door were let loose, in came a puff of furious wind and rain, and our house of canvass, already tottering, starts off first like a balloon, and then turns quietly over on her beam ends. And oh what a sight the lightning flashes revealed to us!

The camp was in the sea, or looked so, that is, what little was left of it the storm was driving the breakers in upon us; the sandhills were sending down their torrents; whole streets of tents were prostrate, yet kept in their order more or less perfectly by their fastenings—officers were running here and there, in dress and undress, looking for the men; the men were intent on saving their muskets and ammunition; and such a scene of confusion, yelling, screaming, laughing, swearing, is rarely to be found in a lifetime. My companion and myself, did the best we could under the circumstances; we mounted guard over our effects, and as the wind would lull, we worked away at our treacherous mansion to right it, which we would have done a dozen times, but as the broad surface was presented to the wind, a fierce puff would destroy our labours. The "glorious 4th," never dawned upon so disconsolate a body of freemen as upon that occasion at Camp Vergara; not a warrior but was wet and dirty, cold and hungry; and, as not a dry stick of wood was to be found, or a place to make a fire, he had to "chew the cud of sweet and bitter fancy" for many an hour before his palate was tickled with anything more nourishing.

Duty calls me to the city daily, and besides my occupations in the camp, which are manifold, I am much engaged in getting supplies of medicines and hospital stores. The army surgeons stationed here, tell me they receive many cases of yellow fever daily; that in good constitutions it is tractable, but very fatal to the debauched and reckless. In the cure, quinine in large doses is their sheet anchor. Several spacious churches are occupied as hospitals.

Vera Cruz has a dilapidated look, independent of the battering it received from the invaders; many buildings yet show the shot-holes made by the combined forces of Scott and Perry. The houses are all of the old Spanish school, flat-roofed, or tiled, quadrangular, with their central courts and balconies. They are built of brick or coral, and whitened. At the landing is a noble mole, over which are now suspended huge canvass awnings. You enter the city from the sea by the mole and an arched gateway passing under the middle of the custom-house, a splendid edifice for this country. Then you have before you the grand plaza, which ought to be daguerreotyped with the motley crowd that enlivens it. "Horse, foot, and dragoons," wagons, carts, artillery-carriages, mules, donkeys, greasers, soldiers, sailors, drunken men, Indian women, boys, musicians, and all kinds of adventurers jostle each other, so that it requires no trifling care to steer your course through them in safety. Out of the great plaza the town looks comparatively dull, except towards the gate leading to the camp, and there two human currents are generally to be found. The city is completely and closely walled; a great disadvantage to it in point of health, for the wall obstructs ventilation; one may constantly enjoy in upper stories an invigorating, health-bringing sea-breeze, while in the streets and on ground-floors, not a breath of air is stirring. *Adios*

CAMP VERGARA (NEAR VERA CRUZ), JULY

Coming into the harbour of Vera Cruz, two remarkable objects strike the eye—Orizaba and the Castle of San Juan de Uloa. I know not in what terms to commemorate the first view of the former. From the moment my eyes rested on it, I threw aside worthy Gil Blas to gaze on this brilliant monument of the almighty Architect. What can be conceived more dazzling, startling, and grand, than an immense snow pyramid, looming up eighteen thousand feet above your level, rearing its lofty head far above the clouds? You see no base, no pedestal, but it towers aloft like the conception of Michael Angelo in regard to the Pantheon, "I will suspend it in middle air" and with its huge base and sides girdled with vapour, one might fancy that He "who holds the earth in the hollow of his hand" held aloft the hoary peak of Orizaba.

The sight of it, however grand, is not always most grateful to the mariner; for glorious as it is, particularly when first impinged by the rays of the morning's sun, to the eye of the practised seaman it bodes disaster. A clear view of it is one of the forerunners of a storm, as we, indeed, experienced.

The Castle of San Juan, a great work in its way, ought scarcely to be mentioned on the same page with Orizaba; it is at best but a work of art, and who compares art with nature ? the created being and his works with the Creator and His? The great castle, the object of so much speculation before it fell, is now in the hands of our troops, and they have found in it another Augean stable. Disease is rife there, and more fatal to the conquerors than the fire of the enemy.

You must give me the liberty of being discursive, and to write always what comes uppermost; my bump of order and arrangement is much smaller than some others that are less valuable. I transport you from the harbour to my tent, where you will find my friend probably having the dinner-table set. The most fastidious can find no fault with our table linen, silver or glass, whatever may be said of the cookery and tin cups. Behold the dinner! One heavy box is set in the middle of the tent and has two smaller ones for flankers. That's the chairs and table. Here comes an attendant with some rashers of pork, a dish of beans, some fried plantains, and hard tack, *i. e.* pilot bread.

"No fresh meat today?"

"No, sir, none to be had."

"I saw chickens and eggs in camp, why did you not buy some?"

"All bought up long before they got here," responds our cook, major *domo*, and *valet de chambre*. Well, we turn to, "with what appetite we may," when, inquiring hopelessly if there's nothing else, our accomplished attendant informs us that he has some soup in the background. "Better late than never," bring it on; and here it comes, sturdy bean soup; a pint of it would nourish a citizen- gentleman for a week. It is coarse but wholesome; so we make no faces, nor even comment on its coming by way of dessert.

But we have something better. The water is very warm, and we fish up a bottle of claret to cool it. Directly, here comes an Indian woman with fruit; will take some of her maumee apples that are no apples at all, some alligator pears as like as the apples, and some bananas, the fruit of the tropics. The alligator pears (somewhat pear-shaped, but not otherwise resembling that fruit) are delicious; they are called with more propriety vegetable marrow,[1] and may be eaten either scooped out from the skin and sprinkled with pepper and salt, or spread on a slice of bread in place of butter.

Now after an average dinner, or perhaps something better, we will sit awhile in the shade, under our own vine and fig-tree, with the tent door tied back, and the whole establishment looped up from below to let the sea-breeze pass through, and to drive off the sand-flies. These little creatures are equal to any of the plagues of Egypt; they get into your nose, ears and mouth, bite your face, neck and fingers, and keep faithfully on duty until relieved at night by mosquitoes. Then for the music; tattoo is nothing to it. Speaking of petty nuisances, I must not overlook the sand-crab. The beach is full of them; you will find a dozen of their holes under your bed, and you must take care at night of fingers and toes, for they some times seize them with the force of a pair of nippers.

Well, after dinner, you can smoke your cigar and look around in your neighbours' tents; there's some aristocrat still at dinner when it is near one o'clock; he drinks out of Britannia instead

---

1. By the Spaniards, *aguacdte*.

of a tin cup, and has his dinner on a barrel-head, while he sits on a camp-stool. What ostentation!

Now a courier, a *rara avis*, passes through the camp to the city. When the sun declines a little we will follow him in for the news. A thousand rumours are afloat, generally spread, doubtless, by the Mexicans, and, perhaps, generally believed by them. Disasters and defeats crowd upon us. All the parties that lately left here to join the main army have been cut up. Their specie wagons, ammunition, and provisions have fallen into the hands of the enemy. It is hard to conceive a situation where it is so hard to get at the truth; we are surrounded by enemies, who take the greatest pains to spread bad news, and to conceal all that we wish to learn. The last information was that General Cadwalader had been overwhelmed and captured, and that General Pillow, who went to the rescue, shared his fate. We have no means of knowing how far these reports are true, but we believe them to be exaggerations and misrepresentations. In addition, sickness is spreading rapidly in the camp.

We have a scorching sun during the day, and rain every night, from neither of which the tents give adequate protection. The men spread their blankets on the sand at night, but the water passes freely under them, besides the leakage of the tent, which is very great. The consequence is, we are beset with camp dysentery, a disease well known in all armies, especially on southern service. The diet is not adapted to the climate, and the water is unendurable, or would be if men were not obliged to drink something. The sick list, as may be supposed, grows rapidly; in one week the patients under my care rose from thirty to upwards of one hundred. We are, however, exempt from the *vomito*. A popular remedy in dysentery is a cold infusion of the *Cactus Opuntia* (prickly pear), of which the men make a mucilaginous drink like *benne*, or gum water; it does not cure, though it has a favourable influence on the disease.

There has been great excitement in the camp in the last few days, from an officer, the adjutant of the 14th Infantry, having fallen into the hands of the Mexicans. He was walking out of the city, accompanied by a single soldier, when they were attacked by a party of *rancheros*, the soldier knocked down, a musket snapped at his head, and the officer captured after a desperate resistance. This happened within pistol-shot of the walls of Vera Cruz. The soldier made his escape and gave the information, when various parties went in pursuit, but they returned without any success. It is supposed the officer has been murdered.[1]

Let us put off our trip to the city to another day. We will rise betimes in the morning, take a sea-bath in the breakers, and then and there enjoy the only luxury known at Camp Vergara.

CAMP NEAR VERA CRUZ, JULY

The news of, Cadwalader's defeat proved to be entirely false; that officer did not reach the main body of the army without considerable skirmishing, but so far as we can learn, he has overcome all obstacles. Such is the first information we got on our visit to Vera Cruz. He ought to have been defeated, no doubt; and the Mexicans, by a figure of speech not described in rhetoric, said he was.

The naval squadron on the coast is doing very efficient service, though less conspicuous than that done by the army. Commodore Perry, than whom there is not a more gallant or energetic officer in either service, has just returned in the steamer Mississippi from the capture of Tobasco. This is not a war favourable to naval distinction, yet the navy has to bear a heavy portion of the most arduous duties. There is no more trying duty than blockading;—spending weeks or months standing on and off shore; looking constantly upon a soil where you are not allowed to plant your foot; suffering for want of water and fresh provisions, with all the dangers of the sea, and a lee shore ever in prospect; no naval forces to contend with, and not allowed to strike a blow landward—these are some of the troubles of blockading. Then a bright look-out must be kept to see that no adventurer from beyond seas eludes your vigilance, and carries "aid and comfort"

---

1. This gentleman, Lieutenant Whipple, was set at liberty at the end of the war. His fortunes during nearly a year of captivity were very varied.

to the enemy. Now our sturdy tars have to expose their lives to a more fearful enemy than Mexican soldiery; every river has to be explored, and every port taken; the stars and stripes are to wave over all the battlements that guard the sea-shore. All service in the *tierras calientes*, the scorching lowlands, is fruitful in disease and death, and the river courses abound in deadly malaria. The garrisons of the enemy are of little importance, compared with the fell power that deals so lightly with those who have been born under its influence, and so fatally with the stranger. It takes stout hearts to face such dangers, where it may be said there are no commensurate honours. The Mexicans, indeed, have said emphatically that the *vomito* would soon end the war, by sweeping off both army and navy.

My occupations do not allow me any intercourse with the Vera-cruzanos, so I cannot say much about them. I occasionally make small purchases from the shopkeepers, who have one peculiarity common to their tribe everywhere, that is, to make strangers pay prices that ought to cover all losses from home-dealers. The shops throughout the town occupy the ground-floor, while the upper stories are used as dwellings. It is amusing to read the signs and advertisements—Joneses, and Smiths, and Johnsons, and Thompsons are planted in and among Crapauds, and Ximenes, and Garcias, Rodriguez, and Minas. For languages, Vera Cruz may be considered at present a miniature Babel.

All the public buildings are in the service of our officials: the quartermaster's department alone occupies a large portion of them. Time is now so precious, and sickness spreading so rapidly, that the most active exertions are being made to get our brigade on its way; but we have a large train to escort up, of provisions and ordnance stores, and as yet we have no teams to haul them. There are, to be sure, a thousand or fifteen hundred mules in the camp for the purpose; but it is as hard to make a wild mule draw as to make a horse drink, the difficulty of which has passed into a proverb. You may see at any time on the long white beach a hundred wagons, with a team of mules and a double team of men to each, some going for wards in a run, some in a trot, some backwards, and some sideways; every way but the right way. The mules go kicking, sprinting, rearing, pitching, running, backing, braying, all without rhyme or reason; and although it looks like a frolic to the spectators, it is anything else to those concerned. Several of the men have been kicked into disability for the campaign. The ambulances and some important wagons have teams of trusty northern horses. The ambulances, light four-horse wagons on springs, invented, as you know, by Baron Larrey, for the benefit of the wounded of the *grande arm*ée, are already kept very busy, carrying the sick from the camp to the general hospitals in the city. I am exceedingly harassed by my duties, not only attending to the sick, which keeps me constantly exposed to the broiling sun, but also in providing stores for them, giving or refusing sick tickets, &c. My fellow *voyageur* and late chum was assigned a place on the personal staff of the general, and for a time I was alone; but again I have a companion, whose intelligence and energy is likely to relieve my labours. These extend far beyond the command to which I am properly attached.

We have had, on more than one occasion, night alarms; indeed, nearly every night some raw sentinel imagines an enemy in a bush, and startles us by his fire. Once we had a general commotion drums beat, and all hands called. Two sentinels gave the alarm at once—"Who goes there?— Speak, or I fire!"

No answer. The same is repeated twice, no answer given, and two muskets are discharged at once. The guards are formed immediately, and the entire camp as soon as possible. The sentinels swore to seeing persons prowling around in the bushes, how many they could not say. The poor fellows indeed were very much exposed; they were on the picket guard, on the hilltops, and their forms projecting against the sky were good marks for invisible *guerrilleros*. The bushes were beat, and no enemy found. Some days later, a poor half-starved white donkey was seen in search of water, badly crippled in the legs. Whether he was a spy or warrior, this deponent does not pretend to say.

I must be drawing to a close my last letter from this place. We are under what is called afloat "sailing orders," that is, we strike tents with the morning's dawn, and take up the line of march for the interior. We are told the road is strewed with dead bodies; and I for one confess to going off with no light heart. Some of us—or may it be all?—will return no more to this our place of rendezvous. We leave home, happiness, and health behind us, to penetrate with hostile intent the land of the stranger. It looks like going into "exterior darkness"—but *allons!* I chose my own profession and my own course; then "let fate do her worst," I mount my charger and pursue my line of duty.

Here we are, on the morning of the 16th, some twenty-five hundred men, new and old troops, artillery, dragoons, marines, infantry, regulars and volunteers, belonging to, filling up, and completing various regiments now in the interior. The men are all under arms; the advance is off, dragoons and artillery; then the trains, ordnance wagons first, with their flankers. There they go, yet so slowly that it will take hours to get fairly under way; men fall in the ranks, overpowered by heat, and the weight and constriction of their belts, muskets, and knapsacks. Those who are waiting suffer much more than their brethren in motion. At last, after many hours, the rear guard moves—the marines, accompanied by one piece of artillery. Good bye; I cannot loiter. A single ambulance and a few fallen stragglers are all that remain on the beach, this morning so populous. I must send you this by the last chance, see the sick stowed, and follow the fortunes of the army.

SAN JUAN, JULY

Having sent back our most unpromising cases to the hospitals at Vera Cruz, the remaining sick were supposed to be able to shoulder their muskets, and march with the column; being allowed such indulgences as their condition required and the nature of the circumstances would permit. It proves an uphill business though, I assure you; in our little command, I prescribe for at least one hundred persons daily, of whom some ninety-eight are cases of dysentery. Other surgeons have still more; and

I hazard nothing in saying, that out of our brigade of twenty-five hundred men, fifteen hundred are suffering more or less from that disease.

The first night, *en route,* we had some experience in a soldier's life; the road for three leagues out from Vera Cruz, is of deep sand, and very heavy; the mules, at first, seemed willing to do their part, and half broken as they are, worked faithfully, but some slight hills over came their good intentions; first, they would pause, then start, then stop still. Now came coaxing, swearing, and pounding from the drivers, but it would not do; when the leaders would pull, the wheel horses wouldn't; when the wheelers were willing, the leaders would turn short round in the road. Directly, one starts to pull honestly, and all the rest hold back; now the refractory parties are coaxed or whipped in, and the one that had just set such a good example stops stock still, to kick for a good half hour.

When such a *contretemps* happens in a narrow pass, all of the train in the rear is brought to a dead halt; the advance moves on, and thus the train becomes extended for miles along the road. There was but one way of getting the wagons up the hills, and that was to double the teams, which was accordingly done, but it was slow work, and night caught the rear-guard not three miles from their starting-place. We had two hours of moonlight, and thought not of rest while we could use our eyes; we were yet in the *tierras calientes,* the domains of the grim ogre, *El Vomito,* and it behooved us to move onward while we could. But darkness put an end to our labours, and at about eleven o'clock, we received orders to bivouac where we stood. Here was a prospect of comfort.

No one knew where to find tent, bed, or provisions. I started forward to look for the wagon that carried my scant equipage, and soon found myself in a gully flanked by tied and loose mules, all ready to use their heels on the least provocation; and not choosing to encounter such a battery, I made a hasty retreat. Returning to the regiment, I found the men stretched out on the road; some talking, some munching bread and bacon from their haversacks (neither officers nor men had had either dinner or supper), and some already in the arms of the god of the wearied and sleepy, sending up to him such hymns of praise and thanks, as only true votaries, the heaviest sleepers, can send.

Such of us as were mounted, had our peculiar troubles. What was to be done with the horses? The men were fagged out, for though they had made but a short march, they had put their shoulders to the wheel, literally, having spent hours in helping the train along. We, of course, could not call on them for assistance. Our own attendants were with our respective wagons, and probably ensconced therein, invisible and intangible. We groped about in the dark, and tied our horses to the bushes. Bah! these tropical twigs are so succulent as to be mere water-tubes—they broke like pipe-stems. But we could not stand up all night, so we blundered about through the undergrowth in search of something to make fast to, when we came to a palisade around a deserted hut, and there we tied our four-footed *companeros*. We took off the saddles, and calling the attention of a sentinel (for both picket and camp-guards were posted) to their position, with the saddles as pillows, we threw ourselves down on the damp ground under cover of the broad canopy of heaven. It was an uneasy rest we had, begirt as we were with belts and bands, for all carried haversacks and canteens, besides their arms; then the horses took to fretting, some broke loose and came trotting in and among us, to the great danger of heads, legs, and arms, there exposed. They were caught and secured, in the darkness, with no little difficulty. The worst part of the story won't bear telling; the army was infected with an infirmity that made beds, taken in the dark, apt to be as uncomfortable as they were unsavoury.

Morning dawned at length; bugles sounded, drums beat, and the first rays of light found the column under arms, and the advance in motion. By the time the sun became oppressive, the marines, forming the rear-guard, had reached Santa Fe—, a deserted hamlet three leagues from Vera Cruz. Here the General called a halt, to let the men rest in the shade during the heat of the day. Some wild cattle, belonging to Santa Anna— for the soil and all thereon for thirty miles on either side of the road are his had been shot by the marksmen, and we were regaled on fresh beef, cooked while the flesh was still quivering with the last vibrations of life. A party of some hundreds of lancers was seen reconnoitering, and not knowing but that it was an advance from a larger force, the troops were drawn up and the dragoons ordered out to meet them. They did not seem to desire any close acquaintance, however, but fled as fast as their horses could carry them. Pursuit was not to be thought of, as the general's first object was to reach the main body of the army, by last accounts at Puebla.

Our beef-steak and coffee breakfasts, and some hours of rest in huts and under guava trees, had sufficiently recruited the command for another start, and we came on in comparatively good style to this place, about seven leagues from Vera Cruz. The road was high and level from Santa Fe, with the firmness of paving, though unpaved. We crossed some ravines, or water-courses, now dry, on good bridges, and swamps on excellent *calzadas*, or causeways. The sun was very powerful, and the men, all debilitated by the few weeks spent in this enervating climate, suffered severely they threw off their encumbrances, first watch-coats, then extra garments, then knapsacks, blankets, many of them—in short, threw away everything but arms and accoutrements. The road was strewed with enough for the outfit of a regiment. I felt for the poor fellows, and in common with other officers, frequently had their knapsacks and other valuables, laid in the troughs behind the wagons.

It was noticeable that the waste was on the part generally of Americans and Irish—rarely or never did a German throw off his pack. Whether they were less exhausted by the climate, or only more provident than the others, is more than I can say. The sick had a trying time of it; the burdens of nearly all of them were stowed in the wagons, but they fell by dozens, or hundreds, I should say, by the roadside. We put as many of them in the ambulances as they would hold, and when possible, we would put a man on top of the stores in the overladen wagons, but they fell too fast for us, and all we could do at last, was to recommend to them to hold on to the tails of the wagons.

Late at night the rear, still the gallant marines, reached this camp-ground, which the men, with sufficient reason, call "The Mud-hole." You have traversed "The Shades of Death" on the National Road, but they are cheerful compared to an Juan. The site is low and swampy, the undergrowth almost impenetrable, and in the midst of woods we can scarcely find two dry sticks to make a fire. The whole camp is knee-deep in mud, inside of the tents as well as out. The men sleep in mud and water.

For myself, I have two boxes in my tent, and a stretcher between them for a bed. The stretcher is a piece of canvass, six feet long, with longer poles at the sides that is, it is a sort of hand-litter for carrying the wounded off the field. Don't be envious, although I sleep high and dry, I cannot turn out except in the mud. Is the "mud-hole" a misnomer?

CAMP, PLAN DEL RIO, JULY

It was no easy matter to get away from San Juan, water-logged as we were, but it was ruinous to stay; so by a vigorous effort, we succeeded in getting the trains under way after a sojourn there of a day and two nights. It rained heavily a great portion of the time, and we were beset by insects, as mosquitoes and ticks,— a little varmint so small that it fixes on you without attracting your notice, until, full of blood, with its head buried in your flesh, you see it on some portion of your person, as large and as round and as red as a cherry.

This is the vaunted "life in the woods;" about equal in charms to that "on the ocean wave." Having tried both, I fancy the poet-authors like the French philosopher, who could only write about "verdant meadows and babbling brooks" when in his garret in Paris, looking over a thousand tiled roofs and smoke-pipes; whereas, when he would paint the charms of city life, it had to be done at some rural retreat far from the haunts of man. Is there no enchantment but that that distance lends?

You may ask, what detained us at such a spot? The answer is easily given. The men and the teams reached there incredibly jaded; unaccustomed to such work as they were, and with so much sickness, the entire brigade was fairly stalled. The mud was deep and slippery; the tents, &c., acquired a double weight from the rain; without the day's rest the teams bid fair to break down altogether.

The day's march from San Juan brought us to Lomo, where we encamped on the brow and sides of a high hill, surrounding the remains of a once famous *venta* and bakery. Over against us, on a neighbouring hill-side, stood the ruins of an old church, that had also been used in its day as garrison and fortress. We had on the march a taste of *guerrilla* fight; divers escopets had been fired on the columns indiscriminately, from the hands of invisible enemies, concealed in the dense *chaparral*. Several of our men were wounded, one poor fellow, a dragoon, so badly as to require amputation at the shoulder joint. He and the others are all doing well, however. Some shots were returned on the part of our troops, but with what effect is not known.

Another day brought us to Tolome; our friends, the *guerrilleros*, still sending us some of their tokens, when, like the kid on the precipice, they could be brave with impunity. Towards night a party of them, mounted, was seen dogging the rear—there were no dragoons at hand to pursue them, but a well-directed round or two from a piece of light artillery, soon relieved us of their company. Tolome has somewhat the air of a town; it has, to be sure, its complement of reed huts, but then it has its square or plaza, upon which are several respectable tenements. They are long, low, one-story houses, plastered and white, with tile roofs and ample *piazzas*. In the *plaza* the artillery was parked, and the houses were occupied by the officers.

It was a beautiful moonlight night; we had for the first time, music by a band; the smiths were busy at their fires repairing tires and traces, and I cannot tell you how cheerful the ringing of their hammers sounded; the men had begun to improve in health and spirits, and from the long lines of their transparent dwellings were heard lively songs and peals of laughter;—the whole was so like a gay panorama, that one might have fancied himself in a Coliseum, admiring the handiwork of a skilful artist, who by the illusion of music and transparencies gave to his work the reality of life.

We found ourselves getting into the region of hills, a pleasant change from the lowlands nearer the sea-shore, and after a hard day's march from Tolome, we came to repose for the night at the *Puente Nacional*, or National Bridge, once known as the King's (*del Rey*). Our advance met with a warm reception from some *guerrilleros* who had planted themselves under shelter, on almost in accessible hill-tops. We expected an engagement here, and great was the excitement among those in the rear when by the peals of the artillery and volleys of small arms we learned it had commenced. Every man wanted to rush forward, but this was not admissible; the immense train (of between two and three hundred wagons) had to be protected, and those in charge could not desert it.

The skirmish waxed quite warm for a while, but shortly the fires began to slacken and then cheers, long and loud, re-sounded along the line. When we got in, we found our people in possession of the heights; a number had been wounded, none killed, and the general himself had escaped with a ball through his hat. It would be difficult to find a place better suited for de-fence than the National Bridge. It is approached by a long, nar-row, winding road, through defiles readily overlooked and com-manded; and the bridge itself is in a deep wild ravine, which can only be left by roads ascending obliquely, and enclosed on all sides by rough, precipitous hills. The scenery is majestic re-minding me forcibly of Harper's Ferry, though more primitive. I called the attention of my veteran friend, Major G— , of the artillery, to this resemblance, he being like myself familiar with the picturesque grandeur of the latter place, and he fully coin-cided with me in opinion.

The bridge is a noble structure, a monument of the old Span-ish *régime*. The village boasts of its ample hotel, and near at hand is a palace-looking building, which is one of the many country-seats of the autocrat, Santa Anna. In the street were found the remains of an American soldier, killed there during a late action (for every passing train has had to fight its way at this point), and most probably under General Cadwalader, who fought his way through at night The soldier had not been stripped, and his fleshless bones were, sticking through his pantaloons, held together only by wasted sinews and dried ligaments. Our troops did not leave without laying him in his last resting-place, on the banks of the river Antigua.

Officers and men took advantage of this fine stream, which looks like our own Shenandoah, to wash off some of the soil accumulated on our persons during the march; and thus refreshed, we resumed our onward course.

The day's march brought us to Plan del Rio, sixteen miles from the bridge. The rear got a parting shot from unseen enemies as they started; the advance had the same reception on their arrival at the camp-ground. On the way, we heard that sixteen hundred men were hovering around, to take us at a disadvantage and do what damage they could. I do not know whether it was a false alarm, or whether they considered their opportunity wanting. Our numbers, and yet more, our artillery, kept them at a respectful distance. It is thought by persons whose opportunities enabled them to judge, that no open or general attack will be made on this column, though we may and do hear, daily, some few exchanges of shots. They have in such cases the trifling advantage of being hidden and sheltered; while we, bound to keep to the open road, afford them a fair mark to try their skill on.

CAMP NEAR JALAPA, JULY

You see, I continue my letters faithfully, though without knowing how or when they can be forwarded. We have no communication in either direction. Not a wayfarer is to be seen on the road; nor have we seen hut or house tenanted. All progress is in one direction—all the tracks go into the lion's den; none can be traced returning. But even Reynard's cunning would fail here, for there are huntsmen on the track behind us, ready at once to pick up spoils or cut off stragglers. If any of our men were to find themselves, like friend Talbot in Japhet, with a stout heart mounted on treacherous legs, that would carry them back in spite of themselves, they would fall certain victims to the *rancheros*[1] on our trail.

Plan del Rio is a plain traversed by two streams within half a mile of each other; the first of which is a mere brook, and the second, a small river, with a depth of some two or three feet in dry weather; during the season of rains, however, it becomes a roaring torrent—fills to overflowing its deep canal-like bed, the sides of which have a perpendicular depth of upwards of twenty feet. Both of these streams have (had) massive stone bridges of a structure, *ære perennius*, intended to rival the days of the great destroyer, Time. As our advance reached the first, descending a long hill by a very rough road cut down the hillside, and overlooked by precipices inaccessible except by a long circuit through dense under growth, they found it heavily barricaded. Shots were exchanged with the guerrilla-men, and the train stopped until the barricades could be removed.

One or two companies were despatched in pursuit of the enemy, who was "*non est inventus.*" The object, on their part, was not to meet our troops, but to harass and annoy them— to kill, maim, or cripple as much as possible, with little or no exposure on the part of the assailants. Their principal arm, the *escopeta* or carbine, has a very long range, and sends a ball nearly the size of a grapeshot; it has not the accuracy of a rifle, to be sure, but that is not important where a host of men is known to occupy a certain extent of road, and the enemy can plant himself behind a bluff or tree, half a mile or a mile off, and his position entirely concealed by the *chaparral*.

Clearing away the barricade, occupied no great deal of time, but a more serious cause of detention was soon discovered. Among the thousand rumours we had heard at Vera Cruz, was one that the Mexicans had destroyed all the bridges. And now, indeed, we found the remains of a noble structure; its buttresses and

1. Country people, inhabitants of the *ranchos*. They follow the various occupations of herdsmen, farmers, and highwaymen, indiscriminately.

pillars standing firm on the banks and in the midst of the stream, but the arches gone, and the signs of destruction evidently recent. The river bank was as steep and as clean cut to a perpendicular depth of twenty feet, as if it had been the work of pick and spade, though the hand of man had not been there.

What was to be done— were we to build a new bridge? Impracticable. Were we to offer libations to Jupiter and Mars, and wait for them to help us out of the scrape and over the river, or should we sensibly take the back track, satisfied with the distinguished services we had already rendered? I don't know that the general thought of either of these expedients, unless it was to offer up the libations, which I am sure all of our pious and gallant fellows did, who had it in their power. This done, it was represented that with our force, a road might be shortly cut down obliquely to the water's edge, and that the river could be forded.

By this time night had come upon us, and after despatching a homely meal, a dinner-supper of bread, beef, and coffee, we went in pursuit of the "sweet restorer." The wagons were not parked as usual, but kept of necessity their positions along the road; and many of us having no tents in convenient distance, had to look for shelter, or sleep without it. In common with a number of officers, I took refuge under one of the arches of the first bridge, and thus saved a ducking, as it came on to rain terribly during the night. I may remark though, *en passant*, that the shelter did us no good; for lying on the cold stones, and exposed to the draught through the arches, many of us took severe colds, which was not the case when we slept in tents or in the open air.

The morning's sun found the men diligently engaged with pick and shovel on the new road. They were superintended by the engineers and some officers, Captain B——, particularly, from "down east," who certainly had a natural turn for everything. The work went on rapidly, and by nightfall the whole train was on the other side, and hard by the base of Cerro Gordo. Now this road was cut by *los Yanquees* with less labour than it had cost the Mexicans to destroy their noble bridge. The destruction, too, was accompanied by loss of life, some of the workmen having been caught in the fall, it was said; some human remains having been found in the ruins.

The Mexicans had argued that, as the Americans were coming up during the rainy season, they would find the river impassable; but it so happened that the rains set in very late, and the river had not yet felt their influence. It is not likely though, that even a Mexican flood would have stopped the march of "progressive" Jonathan. It is true, we would have been detained longer, and thus have given more time for the collection of a force at the pass of Cerro Gordo, if such were the plan. The general ordered a company of dragoons forward in the night for reconnaissance, or to take possession of the heights; they were misled, however, in the darkness, and did not reach the important position. The column started at daylight, and as we were creeping up the mountain, there was more than ordinary silence, every man seeming to be buried in his own reflections. My own were somewhat as follows; what others were thinking of, I cannot say:

"Well, Mister ——, here's a battle before you and, combatant or non-combatant, you may be sent to settle your last accounts. Don't you think you were very sapient to leave your happy, quiet home, in the valley of Virginia, to come wandering over these rivers, plains, and mountains, where you have no business; to be killed by the hands of an enemy with whom you have had no quarrel, or to die of the pestilential diseases of his climate? Suppose you are killed, will your country mourn your loss? Pshaw! nobody but the little home-circle will remember that you ever lived six months hence. Suppose, after hair-breadth 'scapes you survive, what honours are in store for you? A Major-General's commission? No. A Colonel's? No. Even a Major's? No—no. No brevets, no honours. If you carry home a broken limb, or a broken constitution, maybe your pension will keep you and yours from starving Oh L—d!" (Aloud.) "Steward, are your bandages and dressings in order, and where you can get at them?"

"All ready, sir."

"That's right."

Then the current of thought stakes a wholesome change towards the duties likely to be required. But my reflections were uncalled for. If batteries had been planted at many available points, our slowly ascending column, with its heavy train, might have been raked from stem to stern, and the troops mowed down by regiments. We fully expected a severe conflict, and after all, "out crept a mouse;" a few *escopetas* were discharged on the advance, a volley of musketry returned, and light troops sent in pursuit, but unsuccessfully. The road for miles approaching Cerro Gordo, would be impassable if defended by staunch troops; but since the two chiefs tried their strength there, and the American triumphed, the point has been abandoned.

To have an idea of the advantages of the defenders, you must know that the mountain is marked by a deep ravine, that rends it from summit to base, enlarging and deepening as it descends. This offered a sort of natural road to the top of the mountain, but a stream of water occupies its bed generally, and grows to a torrent during the rains. The road was, therefore, very judiciously cut along the side of the ravine, making a long continuous ascent, nowhere very steep. The lightest troops would find great difficulty in advancing at all, through bushes and over rocks, if they attempted ascending out of the road. The artillery, wagons, &c., are limited to the road absolutely; there is no other possible passage for them.

The ascent is on the right side of the ravine; on the left, an *escopeta* might be concealed behind every tree, looking down upon the road, and from half a mile to a mile distant. The trees would protect the enemy from our small arms, and the artillery could not be brought to bear on him to any advantage. But the great stronghold is at the summit, where batteries could be (and were, to receive Scott's army) placed most advantageously. The greater portion of the road is completely commanded from that point. The disadvantages of the invaders are obvious. I have not seen any detailed account of Scott's victory, but it certainly required a master mind to overcome such odds. Santa Anna's positions were well chosen, as is shown by the remaining breastworks and trenches, which extend from the road, across the head of the ravine, to the heights opposite. There are many heavy pieces of ordnance dismantled and useless, lying on the roadside, and hundreds of balls, grape and canister, shot and shells of all sizes. Leaving Cerro Gordo, our eyes were gladdened with the sight of tenanted houses and cultivated fields,—a happy change to him who emerges suddenly from the desert and the wilderness.

CAMP NEAR JALAPA, JULY

The sight of the first *rancho* or hut occupied by human beings was decidedly cheering; though the inhabitants were but a poor old mestizo (half-breed) and his wife. They appeared to be quite destitute, but offered in a spirit of Christian charity, all they had to give, a cup of cold water. It was nectar to many a parched and dusty throat, for the men always empty their canteens (three pints) very early in the day, and then, unless a stream or pond is found, pant for hours in the dust and sun without water.

Cleared fields began to take the place of the wild *chaparral*[1] with its undergrowth of thorns and cactus; enclosed grounds, domestic cattle, and fruit trees, betokened advanced civilization. We encamped at night on the banks of a fine stream three leagues from Jalapa. The camp was much diminished in size, for on the march the teams failed so fast, that tents and tent-poles, bag and baggage, had been thrown out and left on the roadside, that the train might not be delayed. All the wagons had started with teams of six mules; now few had more than four, and some but three; the rest had died, or were turned out to die, on the road. I reached the camp-ground among the first, about the middle of the afternoon, and after waiting long and weary hours for my wagon, it came at last after dark, and you may judge of my vexation when it was announced to me that both tent and mess chest, supper and lodgings, had gone by the board.

I went to look up my friends, and found the most of them

---

1. *Chaparral* means properly a dense growth of stunted evergreen oaks, but it appears to be applied in Mexico to any low dense growth of any kind of trees or bushes.

but half a degree better off than myself. So many tents were missing, that all that were found had double or triple their complement; many of them had no poles, and were hoisted on such sticks as could be found, making all sorts of figures, and as the once bleached canvass had taken all the hues that mud and dust, rain and smoke can give, the camp might have been supposed to belong to an army of gipsies. My chum, wider awake than myself, hired a Mexican camp-follower to take his donkeys and go back to the spot where the wagon had stalled, to bring forward whatever he could find; and towards midnight he returned with the tent, and other articles of less importance.

Meantime the usual shower had fallen, and when we pitched upon the wet grass there was nothing between us and it but an oiled sheet we carried with us, and it was indeed a treasure. On the opposite bank of the river is an extensive *hacienda* (an estate properly, but the word is commonly used to indicate the manor-house), and we are told the residents are not unfriendly. Since we came into a region where there is an appearance of private property, the general has forbidden the shooting of cattle, &c. Some officers, who had perhaps not yet received the order, went out in the afternoon to kill a beef; they ventured too far, were fired on themselves, and one of them severely wounded.

The Mexicans escaped—Upon our departure, the following morning, the general set a trap for the lurking warriors who kept so faithfully on our trail. A company of dragoons was concealed, with orders to wait, after the brigade had gone, long enough for these fellows to come up. Sure enough, when the rear-guard was just far enough off to descry the dust of a party of horse, it was seen; then there was a chase, a sort of steeple-chase, where none had ever been before; but it would not do—they knew their ground and their fastnesses, and having detected from a distance that some little arrangements had been made for their benefit, they took to their heels in time to make a safe retreat.

We marched through the outskirts of Jalapa, a picturesque, old-fashioned Spanish town, embowered in the midst of scenery of surpassing magnificence. There is a beauty in the rugged

JALAPA.

mountains of the background that one can appreciate to the full when he has but recently left the wearisome flats of the *tierras calientes*. Nature is clothed in a new aspect; the very air, lately so dense and suffocating, is now pure, sharp, and bracing, and reminds you that you are coming into the *tierras templadas*, the favourite region of perpetual spring. Hundreds of people stood upon the wayside as we passed the town, to have a near view of *los Yanquees*, the barbarians from the North, and as it was on Sunday, the *Jalapeños* were decked in their best apparel, making themselves an array much more showy than that of the army. Fruits and flowers appear to be highly cultivated about the town; and many trees, embraced, stern and branches, by flowering creepers, were beautiful in the extreme.

I thought that garrisoning Jalapa would have been much better than going farther "to fare worse;" but we are predestined to move onward; the commander-in-chief is no doubt anxiously awaiting his reinforcements, and we marched on to encamp some three miles nearer to his head-quarters.

CAMP NEAR PEROTE, JULY

We all enjoyed a rest of a couple of days near Jalapa exceedingly. On the march, notwithstanding the exposure, sickness had abated considerably, and a little repose, in connexion with pure air and improved diet, recruited the men greatly in health and spirits.

The country people visited the camp in great numbers, bringing with them for sale the various fruits and vegetables that the climate produces; that is to say, the products of both the torrid and temperate zones. Apples, pears, peaches, bananas, plantains, zapote, a species of papaw, the aguacate, or alligator pear, cactus berries, and many other fruits, are all offered by one person, and collected in one vicinity. We had to pay pretty well for our luxuries, however; we bought milk, for instance, at a *medio* the half pint, that is, one dollar a gallon; eggs, from a *cuartillo* (three cents) to a *medio* (six and a quarter) each, and other things in proportion.

Fortunately for those who had money, there was but a short

allowance of it in camp, otherwise the prices would have advanced greatly. One fellow, who came to my tent with supplies, saw there the remnant of a sperm candle; he appeared to have a great desire for it, and I gave it to him; he then displayed a great eagerness to commence a barter for more, and upon inquiry, I found that *spermaceti* has the reputation in this region of being a sovereign remedy for various pulmonary diseases. The Mexican gave his information with some reluctance, only coming out openly when he found he was talking to a medico, from whom he could get advice, if not candles, merely for the asking.

Our time was not all given to rest. A train was sent to the town one morning for supplies; and it was understood that a body of lancers was lying in wait to surprise it. Some four hundred men were consequently ordered out as an escort, and prevention proved better than cure, as no attack was made. We learn that the *guerrilleros* levy upon the town at will, taking what they please, and paying for nothing— they are, in fact, but organized plunderers of their own people.

Our army must offer a remarkable contrast in the eyes of this distracted people—all private property taken by the Americans is honestly paid for, and at fair prices. Now and then, it happens that some act of violence or oppression is laid at the door of an American soldier, but injustice to the unarmed enemy is generally reprobated. Some trivial passes happened between individuals at Jalapa, and, in one instance, at least, that came under my notice, the American was mortally wounded. It appeared that he neglected his duty as sentinel so far as to go to a low *fonda*, or tavern, where he drank freely, without the means of paying for his indulgence. This caused a quarrel; a party of Mexicans surrounded the soldier, who was becoming helplessly drunk, and one of them inflicted upon him several severe stabs, entering his liver and lungs, and causing death in about forty-eight hours.

When brought to me, some hours after the affray, he was still beastly drunk, and apparently without any idea of the extent of his injuries. Several officers had their horses stolen during their short visit to the town. An unfortunate little black boy was severely beaten, and nearly killed, by a bold robber, who rode away in triumph on the noble steed the boy had in charge.

A lot of fresh mules was bought for the trains at Jalapa, and taking up again the line of march, we arrived in good time at the hamlet of *La Hoya* (the pit, or basin). Here General Cadwalader had a severe encounter. The road passes through a mountain gorge of most remarkable appearance, that looks really like a huge trap, set by the war god of the ancient inhabitants, to take in unwary invaders—he, good soul, had never heard of a northern tribe at present of some note, under the cognomen of *los Yanquees*.

Picture to yourself a deep river, with mountain shores narrowing towards a point like a fish-trap; then do away with your river, and let a road occupy its bed; make an imaginary disposition of troops, and you will place them on the sides and tops of the hills, protected by their elevation, the trees, and their breastworks, where a portion of your artillery is planted. So much for the entrance to the pass; at the 'little end of the horn' or the narrowest part of the gorge, cut a ditch across the road, and behind it place a heavy barricade, and let it bristle with artillery. Place some few pieces also at intervals along the converging hillsides, and let them be well supported by a judicious distribution of infantry. With reliable troops, then you might defy Santa Anna, or another lame personage himself, also a distinguished commander, whose general ship is universally admitted. But though these dispositions actually were made, a small American force dislodged and routed the enemy, and passed on triumphantly to join the main army.

We selected rather an unfortunate camp-ground at *La Hoya*; a very pretty green spot, indeed, but it was, I suppose, the basin that gave its name to the village. We spent the night in a hollow that may have been once the bed of a lake before morning we might have fancied ourselves in the lake itself; for it rained in torrents, and all the rain from the hills poured in upon us, so that there was not only water enough in the basin for ordinary ablutions, but many of us were favoured with baths in our tents; and, what was less desirable, our clothes and bedding were soaked by the deluge. Withal, the temperature has changed greatly since we have been ascending the mountains; the nights are very cold to those who have just left the coast, and though the thermometer may not indicate any great change, our feelings do.

We left *La Hoya* bright and early for Perote, which we did not reach until late at night. It was a hard day's march of upwards of twenty miles, a great portion of the road being rough and mountainous. As we advance, however, the country is enlivened by more dense population; ranches, hamlets, chapels, *ventas* (small shops or inns), appear on all sides. Every house displays on its front the holy symbol of the cross— sometimes gilt, sometimes of plain wood or iron; here simply painted on the wall, there represented in stucco. The spires of rustic chapels shoot up from amidst the green trees in every direction, and add much to the beauty of the landscape, though the edifices themselves are generally extremely plain upon a nearer view.

CAMP IN THE PLAZA, PUEBLA, AUGUST

Perote is a dull, uninviting place, of about four thousand inhabitants; it is on an elevation of eight thousand feet above the level of the sea, and is distant from Vera Cruz, by the road, something less than forty leagues.[1] We encamped on a sand-plain, near the great Castle of San Carlos, between it and a field of maize or Indian corn, that upon such soil, gave but poor promise of reward to the cultivator.

The Castle is a very extensive and formidable fortress; its massive walls, its gates and drawbridges, its slopes and ditches, remind one of the boastful English proverb, "The Spaniards to build forts, the French to take them, and the English to keep them." Its site appears a very strange one. Standing as it does in the middle of a great plain, an invading army could always turn it without difficulty; and the only apparent advantage is, that it would be a *point d'appui* from which troops could conveniently

---

1. A Mexican league is equal to about two miles and five furlongs of American statute miles.

take the field, and where, in case of need, they would find a safe retreat. You must always receive, however, my military speculations and descriptions with allowances. I cannot pretend to do more than give such views as present themselves to an observer entirely unlearned in the science of war. Within the gates, I found objects more familiar than moats and drawbridges, ramparts and casemates: the temple of Mars was dedicated to Æsculapius—the great Castle was but a grand hospital.

It was the first and only military station we had arrived at; and I am sorry to say that, even in the occupancy of American troops, it was most horribly filthy. Volunteers are apt to have a false pride as regards the humbler duties of military life, and they are very unwilling to come down to the necessary police duties. The idea of playing scavenger in an old den of Mexican troops, was certainly not agreeable to men, many of whom enjoyed high social position at home, and who entered the ranks believing that fighting and marching were the only legitimate duties of soldiers. Still, after entering upon a new field voluntarily, it became incumbent on them to endure all the contingent obligations.

Besides the troops in charge, principally the 1st Regiment of Pennsylvania Volunteers, and Walker's Company of Mounted Rifles, there were a great many soldiers who had been left sick by bodies of troops, regulars and volunteers, who had passed up previously. Some of these were on duty; others, convalescent, had nothing to do but take care of themselves—while the greater number were confined to their rude couches, bearing it in their expression to the practised eye, that, in the language of Corporal Trim, speaking of poor Lefevre, "they would never march again in this world."

In a ditch within the outer walls of the castle is a cross, around which were strewed human bones: we were told, how truly I know not, that they were the remains of Texans, who had been executed on the spot and left there without sepulchre. Outside of the walls, immediately in rear of our camp, is a double line of mounds, where repose all the perishable parts of hundreds of our brave citizen-soldiers. They have fallen by scores, and not upon the battlefield, but from the ravages of disease; by the hand of the ruthless conqueror, before whom they fell as the grass under the sickle of the mower. Death has been dealing his darts so freely here, that in many cases the only burial was that of taking a dozen bodies at once to be laid in a common grave.

Perote is considered by the natives a healthy place, but the castle, in its present condition, is certainly anything else—yet, it is to be observed, that the diseases which proved so fatal did not originate there, but that it was made the receptacle of all the unpromising cases of each passing portion of the army. Our own command leaves such cases as cannot travel without transportation, and in exchange we take with us such as are sufficiently restored to rejoin their respective regiments. Many a poor fellow, in his anxiety to escape the charnel-house, reports himself well, and anxious to proceed, while his sallow countenance and tottering limbs belie his assertions.

On Sunday, I attended church at Perote not at the castle, for there the chapel, a tasty and handsome apartment, was used as a sick ward—but in the town, at a spacious and time-honoured temple, where there was a large crowd of worshippers. The interior of the church was imposing, but the effect was impaired by a number of coarse paintings and tasteless statuary. Women formed eight-tenths of the assembled congregation.

During our stay at Perote, we were excessively annoyed by the light sand that was carried about in clouds by every breeze; just such as travellers describe of the deserts of Africa though with us, upon a much smaller scale. The sand penetrated into everything; in clothes-bags, sugar, salt into the dishes cooking on the fire; it filled our eyes, ears, and hair, and we inhaled it at every breath.

Our sick list had not diminished in the proportion we anticipated. The march itself involved a great deal of exposure, particularly as it was during the rainy season; all day we are subjected to a scorching sun, while cold and heavy rains are brought with the shades of evening. Few of the men, besides, have due deference to Hygæa—they eat such fruits as they can get, green or ripe, and they drink, when it can be had, something even worse than bad water. If the ——— "takes care of his own," he does it very badly.

Up to the time of reaching Perote, we had not met a human being bound to the coast; there, however, we learned that a number of volunteers whose time of service had expired, were about to make their way to Vera Cruz, homeward bound. We could not go with them, except in spirit, but we left with them tidings to bear to our friends. Then "shaking the dust from our feet," we resumed our onward march in the bold pursuit of—glory!

PUEBLA, AUGUST

A great landmark, long in sight before reaching Perote, there appeared close at hand; I speak of the lofty mountain called the Cofre of Perote, from an arrangement of rock on its summit bearing a resemblance to a huge coffer or trunk. To my eye, it looks more like the hut of a hermit, another Stylites, who had thus planted himself above the cares of earth, to enjoy a nearer view of the visible heavens. The Cofre is of "*basaltic porphyry;*" it presents an elevation of nearly fourteen thousand feet above the level of the sea; but standing as it does between Orizaba and the Puebla mountains, whose towering summits ascend thousands of feet in the region of perpetual snow, its great height is diminished to the eye by comparison.

Our march had hitherto been ascending, but at Perote we stood upon the great central platform of Anahuac. In the ascent of the Cordilleras from the sea, we had passed successively through the *tierras calientes*, the region of perennial summer, where all fruits and flowers of the tropics reach perfection, and where, too, pestilence is condensed and concentrated; through the *tierras templadas,* where the chilling blasts of winter are equally unknown with the scorching heats of summer; and now we entered the *tierras frias*, a region cold indeed, compared with the lowlands behind us, but where there is no winter as we experience it even in our temperate Middle States. When you recollect, however, that this great central plateau is the summit, in fact, of a range of mountains among the most stupendous on earth; that its elevation is more than one half of that required, even in the torrid zone, for perpetual snow; it will be obvious, that in this latitude, it was not at all amiss to christen the table lands, *Tierras Frias*.

Once on the highlands, our average progress was much better than before; we followed a good road over immense plains, occasion ally varied by hill and dale, from Perote to Puebla. Mountains, it is true, presented on every side, rearing their lofty heads towards heaven; but they rise abruptly from the plateau, and we kept our level road, winding around their bases. A great portion of the country is arid, barren, and uncultivated; of forests there are none—we had left them behind us; at times, scarcely a tree was to be seen for miles. Again, we passed through immense fields of the graceful and luxuriant maize: thousands of acres lay spread out before us in uninterrupted tracts of this invaluable grain.

We passed through some thrifty villages, and by great haciendas; the road was enlivened by caravans of mules and donkeys, carrying on a circulation of trade between the cities and country. The *haciendas*, or perhaps better, villas, that is, the abodes of the proprietors and tenements of their dependants, which dot the face of the country, add greatly to the scenery. In the midst of a green field you see an extensive and massive white wall surrounding a large quadrangular building, white also, that looks more like a fortress than a private mansion. Extensive parapets, more for defence than ornament, and loop-holes, smacking of the feudal ages, and rarely seen in modern edifices, out of Mexico, are common enough here, where every man's house is literally his castle.

Dire disease still pursued us. Our ambulances, or avalanches, as the men call them, were full and overfull; the wagons of the train were pressed into the service of transporting sick, in addition to their proper loads; but still many had to drag along their weary limbs as best they could, or drop by the roadside. This was extremely hazardous, on account of the ravening wolves that kept constantly on our trail—near enough to fall upon unwary and exhausted stragglers, and yet always far enough off, or sufficiently out of sight, to save their precious persons. I sometimes found myself miles behind the train, and even behind the rear-guard, trying to restore and bring on the fallen. The best that could be done in such cases was to group a party of the unfortunates, directing them to stand by their arms and by each other, and thus, marching and resting, to follow on to the camp, which they generally reached some hours after their comrades.

I must admit, that on leaving my little squad to ride on un-protected to my own position, it was generally with a feeling of insecurity, as if a silent lasso from behind a hedge might inter-rupt my lonely progress. Sometimes the whole road would be strewed for miles with stragglers, who could get on indifferent-ly well when allowed to go at their own pace, but who could not keep their positions in the ranks under such circumstanc-es, numbers gave security. It is not particularly pleasant, when alone, to pass a way side cross, with a pile of stones around it, and perhaps an inscription— "Don Fulano was murdered on the spot, at such a time, and he who passes, is besought to offer up a Paternoster and an Ave, for the repose of his soul." These memorials abound in this hapless land.

For wheresoe'er the shrieking victim hath
Poured forth his blood beneath the assassin's knife,
Some hand erects a cross of mouldering lath;
And grove and glen with thousand such are rife
Throughout this purple land, where law secures not life.

We reached this fair city, the abode of angels (*Puebla de los An-geles*), about noon on a very bright day, the third out from Per-ote, and after passing a considerable time in search of quarters, our portion of the brigade had to be content in their canvass houses, pitching the camp in a beautiful green and well-shaded *plaza* (square), near the cathedral. The city does not show to advantage as approached from the Vera Cruz road, the site be-ing rather low, but we entered by a splendid macadamized road, passed the *garita*, (guard-station at city gate), and found a city worthy of its aspiring title. Some of the regular troops came out to meet us; I observed particularly, a gallant and dashing general officer (Twiggs), whose staff and dragoon guard with their well-appointed and highly polished equipments, their free use of "pipe-claying and starching," threw our travel-stained and sunburnt warriors deep in the shade. Puebla adorns the plains of the ancient Tlascala. It was founded upwards of three hundred years ago; and a legend is connected with its name and origin, which at some future time I may send you. The angels who tenant it now (to say nothing of those who belong to our army) are the fair *poblanas*, who have some feminine fame through out the republic of Mexico: the better classes at present are as in visible as the celestial spirits who keep watch over them.

The triumphs of our braves have so far been over men only; the smiles of beauty rest not on the victors; even their avowed willingness to surrender to the winning graces of the gentler sex, has not opened to them the doors of the boudoir and the drawing-room. Perhaps the ladies are right; but other reasons than the stately reserve of the old Spanish blood cause them to keep our gallants aloof: the most trivial acts of civility or courtesy are jealously watched by prying eyes; and the *poblana* who once nods her head to an American, is marked by a fierce and cowardly mob for future insult.

San Martin, August

The main body of the army, under the immediate command of its illustrious chief, has passed the summer in Puebla, and this proverbially quiet and provincial town has been converted into another Babel. The rich and sonorous tones of Old *Castile*, so appropriate amidst the venerable temples and antiquated mansions of a city whose foundations are almost coeval with the discovery of the continent, are blended with, or I may say overwhelmed by, the "diverse tongues" of the half of Europe; English, Dutch, French, and the well-known brogue of the gallant son of the Green Isle—who is sure to be found wherever there is lovemaking or fighting all rise at once in confused sounds that almost disguise the pure vernacular of Yankeedom.

Don't suppose for a moment, though, that Jonathan himself is thrown in the shade; by no means. Behold a stately building, that looks like a Neapolitan palace; you can get admission there—for a bit of painted board makes it the "New York Eating House;" the noble pile opposite is the "Soldiers' Home;" and dozens of other stately edifices are reduced, *pro tempore*, into homely restaurants. Enter any of these, and you will find your fellow-citizens, in and out of uniform, discussing politics and the war, just as they do in any bar-room in the States, from Maine to Texas, with only a little less zest than they clear the platters before them.

Our stay in Puebla allowed but little time for observation. General Scott had been anxiously waiting the arrival of reinforcements to set out for the capital. He considered our brigade a sufficient addition to his effective force to move forward. Delay at Puebla was doubly dangerous, for a fatal form of dysentery had carried off, or disabled, a large portion of his army, on the one hand, while on the other, each day was enabling the enemy to increase and discipline his forces, and to perfect his defences.

Our General (Pierce) had brought on his command with remarkable success; our losses on the way, compared with those of other detached commands, had been very trifling; the men had become inured to hardships, and, except those absolutely sick, (no small number, by the way,) our people were merged in the main army in much better fighting condition than when they left the coast. General Pierce was assigned to his proper brigade, and the various regiments and companies lately commanded by him were distributed according to an arrangement already made by the commander-in-chief.

The army is now composed of four general divisions, under the respective commands of as many distinguished generals, *viz.*: Worth, Twiggs, Pillow, and Quitman. The last named, whose reputation is already very enviable, commands the volunteer division, which I will subdivide, as it embraces our own regiment, (and your humble servant being a *voluntario, bongré, malgré*, is to share its triumphs and defeats,) into its component parts, i. e., 1st, New Yorkers, Colonel Burnett; 2nd, Pennsylvanians, Colonel Roberts; the South Carolinians, or "Palmetto" Regiment, Colonel Butler; U. S. Marines, Lieutenant Colonel Watson; a company of light artillery, Captain Steptoe; and a squadron of dragoons, Captain Gaither; the three last-mentioned belonging to the regular service. There is a siege train in company also, of twenty-four pounders, each piece drawn by ten horses, commanded by Captain Huger, of the ordnance.

While in Puebla, I visited a few of the churches. They are famous for their magnificence, especially the cathedral, which is distinguished by its size, its architecture, and its ornaments. The last are at once rich and chaste, of costly construction and material, and withal in excellent taste. It is the more remarkable, as in a large proportion of Mexican churches, there has been a lavish expenditure of money upon objects that a man of cultivated taste would declare at once to be neither seemly nor edifying.

The cathedral occupies one side of the grand plaza; the Governor's palace is opposite, and was occupied by the commander-in-chief of our army during his stay; the other two sides of the square present long ranges of shops on the ground-floor, and dwellings above; and, in common with the palace, uninterrupted *portales* extend their entire length. The construction of the *portales*, or porticoes, is such that the upper front stories of the houses project considerably, and are supported on uniform arches, so that the side-walks, which are within the arches, are protected equally from sun and rain. In the middle of the *plaza* is a splendid fountain; around it are congregated hundreds of country people, seated in stalls, or standing in the open air, offering for sale all the fruits, flowers, and vegetables that the surrounding country produces. In front of the cathedral is a stand for hackney coaches, rare vehicles, perhaps modelled after that of Queen Joanna, the foolish, who, it is said, introduced the first coach into Spain.

So little change has taken place in Spanish fashions and customs for some centuries, that the coaches in actual use here are precisely such as you see in the old illustrated copies of *Gil Blas* and *Don Quixote*—they are the same huge, lumbering vehicles, suspended on leather springs; *el cochero*, on his mule, with postilions where there is a team of four, six, or eight mules, which, though unusual with hackney coaches, is very common with travelling carriages.

We left Puebla on the 8th, with all the "pomp and circumstance" that bands of music, floating banners, flashing bayonets, and rolling drums can produce; the street windows were lined to see the pageant, thousands of spectators, citizens and soldiers, occupied the side-walks, and the scene was really imposing, and not without solemnity. Ardent, and full of hope and bright visions as were the gallant spirits who were about to engage, some for the first time, others for the twentieth, upon scenes that were to try and to prove men—must not the reflection have forced itself on all, that many and who could say how many of the best and the bravest, would never retrace the steps they were now taking; and that no one could say but that a few days or weeks, would find him in a soldier's grave! Motion, however, is adverse to reflection; each step of the road requires some petty attention, and thus the mind is constantly occupied with trifles of the moment, superseding, fortunately perhaps, graver thought.

The four divisions did not start off together, but each on a day assigned. General Twiggs led the way on the 7th, General Quitman followed on the 8th, and we left Generals Worth and Pillow to follow on the 9th and 10th, successively. Scott, the commander of all, and the master-spirit, passed us the first day, hastening on with his dragoon escort to join Twiggs. He was received with "Hail to the Chief," by the music of each regiment as he passed, and deafening cheers. There is something in his ample brow and majestic form that inspires confidence: he looks like a man fit to conduct any great enterprise to a successful issue.

The sick of the army and a small force under Colonel Childs, a distinguished officer, remain to garrison Puebla; the main army, destined to achieve miracles, or to perish, now on the march for the capital, consists of about ten thousand men. The enemy receives us with thirty thousand in the very heart of his own

COLONEL CHILDS.

country—while we are far away from ours, and from all succour. I dare not, I confess it, I dare not dwell on the prospect, opening so like a yawning gulf immediately before us.

BUENA VISTA, AUGUST

You must not think yourself transported to the immortal Taylor's great battle-field because this is headed Buena Vista, which means precisely the same as the French *Bellevue*, and is similarly applied in Mexico, and certainly with great propriety, in innumerable instances. Our present site is no more than a *hacienda*, and a poorly stocked *venta*. We passed the second night out from Puebla, at the antiquated village of San Martin, which stands at the foot of the mountain wall enclosing the valley of Mexico. We traversed to reach it, a fine rolling country in a high state of cultivation, bearing fine crops of corn and barley, and adorned by numerous castellated *haciendas*. The fields are commonly enclosed by ditches and hedges; the latter being frequently of the maguey (*Agave Americana*), are of great value, not only as being impassable, but more for the famous beverage called *pulque*, which is to the Mexican what beer is to the Englishman, cider to the American, and wine to the Frenchman. The maguey plant is used for so many purposes, that it may be worth while to enumerate them, which I will do when a little more at leisure.

We enjoyed, *en route*, a near view of the great volcano, *Popocatepetl*, which, I believe, signifies the Smoke Mountain, and its colossal, but not volcanic neighbour, *Istaccihuatl*, or, the White Woman; the former, a majestic cone, upwards of seventeen thousand feet high, the loftiest peak of North America; the latter, not so high, but extending to a considerable length its rugged spine in the ethereal region of perpetual snow, bearing a far-fetched resemblance to a reclining female figure. At the summit of the sublime *Popocatepetl*, and for three thousand feet down its mighty sides, my poor eyes could discern nothing but spotless snow, sparkling and glittering in the sunbeams; others, keener-sighted, in reality or imagination, could discern a wreath of circling vapour, rising from the concealed depths within. I have seen, when coasting along the western shores of our southern continent, the great chain of the Andes, wearing an unbroken mantle of snow as far as eye could reach, but the impression does not equal that made by these solitary peaks, as they present themselves to the wayfarer on shore; there is a sublimity about them that is, at once, unspeakably glorious and imposing.

From San Martin, we commenced the ascent of the porphyritic mountains which shut us out from "the happy valley." The day was very bright, and old *Sol* darted his rays down upon us, as he did on the unfortunate traveller he uncloaked on a certain memorable occasion; clouds of dust enveloped us, and as the day advanced, the men began to give way in numbers, from exhaustion; we were all the while in constant expectation of a general engagement at any point along the road, though more especially at *Rio Frio*, a strong pass we were approaching.

Suddenly, a few dragoons rode by us most furiously, seeking the general to announce that the rear was attacked. Then the drums commenced to roll along the line; officers and men sprung to their places; the general passed to the rear, and all of us believed that an engagement was at hand; some sharp firing at the rear confirmed the opinion, but the battle was soon over, and resulted in no very great loss; a straggling dragoon had dropped behind from some cause, when he was set on by a company of mounted lancers, who wounded him in several places, but did not take time to finish their work, finding themselves noticed and pursued.

We continued our march to *Rio Frio* (cold stream), where we encamped for the night. At Puebla we had been told to expect a general engagement at this point, on account of its wonderful natural defences. We found, however, no enemy. A *fonda*, kept by a German and his wife, furnished food and lodgings to as many as could be there accommodated. I contented myself with the purchase of a loaf of fresh bread, which was luxury enough for a weary and hungry man, and repaired to my tent to consume a homely meal and to sleep off my fatigue.

I found the night very cold in this aerial region (we had

made a march of upwards of twenty miles during the day, and were ascending at least four-fifths of the way), but wrapping my comfort around me, and laying aside only haver sack, canteen, and spurs, I slept soundly until nearly daybreak, when sufficiently refreshed, and more than sufficiently chilled, I went out to seek comfort by the guard-fire. At dawn we had breakfasted, and were under way; it had rained in the night as usual, and great difficulty was experienced in getting the train and heavy ordnance pieces up the slippery hills; but time and labour brought the usual results, and, about noon, a large portion of the volunteer division stood upon the highest point of road between the two oceans; that is, on the summit of the mountain, the height of which, at that point, falls little short of eleven thousand feet.

Buena Vista, August

During the descent of the mountain, the army enjoyed the sight of scenery of surpassing magnificence; the lovely valley or basin of Mexico, lay spread out like a panorama of fairy-land, opening, closing, and shifting, according to the changing positions of the observers. At times, nothing would be visible but dark recesses in the mountain, or the grim forest that shaded the road, when in a moment, a sudden turn would unfold, as if by magic, a scene that looked too lovely to be real. It was an enchantment in nature; for knowing, as we did, that we beheld *bona fide* lakes and mountains, plains and villages, chapels and hamlets, all so bright, so clear, and so beautiful, it still appeared an illusion of the senses, a dream, or a perfection of art—nay, in the mountain circle, we could see the very picture frame.

I could see nothing of the city, this American Venice, whose tall spires many persons said were visible from certain points. I know not whether the fault was in my own optics, or in the far-sighted imaginations of others.

There is a clearness in this rare and elevated atmosphere, not known on the ordinary level of the earth; and objects, whose distance would make them dim and misty elsewhere, have here a distinctness of outline, that brings them so much in the field of vision, as to give a delusive idea of their proximity. Although we are here in the tropics in the middle of August, we have no reason to complain of the heat of the climate; on the contrary, the nights are really cold, and even during the day, it is quite cool passing through the shady defiles of the mountains.

At noon we feel the sun's power; in the middle of the afternoon, however, the sky becomes overcast, and a cold heavy rain sets in, that lasts until some time in the night: it is then we find it uncomfortably cold in tents; though persons dwelling in comfortable houses probably do not find it so. For myself, I improve in health and strength from the exposure, and so do many officers and men; but others appear to break under it, probably from some original defect of constitution, or yet more likely, from wanton imprudence, super-added. The men threw away watch-coats and blankets freely while passing through the *tierras calientes*. They were mere encumbrances there, but here they suffer much for want of them. Consequently, the diseases commonly incident to camps are ever with us.

The divisions closed up as they reached the valley. When ours was nearly at the foot of the mountain, we could see Twiggs a few miles in advance—the general-in-chief with him still; Worth's as far behind; and although our army is really a very small one, the immense train accompanying it, makes it seem double or quadruple its size. It is a very pretty sight to see the wagons winding down the hills from a distance: with their white canvass covers, they look like flocks bearing ample fleece, and they are visible through trees and-above bushes when no part of their escort is to be seen.

We encamped at Buena Vista on the 11th, and found ricks of barley straw, of which we made beds—the only time I have enjoyed such luxury since leaving the ship at Vera Cruz. On the 12th, Worth's fine division passed us, and on the 13th, Pillow's, to encamp at convenient distances from each other. This last commander is, though a new soldier, second in rank to the commander-in-chief—a most unfortunate circumstance in case any mishap should befall General Scott; for, without any discussion of their relative merits, Scott commands the perfect confidence of the entire army, which the other does not enjoy; and this alone would be enough to change the tide of battle against us under trying circumstances.

Santa Anna is, we learn, at *El Peñon*, a rugged hill ten miles this side of the city of Mexico, immediately on the road thereto. The hill is a solitary cone, upon which he has planted three tiers of guns, and made substantial breastworks; it is surrounded by water, and he has cut ditches of uncertain depth across the road, behind which are barricades strongly fortified; the hill commands the road completely, which is there but a causeway, so that the train cannot leave it to turn the work. From all information, it is very certain that the place, apparently impregnable, can only be taken at a terrible sacrifice of human life on the part of the assailants; while the assailed, behind their defences, will have but a small comparative loss; and it must be kept in mind, that with our small force, every life is valuable, we are far from recruiting depots, nearly three hundred miles from the sea, with but two small garrisons, at Puebla and Perote, upon which we could fall back if necessary; and once commencing a retreat, it is doubtful if we could even reach them.

We hear that General Scott says it will cost him four thousand men to take Peñon; but after this terrible loss, nearly the half of the army, what will be the condition of the remainder? Yet does this army confide most implicitly in his wisdom and skill to conduct it in safety and honour through the fearful crisis now approaching. All things considered, the troops are remarkably confident and cheerful, and there appears to be a general conviction of a successful issue. May it be justified; if not, we may consider defeat another word for annihilation.

The view from the *hacienda* of Buena Vista, which is on a slight elevation, is certainly remarkably fine; but I cannot conceive of any point within this valley where it can be otherwise, there being in so small a space so much variety. I witnessed here a grand sight, a snow-storm on the mountain tops, while it was clear below. You may imagine, but I cannot describe, its sublime beauty.

Our reconnoitering parties are very active, gathering information as to the strength and positions of the enemy. It is a hazardous duty, but the time has come for every man to be willing to make a sacrifice of himself, if necessary, for the good of the whole. The engineers, and others[1] engaged, give daily practical evidence of their ability and devotion in the cause. We know not how soon to expect to meet the enemy; and we would not be surprised at any moment to be ordered forward to the attack. We expect, of course, dreadful carnage, but believe at the same time that the sagacity of the chief will save all unnecessary bloodshed. By the 13th, the anniversary of the triumph of the great Spanish conqueror, we hope to enter the famed capital of Mexico.

CAMP NEAR LAKE CHALCO, AUGUST

On the 15th, we (Quitman's division) left our camp at Buena Vista, where we had lain for several days, and moved to Chalco, an old town of no small note in Mexican history. We started, as if for Peñon, marched several miles, until we reached Twiggs' camp, near Ayotla, when the division was ordered to countermarch, return to a fork of the road, near the point from which it started, and take the road to the left, leading to Chalco. Whether we made the first movement by mistake, or as a feint, I know not, but presume it was the latter.

We made a very slow march, over a road that led through fields of growing corn (maize), and that was probably never travelled before by anything more pretending than the lumbering carts of the country.

We heard considerable firing at one time at a distance behind us, and learned afterwards that Twiggs' division, now coming on in the rear, had a brush with a large column of the enemy, which however soon left the field, and their dead on it. The encounter happened near the fork where we had deviated from the direct road to the capital. At Chalco, we encamped on the ground that

---

1. During one of the reconnaissances, near Mira Flores, several dragoons were killed, and Lieutenant Schuyler Hamilton, a gallant young officer, *aide-de-camp* to General Scott, was severely, if not mortally wounded.

Worth's division left, only in time to allow us to occupy the same spot. Several of our regiments pitched their tents in a grassy and well-shaded enclosure in front of a church, that has stood the buffetings of changing seasons for centuries. Its solid foundations and massive walls look as though intended to rival, in durability, the neighbouring mountains. Besides the church itself, there are various apartments under the same roof, probably intended as a residence for monks, but the only occupant at present is an ancient padre, the parish priest, who, if not so old, is much more tottering than the temple in which he offers sacrifice.

At the head of a flight of steps leading to a suite of rooms, the following inscription is painted on the walls, under the names and times of service of all the curates who have officiated there since the year of our Lord one thousand six hundred and six.

Laudemus viros gloriosos, et parentes nostros in generatione sua.
Omnes isti in generatione suæ gentis gloriam adepti sunt. Eccles.,
Cap. 44.
Animæ eorum per misericordiam Dei requiescant in pace.

Let us praise men of renown, and our fathers in their generation.
All these have gained glory in their generations, and were praised in
their days. From the forty-fourth chapter of Ecclesiasticus.
May their souls, through the mercy of God, rest in peace.

The last is a prayer common to all Catholic Christendom for "those who have gone before" into the realms of the spirit world.

The building is in the form of a cross, and externally, one of the angles is shut up by a monumental-looking wall, upon which is a rough painting of the sufferings of those who left this world with sins not yet atoned for, but whose crimes are not supposed to be so heinous as to merit eternal punishment.

The following inscription, as the voice of one of the sufferers, in old Spanish, accompanies the painting, at once a warning and petition, to half-repentant sinners whose sands are yet running.

Hoy por my, manana por ty—como te beo, me bi—como me bes, te
beras. alibiara por tu amor que otro a ti, te alibiara. cuanto bien hases
for mi, es otro tanto caudal que contrepesado a el, atesoras para ty.

Which may be somewhat freely translated as follows: "I to-day—thou tomorrow—what thou art, I was; as thou seest me, wilt thou be seen thyself. Aid me, for thine own love, that another may aid thee. All the good thou doest for me is so much treasure laid in the balance, in thy favour."

There is an aperture in the wall, partly filled by an image of *Nuestra Señora*, the virgin mother: through the opening may be seen heaps of human bones, and many niches are adorned with human skulls, themselves impressing, without inscription, the solemn *"memento mori."*

General Scott and staff were at Chalco on our arrival, and it was reported he was going to order a portion of the army to the city by way of the lake, in boats found at the town; but no such order was given. He went on to join Worth, and Quitman's division followed in the morning. Our march brought us to a hamlet less than ten miles from Chalco; but on account of the road, it was impossible to go farther. We are close on the heels of Generals Worth and Pillow, as Twiggs is on ours, and we are making a detour around Lake Chalco, so as to turn the formidable Peñon, and thus neutralize Santa Anna's great preparations at that point. The Mexicans not dreaming that with our heavy train we would attempt or could pass along this road, have expended all their time and labour, fortifying that which we have just left.

This valley is marked by numerous truncated cones, varying in height from one to five hundred feet, which are extinct craters. What must have been the condition of the basin when it was, as it were, one huge cauldron, boiling over at so many points! Imagine, if you can, hundreds of these Cyclopean chimneys belching forth at once fire and smoke, sending forth torrents of liquid lava, boiling and raging as it descended to spread over the troubled and trembling plain! And if the pygmy earthquakes and eruptions of this age of the world are accompanied by so fearful a roar, what must it have been when these huge mountains were heaved up to their present wondrous height by the giant throes of earth convulsed! Behold the change. Nature is stilled and hushed—a calm serenity, a death like stillness rests upon the scene once so fearful and man, the creature of yesterday, weak and proud, dares to wake the slumbering hills and dales with his contests; and to announce, upon this spot, through the iron throats of his destroying agents, the story of his ambition and his hate!

IN QUARTERS, SAN AUGUSTIN DE LOS CUEVAS, AUGUST

Our slow progress gave us some opportunity of seeing the cultivation of the country, as we passed through and by many fields and patches that represent the market-gardens near our large cities. The most important article of produce appears to be the *Agave Americana*, or maguey plant, which is the vine of Mexico: it furnishes *pulque*, the wine of the country, and mescal, a strong alcoholic drink, somewhat resembling Irish whiskey. If the Mexicans were a poetic people, many would be the odes, written and sung, in honour of the former, for it receives the devoted attentions of all classes of people, as the numerous signs attest at innumerable *pulquerias*. You are constantly seeing by the roadside, not only men, women, and children, with *pulque* for sale, but at every angle of the road, a hut with tempting invitations, as follows: "*Pulque!! al nectar de los dioses,*" " *pulques fines de* ——," from some particular *hacienda*, as fine wines from some particular vineyard. The walls of the *pulquerias* are commonly adorned with illustrations in *fresco* of the charms of the beverage. It is the fermented juice of the maguey, and varies in strength and condition, like cider.

Our people were at first as much prejudiced against it, as are the natives in its favour; and when one sees the uninviting form in which it is carried to market, it requires a stomach above all squeamishness to acquire a relish for it. A string of dirty and squalid-looking Indians, with long matted hair, garments of the scantiest, leaving the chest and limbs exposed, feet bare, or with the simplest sandals, and the whole person sunburnt almost to blackness, are the *cargadores* of the precious burden, which they bring on their backs in skins. These last preserve the form of the "entire swine" from which they are taken; so that every Indian appears to have a hog on his shoulders, wanting only the head. The tails and legs stand out in bold relief, occasionally moved by the fluctuations of the contained liquid. But campaigning cures fastidiousness so effectually, that dirt becomes a sort of condiment, or at least nobody objects to it; and *pulque* soon obtained favour, in spite of Indians and hog-skins. It is really a most refreshing beverage, with a piquancy peculiar to itself, that becomes by habit very grateful. The immoderate use of it, as of hard cider, causes intoxication. It is obtained somewhat as follows:

About the period of inflorescence, when the plant has reached from five to ten years of its growth, the central leaves are cut, and the juice, which was to have been expended in furnishing the flowers, exudes slowly for some months, when it is daily collected in gourds by the Indians, and kept until it undergoes the necessary fermentation, a process much hastened by the addition of a little old *pulque*. The first liquor is called *agua miel* (honey water); it is rich in sugar and mucilage, and the taste resembles much that of the milk of the green cocoanut, a favourite beverage wherever known.

I have drank the sweet liquid from the cup formed in the plant for receiving it as it exudes; but the Mexicans never use it until after fermentation.

The plant fulfilled various purposes among the Aztecs: it furnished them paper, coverings for their houses, lancets, from the sharp prickles bordering the leaves, needles, cordage and cloth, from the strong fibres which form the texture of the leaves, and, as now, impenetrable hedges. Ropes are still made of the fibres, of such strength that bridges are suspended on them in certain parts of Mexico. Withal, the plant, so rich in juices, will thrive in a soil too arid to produce any of the ordinary fruits of the earth. It has other uses, you see, besides bringing *pulque* and *mescal*.

We passed through immense olive groves: the trees are truly magnificent, but the fruit is small and indifferent;—through fields of corn, beans, tomatoes, peppers, &c., all grown for the city market. We see often the fruit trees of the tropics, but the fruit commonly does not mature, or is in some way defective. We are enabled to get occasionally, supplies of fruits, as apples, pears, peaches, oranges, figs, the fruit of the prickly pear (*Cactus opuntia*), which is in great favour with many persons, alligator pear (*Laurus Persea)*, and others; but they are generally scarce, in great demand, and consequently high. I frequently notice a tree by the roadside producing a berry very like cubebs (*Piper cubeba*), both in appearance and taste; that is, it has a mixed taste of pepper and turpentine. The natives call it the *Arbol del Peru* (tree of Peru); they obtain from it a balsam, which has the common virtues of the terebinthinates.

We had a very tedious time getting here, passing by lakes Chalco and Jochimilco. The road at times appeared almost impassable for foot, to say nothing of wagons, ambulances, and heavy artillery. Sometimes there was scarcely the width of a wagon between the marshy lake on one side, and rough precipitous banks on the other; and again the road was a causeway of rough, shapeless rocks, about as definite in size as the piece of chalk you have heard of, irregularly laid or heaped over a miry bottom. It was a difficult matter to keep on, or pass over them, and fatal to get off. The greatest objection to our delay is that it gives Santa Anna time to make new preparations; but he can make none, it is said, equal to the Peñon defences. He had his emissaries out, obstructing our road by felling trees, rolling down rocks from overhanging banks, &c.; but, though it caused some detention, the obstacles were readily removed by Worth, whose division led the way.

On the 18th, approaching this village, or *Puebla*, we were warned to expect an engagement. Quitman's division encamped, our portion of it in a cornfield, ready to move at a moment's notice. We heard during the day a brisk firing of artillery. I ascended one of the numerous mountain cones not far distant, and found the gallant general there with his staff, overlooking the plains below. From our position we could see distinctly the flash and ascending smoke from the pieces, but nothing in detail, on account of trees, &c. We had a fair view at the same time of Peñon, the terrible, from the summit of which waved the tricolour of the Mexican republic.

The firing became more active as the day advanced, and we were on the tiptoe of expectation, looking for a general engagement. After a while some reports came in, and we learned that, early in the day, Captain Thornton, of the 2nd Dragoons, a Virginian and a gallant officer, had been killed by a cannon-ball, the first, I believe, that was fired, while escorting Major Smith and other engineers on a bold reconnaissance: their interpreter was severely wounded. The continued fire was on Worth's division, engaged in planting batteries against the fortified *hacienda* of San Antonio. The excitement among us became intense, I assure you; the men crowded the hill tops, looking for what was to be seen, and expressing most ardently their desire to be led at once to battle action is so much better than suspense; and the Mexicans rushed to their house-tops, burning, no doubt, with feelings they were too wise to express so near the daring enemy.

San Augustin de las Cuevas, August

This is quite a pretty village, some ten miles from the capital, on the road to Acapulco, the principal port on the west or Pacific coast of Mexico; its name under the former rulers was Tlalpam; but the Spaniards rechristened even the heathen towns in their zeal to blot out the remembrance of the religion and the power they were then levelling to the earth; and Tlalpam bears the title imposed on it by the Christian conquerors. The hideous god of war, old Huitzlipochtli, is once more awake in his favourite valley, and receives again his hecatombs of human victims. Since my last, a bloody battle has been fought, and the din of war still resounds in my ears.

There are, it seems, in all directions leading out from the capital, three separate fortifications on each road or causeway; each of which has to be carried successively, before the army can reach the city; the first of these, on this road, is at the *hacienda* of San Antonio. As commonly understood among us here (in a chafing reserve), Worth's division was planted before the *hacienda*, and Pillow's ordered, by a detour of several miles, to fall upon it, a *tergo*, or as soldiers say, in reverse. The division sallied out on the 19th, expecting something of a brush at a point about four miles distant. A laborious march, great natural difficulties in opening the road, &c., brought them in the afternoon within the range of the Mexican batteries, and it soon appeared that the brush would result in a great battle.

The Mexicans were established in great force on a commanding hill near the village of Contreras, under the command of General Valencia, second in rank to his excellency the President, and commander-in-chief of the forces. Pillow and Twiggs were to carry Contreras, en passant, and pursue their course to the main road beyond San Antonio. This was easier said than done. Our troops had to make a road as they marched; and their difficulties, to most persons, would have appeared insuperable.

The course lay over what is here called "*Pedregal*" or field of lava. It is a mass of irregular uninterrupted rocks, nearly a mile wide at the point crossed by the army. At many points, there are perpendicular barriers of rock, some firm, others loose, and all impracticable for the motions of dragoons or artillery; yet so indispensable was the agency of the latter, that two batteries (Magruder's light, and Callender's howitzer) were dragged into position by the hands of the troops, so as to play on the camp at Contreras. All this was not only great labour, but it caused much delay, and that was a period of no little suspense and suffering among our troops.

The Mexicans, safely ensconced behind their entrenchments, played away on our fellows, without let or hindrance. They were entirely out of our reach: musketry would not touch them; and for weary hours were our men lifting and hauling the unwieldy pieces of artillery, exposed fully to the iron hail that fell around them, with no more power to return it than has the stricken wayfarer to send back the shower from heaven. Slowly and wearily did the Americans clear obstructions, and advance upon the enemy.

There was no rush, no charge, none of that brisk stirring

excitement that keeps men in heart; the only virtues called for were steady labour, and patient endurance. With others not participating in the fight, I stood in the belfry of a church, looking on in a state of the most intense excitement. The scene was not clear, on account of the distance, and the rocks, bushes, &c., which concealed almost entirely the motion and progress of the troops; but we could see and hear every shot fired by the Mexicans, while, for hours, it was but too evident there was no return from the Americans.

My own mind was in torture. Why should the Americans stand back as they did to be mowed down, instead of rushing to the charge, and carrying all before them? Were they kept at bay by the overwhelming force of the enemy? Why, then was not our whole army ordered out to decide the contest at once? These, and a thousand impatient questions were in every man's mouth, for the delay was certain, the cause entirely unknown. It showed the anxiety of the spectators, if not their judgement. My eyes would wander from the battle-field to the towers and spires of the distant city, and I asked myself when we would be there, and at what sacrifice?

During the afternoon the batteries were successfully planted, and commenced their deadly work, but at great disadvantage. They were small pieces, but few of them, and entirely exposed, while the enemies , *per contra,* were large, numerous, and protected. They, however, played their part faithfully, though with heavy losses. Meantime the battle, so far one-sided, continued until the dark mantle of night covered over the contending hosts. It was a dreadful night. I was in pursuit of quarters at a late hour, when I fell upon a house occupied by a reserve of New Yorkers. After a while, one of the followers of the army came in, who gave a sad picture of the prospects and condition of our army. He left the field at dark the men were ready to drop where they stood, "The weary to sleep and the wounded to die."

They were suffering with cold, hunger, thirst, and want of rest they were, withal, disheartened, because they had suffered without the power of retaliation, while the Mexicans were in a perfect gale at their astonishing success. This was shown by the spirit and clangour of their martial music and their shouts of joy—"*vivas*." During the night the rain fell in torrents—indeed, it appeared to me to exceed the heaviest showers I had known in Mexico; and as it was very cold, you may judge what they suffered, who, faint and exhausted, had to bear its peltings as they lay on the wet sod, or on the rocks of the Pedregal.

The conflict had become so desperate that Garland's brigade of Worth's division, had been ordered to the scene of action by the commander-in-chief; and early next morning (20th) the reserve at San Augustin was directed to move to participate in the fortunes of the day. As we approached the field, however, loud shouts, that were not "*vivas*," indicated that our people were in high spirits; and very shortly our march was arrested, and the brigade ordered to counter-march, as Contreras was won. We were obliged to retrace our steps, though most reluctantly; but General Scott considered San Augustin too important a point to be abandoned, and as it was the depot of ordnance stores, &c., its protection was of prime importance. General Quitman was, therefore, left in command, with a portion of his division.

It was a hard infliction on a man of his temperament, and he did not submit without using every exertion to get on active service. Scott was inexorable. Some one must be left, and there was great danger of -an attack at that point, the enemy knowing it to be our great depot. No one could be better trusted than Quitman for the defence; and he had to subject his inclinations to his sense of duty.

The taking of Contreras was "honour enough for one day;" but the din of battle continued. Our troops followed the fugitives to another stronghold on the main road, and in the mean time hundreds of prisoners, including the notorious General Salas, late Vice-President of the Republic, who had announced "no quarters" when elated with the prospect of victory, were brought in to this place for safe keeping.

The Battle of Contreras, at first so threatening, not only to the honour but to the very existence of the invading army, now stands recorded, surrounded by a halo of glory, upon our national archives. A detailed account of it, as of battles generally, can only be given by a man versed in the art of war and military literature; but an outline sketch for the general reader, taken from some of the leading reports, may not prove unacceptable, nor, in this connexion, inappropriate.

On the morning of the 19th of August, the four divisions of the American army were at or near the town of San Augustin, with the commander-in-chief. Worth's division was engaged at San Antonio, the first obstruction on the highroad to the capital; Twiggs' and Pillow's were in the town; and Quitman's was approaching from the last night's encampment. General Scott, deeming it highly important to throw a force between San Antonio and the city, ordered careful reconnaissances of the surrounding country, for the purpose of turning, if possible, this strong point; the information he received was, that it was practicable to open a road across the country to intersect a road leading through the village of San Angel to the city. He learned, at the same time, that in anticipation of this attempt, the Mexicans had fortified a commanding eminence, overlooking the proposed route.

Generals Pillow and Twiggs were ordered with their divisions to proceed by the course indicated by the engineers, and while engaged in the laborious duty of opening the road, they became exposed to the murderous fire of the enemy. The Mexicans in their entrenched camp, with nearly thirty pieces of artillery planted, ranging in calibre from six to sixteen-pounders, had a fair sweep at our advancing columns; while, from the nature of the ground over which our troops were moving, (" a vast plain of broken volcanic stone and lava, rent into deep chasms and fissures, effectually preventing any advance except under his direct fire," Pillow's Report,) it was impossible to bring up the few pieces of artillery, except by the actual and laborious transportation effected by the soldiers; and even the light troops advanced with great difficulty. A very brief notice of the topography of the region will give some idea of the relative positions of the contending parties.

To begin at San Augustin, which lies from the capital about south by west, you find the main road to the city winding north, north-east, north by east and north-west, that is, describing a sort of semicircle, of four or five miles in extent, to avoid the Pedregal, the right of which extends to the road, and gives it its form: leaving the Pedregal, the direction is nearly due north to the city. The *hacienda* of San Antonio is at the extreme east of the Pedregal, and about north-north east of San Augustin. The Pedregal extends thus from San Antonio northward for five or six miles, where it connects with the mountains. It lies north, a little way to the east, and a long way to the west of San Augustin, while Contreras is beyond it, bearing about west-north-west from that town. The Pedregal is impassable for all wheeled vehicles, though there are some winding paths through it, which may be traversed afoot, or on horseback.

Now the Mexican camp at Contreras was on the summit of a lofty hill, communicating by a good road, which passed immediately by it, with the city, through San Angel; but it was inaccessible, apparently, from the side of the Pedregal, overlooking the last completely: there was, in fact, no advance except under the direct fire from it. The site was chosen with great judgement; for it was but reasonable to suppose that the natural impediments in the way of the attacking army, would keep it. long enough exposed to the point-blank range from the camp, to cut it up completely, before the artillery could be got in place, if it could be done at all, or before small-arms could be made available. If the Mexicans had fought as well as they reasoned in the case, they would have remained masters of the field. Their fighting, indeed, was unexceptionable while their advantages served.

When night suspended the combat, our army had suffered seriously; the enemy little or none. During the evening, two small batteries, Captain Magruder's twelve-pounders, and Lieu-

BRIGADIER-GENERAL GEORGE CADWALADER.

tenant Callender's mountain-howitzers, had been planted in front of Contreras, but, attracting the fire from the heavier and more numerous pieces of the enemy, they were soon disabled. Lieutenant Callender was seriously wounded, Lieutenant Johnstone mortally, and many of the cannoneers were killed at their guns. General Scott was on the ground until the darkness made his presence useless, when he re turned to his quarters, but not to rest, in San Augustin.

As the contest waxed hot in the afternoon, he ordered out Shields' brigade. At a moment's warning, all hands were ready; and when in line, the officers of the Marine regiment had the mortification to learn that they were to remain, while the New Yorkers and South Carolinians, both already covered with laurels, were to join in the strife.

At nightfall, the following troops were on the field, *viz.*: the 2nd, or Twiggs' division of regulars, composed of Smith's brigade of mounted rifles, 1st Artillery, and 3rd Infantry, and of Riley's brigade of 4th Artillery, 2nd and 7th Infantry; the 3rd, or Pillow's division of regulars, (new regiments,) composed of Pierce's brigade, of the 9th, 12th, and 15th infantry; and Cadwalader's brigade, of the 11th and 14th Infantry, and regiment of voltigeurs. The light battery of Captain Magruder of 1st Artillery, and the mountain-howitzer battery, under Lieutenant Callender of the ordnance, were also attached to Pillow's division, but were temporarily assigned to Twiggs. Quitman's division of volunteers was represented, as stated above, by General Shields, with two regiments of his brigade, that is, the New York and "Palmetto" regiments.

The general distribution of these troops was somewhat as follows, *viz.*: the batteries were planted in front of the enemy, partially covered by a ledge of rocks. General Smith's brigade was to support them, and to cover the advance of the party making the road. Riley' s brigade was ordered to the right, to get between Contreras and any forces coming from the direction of the city, to support Valencia, there in command. As large bodies of troops made their appearance, Cadwalader's brigade was ordered to get to the rear of Contreras, to support Riley and check the Mexican cavalry. Pierce' s brigade covered Smith's; and Shields' two regiments were ordered out to the support of Riley and Cadwalader. The Mexican forces occupied the entrenched camp, flanked by large bodies of infantry with a strong cavalry force in the rear.

The hero of Contreras may tell the rest of the story.

Between us, (his own position and the Mexican batteries,) was about half a mile of lava rocks, almost impassable for a single foot man, then a slope down towards a ravine; on the opposite bank of which, were the road and the enemy's works, on a height called Contreras. The front faced us, and the left flank swept the road below it, a turn forwards in the road bringing the work directly in the prolongation of the lower part of the road. The work had upwards of twenty large guns, was full of infantry, and large masses of infantry and cavalry were behind it, and on its flanks.

He then went to the support of the batteries, which he says were soon disabled, Riley at the same time going to the right.

On examining the ground, it was evident we were advancing by the only path that crossed the broken bed of lava, and on which the enemy were prepared to receive us, having cleared away all the bushes that obstructed their view.
The guns could go no further, and the infantry would, on its march down the slope, be exposed to a terrible fire, without knowing whether crossing the ravine below was possible. Being isolated from the division, I determined to try one of the enemy's flanks; and that on our right being preferable, as it would cut off his retreat, I determined to move in that direction. Captain Magruder was directed to open his fire as we passed his rear, to occupy the enemy and mask our movements to the right. This he did most effectually, though suffering from a great loss, especially of officers.

Leaving Lieutenant Haskins and twenty men of Major Dimick's regiment to supply the loss in a measure, and a supporting party of three companies of the 3rd infantry, General Smith moved with his brigade, crossing two streams and deep and difficult gullies, to the village of Encelda (or Contreras), where he found General Cadwalader with four regiments of Pillow's division. Observing large bodies of troops coming from the city, General Smith prepared to meet them, forming the three brigades, Cadwalader's, Riley's, which arrived about sunset, and his own, to meet them—

> ....formed in front, opposite to us in two lines, the infantry in front, and cavalry in the rear, about ten thousand strong.

Smith ordered an attack; but it soon became so dark that the enemy's line could not be seen, and the order was countermanded. It rained heavily all night, and the troops were without fire or shelter. Lieutenant Tower, of the engineers, came in during the night, and reported that infantry might, by following a ravine passing between the village and the main road, get to the rear of the enemy's works at the entrenched camp, but that it would be very difficult.

> We had now in front and on our left flank, eighteen thousand Mexicans, with between twenty-five and thirty guns; among the troops, six or seven thousand cavalry.
> We were, at most, three thousand three hundred strong, and without artillery or cavalry; and it was evident that we could only maintain our position, which was of the utmost importance to the commanding general, by the most prompt and energetic action. I therefore directed an attack on the works at Contreras, by turning their rear before day.

Captain Lee, of the engineers, undertook the bold and difficult task of returning to General Scott, to give him information of Smith's proceedings, and to ask that a powerful diversion be made against the centre of the entrenched camp towards morning. Captain Lee succeeded, and received General Scott's thanks, with the highest compliments.

At 3 o'clock on the morning of the 20th, the troops left their wet bed, and in the densest darkness followed up the ravine under the guidance of Lieutenants Tower and Brooks, through mud and over rocks until daylight, when Riley's and Cadwalader's brigades rushed to the charge, carrying everything before them.

Riley's first cleared the work and planted their colours on it.

Smith's brigade, under temporary command of Major Dimick, was on the track of the others, but—

.... when nearly opposite the work, seeing a large body of the enemy on its left flank, I ordered Major Dimick to face the brigade to the left, and, advancing in line, to attack this force in flank. This was done in the finest style, and the 1st Artillery and 3rd Infantry, mounting the bank of the ravine, rushing down the next and up its opposite bank, met the enemy outside of the work, just as Riley's brigade poured into it, the whole giving way. Cavalry formed in line for the charge, yielding to the bayonet of our foot, the rout was complete, while Riley's brigade cleared the work.

Colonel Morgan's regiment (15th Infantry) had been ordered on the evening of the 19th by General Scott (through General Pillow, to whose division it belonged) to the hamlet of Contreras, to check the reinforcements coming to the enemy from the city. When Shields came up from San Augustin, General Scott ordered him to the support of Morgan. Shields, with his New York and Palmetto regiments, reached the village about midnight, but finding Smith, though the senior officer in the village—

.... had made the most judicious arrangement for turning and surprising the Mexican position about daybreak, was not willing to interfere. (Shield's Report)

He reserved to himself the double task of holding the hamlet with his two regiments against ten times his numbers on the side of the city, including the slopes on his left, and in case the camp in his rear should be carried, to face about and cut off the flying enemy. (Scott)

While Riley's brigade, conducted by Lieutenant Tower, of the engineers, and Cadwalader's, conducted by Lieutenants Beauregard, of the engineers, and Brooks, of General Twiggs' staff, were attacking on one side, under General Smith, Colonel Ransom, with his own (9th) regiment, and portions of the 3rd, 12th, and Rifles, conducted by Captain Lee, from the side opposite the Mexican front and centre—

> .... made the movement to distract and divert the enemy; but, after crossing the deep ravine in his front, advanced and poured into the works, and upon the fugitives, many volleys from his destructive musketry. (Scott)

Upon Smith's leaving the village with his temporary division for attacking the camp from the rear, Shields very skilfully spread out his handful of men (5 or 600) over the ground occupied at nightfall by the various brigades and regiments there assembled. He had fires made at daybreak, as though the men were preparing their break fasts. The Mexicans in camp seeing at that hour a force descending upon them, and no apparent diminution of troops in the village, thought the Americans had received considerable reinforcements, which added greatly to their confusion and alarm. During the retreat, Shields fell upon them:

> .... the Palmetto regiment, crossing a deep ravine, deployed on both sides of the road, and opened a most destructive fire upon the mingled masses of infantry and cavalry; and the New York regiment, brought into line lower down on the roadside, delivered its fire with like effect. At this point many of the enemy were killed and wounded, some three hundred and sixty-five captured, of which twenty-five were officers, and amongst the latter was General Nicolas Mendoza. (Shields.)

Upon the capture of the works at Contreras, the 4th Regiment of Artillery had the extreme gratification of recovering the two brass six-pounders lost by them at Buena Vista, though "without loss of honour;" for it will be remembered that the gallant O'Brien fought them until not a man was left at the guns, and himself crawled away crippled, after contributing so greatly, by losing his guns, to saving the day. There were taken, in all—

> .... twenty-two pieces of brass ordnance, *viz.*, four Spanish sixteen-pounders, seven hundred pack mules, and many horses, and an immense number of small arms, which we destroyed. After directing the prisoners and property to be collected, I directed the pursuit to be continued,. We killed seven hundred, took fifteen hundred prisoners, among them several generals.

Among the killed on our side, were Captain Hanson of the 7th Infantry, and Lieutenant Johnstone of Magruder's battery, both of whom were highly esteemed officers.

The force present on our side at Contreras, including General Shields, was about 3650 men; that of the enemy about the works, 7000, under Valencia, and in their reserve 12,000, under the President, Santa Anna.

Such is the rather extended sketch of this great victory. The quotations, not credited, are from the perspicuous report of Brigadier-General (now Major-General) Persifer F. Smith, who did so much on that occasion for his own and his country's glory.

SAN AUGUSTIN, VALLEY OF MEXICO, AUGUST

When it was known that Contreras was taken, the Marines and 2nd Pennsylvanians returned to this place, while the victorious divisions of Pillow and Twiggs, and Shields' brigade, continued in pursuit of the enemy. The brigade detached from Worth's command, like ourselves, reached the ground after the conflict was over, and returned to the body of the division before San Antonio. In the mean time Worth had been by no means idle; he was left with his single division to take San Antonio with its strong garrison.

It was very difficult of access, for he had to approach by the open road, to be enfiladed by the batteries from the fortification, or turn, on the one hand over the Pedregal, or on the other over a low, swampy plain,, intersected by ditches. He sent a brigade (Clarke's) to cross the head of the Pedregal, while the other (Garland's) he ordered to attack by the road, when the former was ascertained to be in position for turning the works, attacking in the rear, and cutting off the enemy's retreat. His success proved the judiciousness of his arrangements; and after news reached the Mexicans of Valencia's defeat at Contreras, the contest was soon decided.

Worth captured a number of pieces of artillery, *inter alia*, and, what was more important, large supplies of ammunition, desirable in the extreme to our army, whose supply was comparatively very limited, at the same time that we had the advantage of finding it exactly where most wanted, thus saving the labour, expense, and risk of transportation.

Our portion of Quitman's division, which had been temporarily relieved by Harney's dragoon brigade, remained in charge of prisoners, stores, &c., during the continuance of the bloody fight, which continued from Contreras and San Antonio to the fall of Churubusco. During these contests, we were in constant expectation of an attack for the capture of the valuable munitions of war under our charge, the recapture of prisoners, &c. In the afternoon, a squadron of our dragoons had a brush with a large irregular force, some two miles distant from the village. We were ordered out to the support; but the enemy fled, and dispersed as we approached. In the mean time San Augustin was becoming a grand hospital. The surgeons, following the movements of the army, did all that men could do in the field for the wounded—night and day, without shelter, in sun and rain, they gave their devoted attentions. After the first temporary dressings, they sent their wounded to the various establishments converted for the time into hospitals.

An incessant roar of artillery, and rattling volleys of small arms, gave us constant tidings of the work going on during the 20th of August; but how the tide of battle was running, we knew not: we augured well, however, of the present and future, from the past. The troops in reserve were fretting and fuming that they were not allowed to participate in the bloody strife; for, fearful as are the horrors of war and the details of the battle-

BATTLE OF CHURUBUSCO.

field, he has no soldier's heart who can hear the clang of arms, and look upon the wreathing smoke as it ascends from the scene of slaughter, where his compatriots are battling and shedding their life's blood, without wishing to share at once their dangers and their triumphs. Occasional rumours reached us, giving uncertain information of the course of events. Among others, we learned that the South Carolina and New York regiments, with which we had been so much associated, had each lost, during the day, one-half of their already diminished numbers, and that the gallant Colonel Butler, of the former, who had left his sick bed to lead his regiment, was among the slain. They are noble fellows, those "Palmettos" as brave as they are polite and generous, and withal possessed of a vein of chivalry that seems to belong to a past age. The rumours proved nearly correct; both of these gallant regiments suffered severely, both in officers and men—the colonel of the one killed, the lieutenant-colonel severely wounded,[1] and the Colonel (Burnett) of the New Yorkers wounded also, very dangerously.

So great was the anxiety of the officers of marines to take part in the engagement going on, that they drew up a most earnest petition to the commander-in-chief, representing their peculiar position, how they had left their regular line of service to participate in the for tunes of the army, and how deeply they felt being left in a position of inactivity during scenes so exciting. Colonel Watson called on General Quitman in relation to it; but from the conference with that officer, who was lamenting the necessity that kept him also in the background, he was deterred from sending the petition. General Quitman thought there was yet much to be done, and that he would be enabled to give his division an opportunity to win soldiers' laurels, or soldiers' graves. The marines consequently continued in the discharge of the duty assigned them.

The battle continued to rage until Churubusco shared the fate of Contreras and San Antonio. Our people fought like lions, braving danger at the very cannon's mouth. Our entire army,

---

1. The brave Lieutenant-Colonel Dickinson; his wound proved mortal.

under its immortal chief, was in at the death, except the fragment of it remaining here; and none can say which portion fought best. There stood, side by side, regulars and volunteers, new regiments and old, all daring everything, accomplishing everything. The conduct of the old army is an imperishable eulogy on the system of military education given to the officers at the sterling school, so justly prized and cherished by the nation; the conduct of the new troops proves that our great country bears in its bosom the natural materiel for war, as abundantly as for the prosperous arts of peace.

One great secret, undoubtedly, of our success, is owing to the unity of feeling that pervades the army. We are but a handful here, far from home, and surrounded by thousands, aye, millions of enemies. Defeat is annihilation;—we may therefore die, arms in hands, but we must not be defeated. The question is equally of life and death, as of honour and glory; and victory is the only road to self-preservation. Here we are, from all quarters of our glorious Union, acting in the same concert as if all were the children of one state, or one family. May the Ruler of nations grant that it be ever so with our beloved country; that wisdom and harmony govern her councils; and we have nothing to fear from any human power.

In my travels, which you know have been somewhat extended, never have I seen the peace, happiness, and prosperity that rests upon the soil of our great republic. Would to God every man, woman, and child nurtured in its bosom could see and know the difference between their own favoured condition and that of those not enlightened by the broad, diffusive beams of universal education, nor cheered by the blessings of civil liberty! The blighting spirit of discord could then never find a resting-place among a people knowing, by comparison, their strength and their happiness.

In this country, Mexico, so far as my observation goes, there is wanting the first element of national greatness, i. e. a people. What matters it that a population of seven or nine millions of human beings occupy the same soil, if between them there is no harmony, no fellowship? Such is the condition of things here—aristocracy and dregs—the sturdy middle class, the bone and sinew, aye, the vital element, exists not here. The most important link in the social chain is wanting or defective; the Nation's Heart, for I may term it so, scarcely throbs. What marvel, then, that the body is puny and sickly?

VICTORIES

20th August, 1847, stands upon the annals of our history, marked by a victory, or a series of victories, as brilliant as any known in the records of wars. The Mexican forces averaged with the Americans as three to one; at San Antonio, Contreras, Churubusco, (the church, and the *Tête du pont*, or bridge head,) they had strong fortifications, exceedingly difficult of approach; with heavy batteries mounted, with sufficient skill to make good use of them; they fought in sight of their large and beautiful capital; on their own plains, surrounded by their altars, their homes, and their families; with the greatest advantages, natural and artificial, and with all incentives to a glorious defence; yet, with not enough to repel a handful of bold invaders, or to save themselves from an overwhelming defeat.

General Scott, in his report of the "Battle of Mexico," divides this great victory into five brilliant parts, as follows, *viz.*: the first, the taking of Contreras; from which the victors passed on, one portion under Twiggs, to the attack on Churubusco, the other, under Pillow, to the assistance of Worth, at San Antonio: before reaching that point, however, Worth had turned and captured the fortification, making the second great act of the drama, and was on his way, in pursuit of the retreating enemy, to the important defences at Churubusco. On the road directly before him, lay the formidable *Tête du pont,* or head of the bridge crossing the Rio Churubusco, where there was a "strong field-work with regular bastions and curtains," surrounded by a deep wet ditch.

While Worth's division and a portion of Pillow's were attacking the *Tête du pont,* the battle was raging at two other points;

that is, at the church or convent of San Pablo, and on the main road to the city beyond the bridge. When the body of the army from Contreras reached Coyoacan, a village some two miles from San Antonio, and one from Churubusco, the commander-in-chief made the following disposition of his forces. By a road leading to the former, he directed General Pillow to proceed with Cadwalader's brigade to attack that place in the rear, and to cut off the retreat of the enemy; by the road to the hamlet of Churubusco, on the side of the fortified church, he sent Twiggs with his division, preceded by Lieutenants Stevens and Smith of the engineers, with a company of sappers and miners, and accompanied by Captain Taylor's field battery, to attack the convent, beyond which the road debouched at the bridgehead, some two hundred and fifty yards distant.

The two roads just indicated, with one leading direct (the main road) from San Antonio through the hamlet, and by the church to the bridge, (continuing on to the city,) made an irregular triangle, of which Coyoacan was at one angle, San Antonio at another, and the works of Churubusco at the third. While Pillow and Twiggs were pursuing their respective courses, the general-in-chief sent first, General Pierce with his brigade, and shortly after, Shields with his, by a road indicated by Captain Lee, to the left of that taken by Twiggs, "to attack the enemy's right and rear, in order to favour the movement upon the convent, and to cut off the retreat towards the capital."

The third, fourth, and fifth, "brilliant events" of the day, then, were successively, the taking of the bridge head by Worth's division, and Cadwalader's brigade of Pillow's; the taking of the church by Twiggs' division; and Shields' victory, with his temporary division of Pierce's brigade of Pillow's, his own brigade of South Carolinians and New Yorkers, and Twiggs' reserve under Major Sumner, of the Rifles, and Sibley's company of dragoons, over a force of four thousand infantry, and three thousand cavalry. It should have been mentioned that Pillow, finding Worth had carried San Antonio, did not proceed to that place, but under instructions from the commander-in-chief, leaving the road, "immediately turned to the left, and, though much impeded by ditches and swamps, hastened to the attack of Churubusco."

After the works were taken at the bridgehead, Pillow and Worth pursued the retreating enemy on the main road, where they fell in with Shields, who had completed his achievement. A spirited chase was kept up, for some miles, led by Kearney's company of Harney's dragoons, the brigade having been ordered up by General Scott before he left Coyoacan. Kearney heard not, or heeded not, the recall when sounded, and charged, with the squadron, to the defences at the gate of the city, where he was severely wounded, (losing his left arm,) as were many of the officers and men with him.

The whole remaining force of the Mexican army, of all arms, amounting to about 27,000 men, was assembled at Churubusco "in, on the flanks, or within supporting distance of the works," while the American army at that point, (deducting the reserve at San Augustin, the troops left in charge at Contreras, sick, wounded, &c.,) amounted only to between eight and nine thousand.

The general results of the day are thus stated in the report of the commander-in-chief. "It (our army) has in a single day in many battles defeated 32,000 men; made about 3000 prisoners, including eight generals, (two of them, ex-presidents,) and 205 other officers; killed or wounded 4000 of all ranks—besides entire corps dispersed and dissolved—captured 37 pieces of ordnance—more than trebling our field train and siege batteries—with a large number of small-arms, a full supply of ammunition of every kind, &c., &c.

> These great results have overwhelmed the enemy. Our loss amounts to 1053; (killed, 139, including sixteen officers; wounded, 876, with 60 officers.) The greater number of the dead and disabled were of the highest worth. Those under treatment, thanks to our very able medical officers, are generally doing well.

The party left under General Quitman, at San Augustin, is noticed in the same report as follows:

I regret having been obliged, on the 20th, to leave Major-General Quitman, an able commander, with a part of his division—the fine 2nd Pennsylvania volunteers, and the veteran detachment of United States Marines—at our important depot, San Augustin. It was there that I placed our sick and wounded, the siege, supply and baggage trains. If these had been lost, the army would have been driven almost to despair; and considering the enemy's very great excess of numbers, and the many approaches to the depot, it might well have become emphatically, the post of honour.

In a sketch like the above, it cannot be expected that justice should be done the respective divisions, brigades, and regiments, much less to individuals concerned, distinguished on that remarkable day—the only aim of the author of the letters has been to give some general information, accurate, so far as it goes, because drawn from the best sources, of the current and permanent events of that important part of the war. He will, in an appendix, give the names of such officers as distinguished themselves, with a notice of the honours bestowed upon them by the government. He does not doubt but that some one, more competent than himself, will one day give, what is very desirable, a complete military history of the war.

San Augustin, Valley of Mexico, August, 1847

The troops, though much fatigued with their labours, watchings, and fastings, on the evening of the 20th might no doubt have carried the defences at the *garitas* (city gates) with ease, and entered the capital in triumph; but Mr. Trist, United States Commissioner, and General Scott, thought a peace could be concluded the more readily for not inflicting that additional humiliation upon the Mexican people. Notwithstanding our loss of men, which, though small comparatively, is very considerable, the large number of heavy pieces of ordnance and the immense supplies of ammunition taken at the various points of defence, have afforded us some material advantages for siege or bombardment; besides taking so much from the efficiency of the enemy. When fully expecting to enter the city at once, it was announced to the army that a treaty was pending for peace, during which time there would be a suspension of hostilities: in consequence, we are now lying idle.

The commanding General is at Tacubaya, a suburban village two or three miles from the capital; Mr. Trist is with him; and General Worth with his division is quartered there. The remaining divisions of the army are quartered in other pretty and pleasant villages between this and Tacubaya. I should not have said we were idle—our corps is fully engaged. We have not only a large number of wounded in the hospitals, but the great exposure of the men at the time of the battles had its influence, though not felt immediately. A great many persons, officers and men, were out night and day, without provisions, blankets, or shelter; and though they bore the vicissitudes of the weather, the midday sun and the midnight shower, with apparent immunity, the effects are felt now that the excitement is over.

There are enough of such diseases as are incident to camps to keep the surgeons employed, even if there were no wounded. These are contingencies of war that are not often set down in the reckoning, though they should be always. Many a valuable life is sacrificed, and many more constitutions broken in war, besides those given up on the battle-field.

The armistice, let it result as it may, gives us a little breathing time, and some opportunities of looking around us. It is tantalizing, indeed, to look upon the great city in the distance which we may never enter; but a general impression is abroad in the army, of Punic faith on the part of the enemy, and that there will be no peace until the capital is in our possession. We have daily, almost hourly, flying reports, of what is to be done;—one day, peace is certain, and we return shortly to our homes—the next day, or hour, informs us that, hopeless of peace, General Scott is about to make immediate arrangements for an active bombardment.

These conflicting rumours keep up a perpetual suspense; but there are few besides the commissioner, who would not rather take up arms again, than leave without entering the capital. Our people are not willing now to turn their backs on the "halls of the Montezumas," without the revel for which they have toiled and fought so hard.

My host, that is, the person whose house gives me present shelter, is a very respectable and intelligent old gentleman, from the city. He informs me that there all the better people desire peace, almost on any terms; that the common people are too ignorant to have an opinion (worth the name) about it, but that they are essentially pacific; and that the war men are adventurers and employes of the government, or of factions, having nothing to lose, and who can only hope, like scum, to keep on the surface during commotion.

Circumstances have thrown me considerably into the society of residents here, and among the better classes I find a high degree of intelligence, refinement, and good breeding—in this village we found a large proportion of well-dressed and educated people; they, however, are from the city, and came out as to a place of refuge, supposing themselves safe from witnessing the horrors of war. They found themselves, however in the midst, at different times, of both armies; first, the Mexican, which moved here to meet us, when it was discovered that we were taking this route; and then ours occupying the town as they vacated it. Coming here was a sad mistake, for between Santa Anna's levies, and the approach of our army, supplies were cut off from the citizens, and some of them before the armistice went into operation, were likely to die of starvation. Some persons, apparently in good circumstances, applied to myself and others, for fragments of the hard, dry bread used in the army, for the nourishment of their families.

None of the *upper ten* reside in villages, or small towns. My first impression on reaching this place was that it was well supplied with gentry, but I soon learned that the greater portion were mere visitors, fled temporarily from the city, while others have their *casas de campo* (country-seats) here, to which they repair for a season every year. The villages have no residents pretending to social rank; the *padre*, or curate, and the *alcalde*, who is generally a small shop-keeper, are the most important personages. The remaining inhabitants are principally *mestizos*, in whom the aboriginal traits preponderate greatly.

A little politeness on my part, together with my lame Spanish, soon put me on a friendly footing with the proprietor of this house, and his family, that is, the male portion of it. The old gentleman, though a native of this country, was educated in Spain, married there, and held a colonel's commission in the Spanish army during the Peninsular war. He there saw active service under his personal friend Espartero, and acquired that knowledge which marks and distinguishes the man of the world. He was wounded at length in a charge of cavalry, trodden down by a troop of horse, taken prisoner by the French, and detained to the end of the war.

His sufferings brought on a disease of the chest, which obliged him to return to his native country; though he was called at the same time by another motive, to prevent the threatened confiscation of his Mexican estates. He has about him here all the appendages of wealth; that is, beautiful grounds, highly ornamented, coaches, horses, mules, servants, &c., &c. His two sons, with their wives, young and handsome women, and their sweet, bright, and ruddy children; a niece, a *soltera* (spinster), as fair as the morning, and a nephew, her brother, constitute his present family.

They looked upon my entering the house, as a disagreeable intrusion which had to be endured, but finding I spoke their language, and that I carefully abstained from intruding upon their privacy, they soon became sociable, and then intimate. They authorized me to invite any of my friends to take apartments in their spacious house, upon which I brought three reliable gentlemen, who with myself, constituted a mess. They treated us with all politeness, except introducing us to the ladies; that, however, we could not but pardon, as we were such entire strangers; bearded worse than the *pard* (for few used the razor on the march), and dressed as people might be, whose scanty wardrobe had been soaked with water, saturated with dust, and rolled in the mud, times and again. But woman is woman the, world over. A young officer of marines was brought to the house, ill, dying; the "ministering angel" saw not her country's enemy, but a suffering brother far from home and friends; she felt for the young and hapless wanderer; for the fond mother, who knew not her impending loss; for the tender sister, who looked with feelings, perhaps of exultation and pride, to the joyful day of her brother's return; she saw the tears of their disappointment and grief; and she, a high-born and lovely Mexican woman, prepared with her own hands such little delicacies as only the skilful hand of gentle woman can make acceptable to the perverted palate of the victim of disease.

I had heard much of the kind-heartedness of Mexican women—here was a practical proof; and the lady's frequent application to me to know what she could do, and what would be suitable, exposed the deep sensibility of her feeling heart. The youth died; and though far away from those who loved him best, he had at least the gentle ministering of this kind family; and soldiers' tears accompanied the volleys that were fired over his grave.

San Augustin, Valley of Mexico

When the armistice went into effect, nearly all the good folks from the city repaired to their homes; the village was enlivened by dozens of *diligencias* that is, the regular stage-coaches of our States, reminding one much of home, and differing only in the teams, which are here of six mules, four leaders abreast. There was a general breakup, leaving only the permanent residents, a poor set, our division, and the prisoners of war. Among the latter are some forty deserters, who fought desperately at Churubusco and elsewhere, under Major Riley, who deserted from our army about the beginning of the war. He expects to be hung, but denies the justice of it, as he calls himself a British subject.

Our kind friends left with the rest, inviting us to their home in case of ever reaching the city. The place of their residence is somewhat remarkable—*Calle del Puente de Jesus* (Jesus Bridge

Street). While here, they showed their goodwill by bringing us many little luxuries money could not pro cure, from their own stores invited us at times to their table, which was set with Gralicia ham, cakes, the never-failing *dulces* (sweet meats), chocolate, wines, &c. We had nothing to offer in return but a little civility.—I mentioned that this might be considered a very pretty village, and will give a slight description of it, as it may answer as a general type of most places of its class. It has then, first, its *plaza*, or square, in the centre, with a large church and enclosure on the east side, a large fonda with its portales, and some private mansions on the north; *pulquerias, tiendas* (shops), &c., on the west and south sides. The whole is about 400 feet square. Beautiful shade-trees are set uniformly through it, so that it is a pleasant walk, even during the heat of summer. The streets are rectangular, and there are many handsome houses, generally of one story, and never over two. They are of stone, plastered, white or light-coloured, with flat roofs and parapets; large windows opening to the floor, having iron balconies in front on the second floor, or a close grating on the lower—a necessary precaution against the various classes who have not a proper regard for the tenth commandment.

The outside rarely gives an idea of what is within, not, indeed, that the houses are handsomely furnished; on the contrary, they are almost bare; but of the courts, gardens, fruits, flowers, and fountains, which are universal. The house we occupy may be taken as a specimen of the whole. The entrance is by a *porte-cochère* from the street. As the house is quadrangular, you find yourself in a clean square court, well paved with smooth flag stones; in the middle of the court is a fountain, garnished with vases of growing flowers. Four well-trimmed orange trees adorn the angles. Within, the rooms all communicate with each, other by doors; there are no passages, but on the sides presenting to the court are covered balconies, communicating with some of the rooms.

One of the peculiarities of the houses, and a very awkward one, is that of passing through a suite of rooms to get at those towards the remote end. It not unfrequently happens that you pass through the family bed-chambers to reach the parlour. In the best houses, however, the difficulty is corrected generally by *piazzas* or balconies, as in this case. In rear and to the right of the dwelling are the stables, coach-house, and other outhouses. Immediately in rear of the house, and extending, indeed, largely on both sides, is a noble garden of a couple of acres, teeming with fruits and flowers. It is beautifully laid off in squares, is adorned with summer-houses and sparkling fountains; a great variety of fruits now hang on the trees. There are fine apples, peaches, pomegranates, alligator pears, mangoes, oranges, &c., &c.,—not, however, all in equal perfection. The oranges, for instance, are only ornamental, being both bitter and sour; all that are good in the market come from the *tierras calientes*.

Our host enjoined it upon us at his departure to use all the fruits of this paradise as if our own; he cautioned us against the oranges, but we tried them for ourselves, without the solicitations of any curious Eve, and were soon satisfied. An old gardener and his family hold the place divided with us. The house itself has little that is ornamental; a little *fresco* painting adorns the walls of the *piazzas*. Among the views is one of the castle of Chapultepec, a powerful fortification, built by the Count of Galves, when viceroy, and now used as a military school, at the same time that it is the most formidable work that guards any of the entrances to the city. Our house has no chimneys nor fire-places, not even in the kitchen; the cooking is done with charcoal fires, on ranges of small furnaces, built up in the middle of the floor.

The common houses are built of *adobes*, or large sun-dried bricks, which answer very well in this climate, and look well, too, when whitened. All the fine houses, it must be recollected, are the country-seats of people of wealth from the city. San Augustin is distinguished for its fine gardens, but more for an annual fiesta of gambling, when all classes repair here, from the president to the squalid *lepero*, and spend, in various forms of gaming, at the monte table, cockpit, &c., from thousands of ounces of gold and large estates, down to handfuls of miserable coppers.

Lieutenant-Colonel Watson, the estimable commander of the Marines, is acting military governor of this place—no sinecure, considering it devolves on him to sit as *oidor*, or judge, in the endless disputes between the residents and certain restless followers of the army.

SAN AUGUSTIN, VALLEY OF MEXICO

"Misery makes strange bedfellows" and war strange associations. There may be found in our little army representatives of every profession, trade, and calling, practised in civilized life. The ranks present not only the drainings from the worthless and bad of our towns and villages, which may be expected, but also persons well to do in the world, well-informed, skilful in the mechanic arts, respectable husbandmen, doctors, lawyers, engineers, merchants, &c., some of whom have been reduced by misfortune, or intemperance, while others assumed their position from mere love of adventure. This admixture is most remarkable among the volunteers, many of whom gave up the comforts and even the elegances of civil life, for the variety and novelty of a distant and dangerous campaign.

The army followers are yet more varied: thus we have sutlers, and their stores; printers, with their presses; editors, reporters, players, circus-riders, with their fancy horses; gamblers, jobbers, speculators, brokers, and certain frail but daring fair ones, *damas cortesanas,* who venture to face the dangers of war; besides a variety of nondescript characters: sailors turned teamsters; discharged soldiers, proposing to be landlords, &c., &c.,—so that even in our diminutive army, we have a little world; all of which must be considered mere miniature of the immense bodies brought into the field during the great wars of nations beyond the Atlantic. We have only enough with us to give the idea of an army, that is, of a vagrant world.

It is but just to say that many of the citizens accompanying the army, indeed a large majority of them, took an active part during the battles: some acted on the staff of generals and commanding officers; others enrolled themselves under Captain M'Kinstry, of the quartermaster's department, and did good service as volunteer cavalry—every American, indeed, was a man in trying times; and it required no articles of enlistment to wield the sabre, or shoulder the musket, during the emergencies of the battle-grounds.

Our time has been passed here comfortably in some respects, but the busy tongue of Madame Rumour has always kept up a restless *qui vive,* that dispelled easy tranquillity. We are at once, too near the capital, and too far from it. We are in the paradoxical condition of the Irishman who is never at peace, except when fighting. Apparently, there is something now brewing which will bring affairs to a crisis. The conditions of the armistice required, *inter alia*, a free exchange of supplies between city and country, and between our army and citizens; and, not only a suspension of hostilities, but of all offensive and defensive works, &c.; both armies were to remain precisely in *statu quo*; we were to be allowed to purchase, on fair terms, the necessary provisions, but were not to receive reinforcements, (a condition binding on both, of course,) during the session of the commissioners to adjust a treaty of peace.

An infraction was soon made by the Mexican mob. A train of wagons was sent to the city for supplies: the teamsters were set on, stoned, and dreadfully maltreated and injured; but the mob was not responsible, and the parties in power disapproved, or pretended to disapprove of the attack, and there it seems the matter dropped; but a more serious infraction has since come to light: the enemy has taken advantage of the lull to prepare defences, collect ammunition, cast guns, &c.

The armistice, of course, died a natural death, as soon as these facts became known, and this day, (September 7th,) an express came from General Scott for the division to move on to some point near the city, for the purpose of attack. We will have bloody work, doubt less; but the troops appear to be anxious for it, and bent on entering the city: they are full of hope and confidence; and though it seems impossible that that great capital should fall before such a mere handful yet the past, promises unbounded success. My own convictions of a favourable issue have been much strengthened by reading a report made to General Jackson by a commissioner he appointed for inquiring into the contest between Texas and this country. The superiority of the Anglo-American race over the mongrel breed of Mexico, is there set forth in unmistakeable characters the Americans beat them against all odds, and excelled them as much in the art of war as in the arts of peace. For this gratifying information, I am indebted to the Hon. Waddy Thompson's interesting *Recollections of Mexico*, of which I have just finished a hasty perusal.

Tomorrow morning, the volunteer division leaves San Augustin for another trial of prowess. Though anxious to move onward, I cannot leave without some regrets, as my associations here are agreeable; but this is a life that breaks up all ties, beginning with the nearest and dearest, from the day a man leaves his own cherished fireside; and snapping daily the feebler cords, made by transient fellowship and mutual good-will. The vicissitudes of fortune, how ever, cannot sever the invisible chain that connects one, at any distance, with the beloved home circle; nor dispel the visions of hope, sweet hope, the true life-preserver, that buoys us up against the tide of adverse fate, until we are called to settle that reckoning to which we are hurrying, it matters not, whether by the battle-field, or on the bed of down, surrounded, if not sustained, by all known consolations.

Santa Catalina

On the morning of the 8th, our division resumed the march, escorting a large train, and hundreds of prisoners. A set of voluntary captives, wives, or *queridas*, accompanied the poor fellows, ministering to their wants as well as they were able. They were for the most part bareheaded and barefoot, with garments scant enough to show their limbs and busts of bronze, laden, some with infants, strapped on their shoulders; others with such scant stores as they could command, for their husbands or themselves. They were uninteresting enough, except as displaying the beautiful feminine trait of fidelity in misfortune.

A rapid and fierce firing of artillery and small-arms gave us notice that we were approaching the scene of a hot engagement; but by the time our rear reached the hacienda of San Antonio, the contest appeared to be decided. A glowing account soon reached us of a battle won at *Molinos del Rey* (King's Mill), near the great fortress of Chapultepec; but as we advanced, the pleasure of triumph was shorn by the accounts of our heavy losses. Worth's division and a portion of Pillow's shared the laurels and the cypress. Dreadful havoc had been made in the very flower of our army; and many of our bravest and best lay stretched upon the battle-field. American valour had triumphed, and the victory was complete, but at so great a sacrifice, that we might almost say, with the famous king of Epirus, "Another such would be fatal to us."

During a temporary repulse, the ignoble hosts of the enemy sallied forth from their shelter to slay the wounded and mutilate the dead, as they lay where they had fallen. A feeling of exasperation, not unmixed with gloom, took possession of our people as this news reached them; and there was that in their countenances that gave promise of more than avenging retribution.

We passed through the venerable village of Coyoacan, and took quarters in the hamlet of Santa Catalina, which extends by straggling houses along the roadside, from the former place to the town of San Angel, where Twiggs' division was quartered. We had nothing to do but await the results of the reconnaissances going on for future operations. Meantime a disposition was made of a portion of the captured deserters. Sixteen of them paid the forfeit of their lives on the gallows, at the same moment, between this place and San Angel, about half a mile from my quarters. They had deserted and gone over to the enemy during the war. Others, including Riley, who had deserted before the war, had the letter D branded on their cheeks, were whipped, are to be kept in irons until the war is ended, and then drummed out of the service. And all this was for giving up substance for shadow: they were lured from their duty by the magnificent promises of Santa Anna, bore the brunt of his battles, were poorly paid, and finished their career in damning ignominy. I have more than once seen the circulars of the crafty Mexican distributed by the roadside where our army was to pass, proposing the most tempting offers to the unprincipled and the unwise. However, though "many were called," few were found to be misled by the seducer.

I visited San Angel on several occasions: it is a beautiful place, differing from San Augustin in being located on a commanding eminence, which gives a fine view of the city and surrounding country. The hill is crowned by a large church and convent, be longing to the Carmelite order, reminding one, like so many objects in Mexico, of the middle age. The whole country, indeed, seems to be centuries behind ours. I sauntered through the buildings, and was pleased with the general air of neatness and order everywhere apparent. Still the cloisters are dank and gloomy, striking a chill through you as you traverse the long corridors. Without, however, the gardens and grounds, well kept and highly cultivated, with their avenues of shade-trees, looked very cheerful and inviting. The towers and dome of the church are enamelled with a mosaic-work of porcelain, the belfries laden with bells of many sizes, of various tones and richness, and the walls are adorned with many large and some fine paintings.

I conversed a little with the monks, who were civil, polite, and sociable. While there, an American officer, professing the ancient faith, asked me to inquire whether he could be shriven, he speaking not a word of Spanish, and the *padres* as little English. After some consultation, an affirmative answer was given; he confessed, and I afterwards was curious to know the *modus*. He informed me he was assisted by an invisible interpreter, who read slowly through the tables of sins, as infractions of the commandments, &c., each and every one separately, first in English, then in Spanish; the penitent held the confessor's hand, unseen by the interpreter, which he pressed whenever he wished to admit a particular dereliction. By this complex process he relieved his oppressed conscience, and, I suppose, was absolved.

Not a day has passed since the conclusion of the truce, without our ears being occasionally assailed by the boom of artillery. The firing is generally directed on reconnoitering, or other small parties, on exposed duty.

We have had worse than soldier's fare of late: it is only with great difficulty we could obtain the commonest articles of subsistence. We learned that Santa Anna has had large foraging parties out, whose business was not more to supply themselves, than to prevent supplies from coming to us, by driving off cattle, &c. We have now an illustration of Scott's sagacity, as well as his honesty, in ordering all articles obtained to be fairly paid for. Had he adopted another policy, his army would probably have been disbanded before this, and roaming over the country in search of subsistence; but the fact is, sellers find it to their interest to furnish us, and they will do it, in spite of Santa Anna.

On the afternoon of the 11th, preparations were made for another move; and when the day was well spent, the division was in motion, standing directly for the *garita del niño perdido,* or the entrance from the village of San Angel. Our progress was very slow remarkably; we made frequent halts as soon as the darkness set in, and somewhere about midnight we passed Pillow's division, where his fires were burning as quietly as if there was nothing to be done but to cheer the guard with hot coffee. We had deviated from the direct road, but wherefore, or whither bound, was left to conjecture. Silence was enjoined, and we knew only there was a ruse de guerre, in which we were *particeps.*

The night was quite cool, but dry; and whenever a halt was called, officers and men lay down on their arms by the roadside, ready at a whisper to rise for marching or assaulting. I was expecting a night attack on some *garita* where we were least expected. My attendant, as usual, was out of the way when wanted, and I had to take my snatches of rest wrapped in the oiled sheet I carried on my saddle, holding my horse by the long reins, and jerking at him every few minutes to keep him from treading on me. I soon found a friend in the same predicament, and we agreed to hold each other's horses, and sleep by turns. After that I enjoyed some half hours of repose. One had to choose his resting-place with great precaution; a poor fellow, who did not distinguish the road from the barren soil at the sides, had the misfortune to have his legs crushed by the passage of a heavy piece of ordnance. His sufferings appeared to be awful, but I have heard nothing of him since. Towards daylight we found ourselves passing through the smart town of Tacubaya. As the day broke, we saw the great key to Mexico, frowning Chapultepec, standing over and against us. The mystery of the night march was solved.

MOLINO DEL REY

General Scott, having sufficient proof of the double-dealing and treachery of his adversary, ordered reconnaissances to be resumed on the 7th of September, for the purpose of arranging his plans of attack on the city. During the afternoon of that day, large bodies of Mexican troops were seen hanging around the Molinos del Rey, something more than a mile from Tacubaya, and about one-fourth or third of a mile from the works at Chapultepec. The commander- in-chief had learned that the mills contained a cannon foundry, while near them, in a stone building called Casa Mata, there was a large deposit of powder; and "having heard, two days before, that many church bells had been sent out to be cast into guns," the general understood the object of the enemy's presence there, and determined to "drive him off early the next morning, seize the powder, and destroy the foundry."

He was impelled to this decision because he knew there was no cutting off communications between the foundry and city until Chapultepec was taken, which was on the direct road and overlooking both of them; and he hoped further reconnaissances would enable him to turn Chapultepec, and enter the city by one of the southern entrances. The destruction of the foundry was of extreme importance, as "our recent captures had not left the enemy one-fourth of the guns necessary to arm, all at the same time, the strong works at each of the eight city gates."

He accordingly ordered General Worth, with his division, "reinforced with Cadwalader's brigade, of Pillow's, three squadrons of dragoons under Major Sumner, and some heavy guns of the siege train under Captain Huger, of the ordnance, and Captain Drum, of the 4th Artillery" to carry his designs into execution.

As the engagement became more general than had been anticipated, and the enemy received reinforcements at various times, General Scott ordered up Pillow with the rest of his division (Pierce's brigade), and Riley's brigade of Twiggs'; but "the battle was won just as General Pierce reached the ground" &c. (Scott.)

Generals Scott and Worth made in person reconnaissances about and around the works at Chapultepec, &c., and Captain Mason, of the Engineers, a "close and daring reconnaissance," immediately about the present point of attack at Molino del Rey, &c. He discovered that the enemy's line extended from that point to the strong stone building, the Casa Mata, on the right that "midway between the buildings was the enemy's field battery, and his infantry forces were disposed on either side to support it." El Molino itself is "a group of strong stone buildings, adjoining the grove at the foot of the hill of Chapultepec, and directly under the guns of the castle which crowns its summit."

General Worth's first object was to isolate the point of attack from Chapultepec and its immediate defences. Before day, on the morning of the 8th, he commenced his operations. Hot work was expected, but the full extent of the enemy's defences had been skilfully masked; so that our troops only learned what they had to meet during the charge. General Worth had planted his batteries (the artillery under the general superintendence of Lieutenant-Colonel Duncan), detailed his storming party, assigned their parts to the different brigades, &c., and, as day broke, they were found as "accurately in position as if posted in midday for review."

At dawn, Huger's heavy guns opened on the Mills. Wright's storming party, guided by Captain Mason and Lieutenant Foster, of the Engineers, charged upon the enemy's column, crossed bayonets with more than quadruple their numbers, drove them off, and got possession of the enemy's field battery; the latter, however, seeing what a mere handful was opposed to them, re-turned, and aided by a plunging and murderous fire from behind the parapets on the house-tops, struck down "eleven out of the fourteen officers of the command, and non-commissioned officers and men in proportion, including Major Wright, the commander, and Captain Mason and Lieutenant Foster, engineers, all severely wounded."

This severe loss paralysed, for a while, the assailants; but aided by the artillery, and supported by Cadwalader's brigade, the attack was resumed with fresh vigour. The buildings were carried by assault, our troops advancing by perforating the walls within, and mounting to the roof without, driving the immense superiority of numbers against them at the point of the bayonet.

Meantime a desperate contest was going on at Casa Mata, "which, instead of an ordinary field entrenchment, as was supposed, proved to be a strong stone citadel, surrounded with bastioned entrenchments, and impassable ditches an old Spanish work recently repaired and enlarged." Our troops, entirely exposed, charged boldly up to it, though suffering most severely; of the three senior officers present, Lieutenant-Colonel Martin Scott was killed, Colonel McIntosh, mortally, and Major Waite severely, wounded. The havoc, was so great, that the command fell into some temporary disorder. It fell back on Duncan's battery, and there rallied. Returning to the charge, it masked the battery, which was supported by the Voltigeur regiment; and at the same time, large forces of infantry and cavalry were approaching on the American left flank, to support and reinforce the Mexican right. Duncan's battery, with the Voltigeurs "moved rapidly to the left to intercept them; the cavalry came within canister range, when the whole battery opened a most effective fire, soon broke the squadrons, and drove them back in disorder."

Major Sumner's command of dragoons and mounted rifles at this time crossed the ravine to the left of Duncan's battery (passing under a most appalling fire from the Casa Mata),

FORTRESS OF CHAPULTEPEC.

"where it remained, doing noble service, during the rest of the action." As the cavalry was repulsed, the Americans drew back from before Casa Mata, enabling Duncan's battery to open fairly upon it, until the enemy was dislodged.

The guns of the battery were then turned upon the retreating columns, and continued to play upon them until beyond reach. The enemy was now driven from every point in the field, and his strong lines, which he certainly had defended well, were in our possession. In fulfilment of the instructions of the commander-in-chief, the Casa Mata was blown up, and such of the captured ammunition as was useless to us, as well as the cannon-moulds found in El Molino del Rey, were destroyed.

The command returned to quarters in Tacubaya, "with three of the enemy's four guns (the fourth having been spiked and rendered unserviceable), as also a large quantity of small-arms, with gun and musket ammunition, and exceeding eight hundred prisoners, including fifty-two commissioned officers.

The enemy's forces engaged on the occasion—

.... exceeded 14,000 men, commanded by General Santa Anna in person. His total less, killed (including the second and third in command, Generals Valdarg and Leon), wounded and prisoners amounts to 3000, exclusive of some 2000 who deserted after the rout. (The American forces) .... only reached 3100 men of all arms. The contest continued two hours, and its severity is painfully attested by our heavy loss of officers, non-commissioned officers, and privates, including in the first two classes, some of the brightest ornaments of the service. (Worth.)

The above is an extremely condensed account of this remarkable engagement. The reports of the subordinate commanders are highly interesting, and the author of the letters has to regret that his limits do not allow him to draw from them. Our entire loss upon that occasion, amounted to, in the aggregate, seven hundred and eighty-seven men, including nine officers killed on the ground, and fifty wounded, some of them mortally. To name all who distinguished themselves, is out of the question; it would be merely to publish the names of all present; but the names of the gallant dead, who on that day offered up their lives to their country, may be here properly commemorated, *viz.*, Lieutenant-Colonel Martin Scott, 5th Infantry; Lieutenant-Colonel William Montrose Graham, 11th Infantry; Captain M. E. Merrill, 5th Infantry; Lieutenant W. S. Burwell, Lieutenant C. B. Strong, 5th Infantry; Captain Gr. W. Ayres, 3rd Artillery; Lieutenant W. Armstrong, 2nd Artillery; Lieutenant J. F. Farry, 3rd Artillery; Lieutenant R. H. L. Johnston, 11th Infantry. Those who died eventually of their wounds then and there received were, Colonel McIntosh, 5th Infantry; Captain E. K. Smith, 5th Infantry; Assistant Surgeon William Roberts, serving with 5th Infantry; Lieutenant M. L. Shackelford, 2nd artillery; Lieutenant C. B. Daniels, 2nd Artillery; Lieutenant J. Gr. Burbank, 8th Infantry; Lieutenant C. F. Morris, 8th Infantry; Lieutenant R. F. Ernst, 6th Infantry.

They died as the patriot soldier should die, on the true field of honour, while gallantly engaged in the line of arduous and desperate duty; and they left behind them a bright and glorious example to those who, entering their country's service, are willing to follow in their footsteps.

City of Mexico, September, 1847

For the last few days we have all been in a whirl of intense excitement. On Sunday morning (12th), our batteries, which had been planted during the night, opened on the dread castle of Chapultepec, and kept up all day a ceaseless cannonading. The Mexicans returned it with spirit, but without doing any execution, while nearly every shot from our side told upon their works.

The castle, or fortress, is a magnificent building, crowning the summit of one of the natural mounds so common in this country. It is doubly strong, by its own strength and by its elevation, which puts assailants at a great disadvantage. At many points the castle is utterly inaccessible, because mounted on a natural wall of perpendicular rocks, surmounted by an artificial one: elsewhere the ascent is rugged, broken, now steep, now perpendicular for some feet, now over loose rocks lying on a slope, and intersected by rents and chasms. High walls and deep ditches first intercept assailants at the base of the hill, to reach which, when the narrow highway is obstructed, it is necessary to traverse low swampy meadows.

Being stationed near the gallant Drum's battery, with other in cautious Americans, led by momentary excitement, I went several times to a point nearly in rear of his guns to observe the course of things, but as a crowd collected, including some horsemen, near the same spot, we were warned off, as giving the enemy a fair mark to shoot at. The marines were located, *pro tempore*, in line-shot with the batteries. I repaired there momentarily, until I learned that a house about a square distant had been selected for the temporary hospital of the division, where the surgeons were to assemble.

I went to my post, and perhaps not too soon: a large ball from the castle passed through the centre of the house occupied by the Marines, over the heads of most of them, and below Captain Terrett and others, on the house-top, making observations. I found my professional brethren getting out their instruments and dressings, arranging tables for operations, &c., and having done the same, I mounted to the roof, to gaze at the rare spectacle before me, until my services should be called into operation. That was not soon, so I passed hours watching the shots as they took effect on the walls of the castle, which they did in a way very gratifying to us. Meantime parties of observation were out skirmishing with the enemy, and keeping up a perpetual ringing of musketry.

Our own gallant Quitman was actively engaged, in person, making reconnaissances. Towards night the castle was pretty well riddled, but it was understood that the next day the bayonet was to finish the work commenced by mortar and cannon. During the day, our brigadier, Shields, who seems to bear a charmed life, came into our apartment, and threw himself exhausted and cov-

FIELD AFTER THE BATTLE.

ered with dirt, upon a rough bench prepared for the wounded. He did not get his fill of cannonading at Cerro Gordo, where he was shot through the chest, and received a wound that would have killed any but another Achilles. He took position on this occasion by the side of Captain Drum, and there stood, until knocked over by a maguey plant and soil, torn up by a ball that made directly for them. Weakened still from loss of blood and suffering, he was glad to find any resting-place until he could expose himself more profitably.

Leading the storming party for the next day, was a duty scarcely desirable for the bravest; yet this gallant Irishman entreated to be allowed to command it—to lead the forlorn hope, in person. At one time he thought his wishes would be granted; he communicated the fact to his aids, telling them, with flashing eyes, that on the morrow they might expect such work as had not yet been seen in Mexico.

At night people are wont to sleep, to rest from their labours, but not so now—"the times have been that when the brains were out the man would die,"—but the times have changed; night marches, night watchings, fighting, caring for the wounded, &c., for many successive nights, seem to have changed the order of nature.

On the night of the 12th, both parties laboured diligently in raising breastworks, repairing batteries, and so forth; the Mexicans were fortifying the road to the city, sending or endeavouring to send, reinforcements to the castle, while ours had to check and repel them, thus keeping up skirmishing until a very late hour. As the day dawned, the work was resumed, at first by the batteries, but at the same time a general preparation was making for assault. When our troops were first seen at the foot of the hill, all around me stood in breathless silence; directly, they commenced the ascent, and the scene, hitherto so deeply interesting, now became intensely so.

I was again on the house-top, heeding not the occasional wild shots from the castle, that seemed to be intended for the American troops, yet not engaged, about us; but gazing most intently on the motions of the contending columns, I scarcely dared to breathe. The guns from the castle were in full blast; the hillsides and summit were alive with the enemy's light troops, pouring destruction into our slowly ascending columns. But mark the course of things: onward and upward, slowly yet surely, moves the American host; an irregular, but fatal fire for the enemy, is heard; irregular, because each individual, or squad, seems to fire and climb, loading as he can.

Is not the enemy falling back towards his strong defences? Certainly. See! first one spot is vacated, then another—they are falling back, decidedly, clearly! Behold, a villainous piece, at a redoubt half way or more up the steep—a long twelve, apparently—that is never silent; it seemed at every shot to plough a way through the assailing column. The deepest pain was expressed in the countenance of every beholder about me. When noticing that piece, every man of us felt himself in personal torture. We could not see exactly its effects, for a turn of the hill; but imagination filled out the picture. Like some insatiate monster, it passed through the throng of human beings, eating its way and leaving a great gap behind. But the column, undaunted, moved steadily onward; sometimes there was a momentary suspense, but it was for physical obstacles; directly again, the onward, upward motion was resumed.

You may imagine, but I cannot describe, what the feelings of the spectators were. I thought of all excitements I had ever known, or witnessed, and felt how far they fell short of this most engrossing spectacle. There were some scores of Americans perched up in trees, and on various house-tops, looking over the scene; but the spectators of the other side were in numbers beyond all calculation, surely there were up wards of one hundred thousand. I looked at the city, where the domes and towers of the cathedral, the churches, and convents, were blackened with myriads of people—hosts stood upon the house-tops, and dense clusters of human beings on every elevation. All the while the work at the castle was going on. The hated piece was captured, and heads of regiments and companies were seen to sink in the ditch, then mount the walls. See them—they stop to wave the regimental flags, as they go over, then a period of the closest fighting, and shortly, the tricolour falls, and the American ensign waves over the proud Castle of Chapultepec.

The troops most under my eye were of the 3rd division of regulars, with a brigade of the 1st; the operations of our own division, with Smith's brigade of the 2nd, were scarcely to be seen from my point of observation. We (surgeons) were immediately engrossed in our bloody work, when an express came for assistance at the castle. Meantime, accounts were coming in to us rapidly, of our losses in capturing that great work; and the first death I heard of was that of the gallant and high-souled Major Twiggs, of the Marine corps, who received his death-wound through the heart, at the head of a storming party, of which he was commander. In early life he earned merited distinction under the immortal Decatur, when his frigate, the *President*, after having whipped the *Endymion* frigate, fell a prey to the British fleet.

I volunteered for the castle, set out immediately, and reached there at the *finale*, when the last shots were being exchanged at the base with the retreating enemy. I had very soon the satisfaction of learning that the active piece at the redoubt had done no execution whatever, as every shot passed over the heads of the assailants. It was not, and perhaps could not have been, sufficiently depressed to clear the steep hill below it.

CITY OF MEXICO, SEPTEMBER, 1847

Heaps of dead and wounded presented themselves to my vision on every hand as I approached the castle. The wounded Americans were carried in as fast as possible; the Mexicans, though there was every disposition to give them the attention humanity required, had to bide their time. Our losses had been heavy, but theirs greater incomparably, notwithstanding the shelter they had enjoyed to the last moment from their defences. Their dead bodies lay in masses of tens, twenties, or more, wherever there had been concentration; some there were gasping in the last agonies, with their dark faces upturned to the sun, like fish thrown on shore by the angler, writhing and struggling in death; others lay motionless, but an occasional gasp, an up-heaving of the chest, alone gave evidence that the vital spark had not entirely fled.

Upon entering the castle, I was arrested by some Mexican officers, who besought me to see a person, apparently a general officer, to whom they were attending. One moment sufficed. A ball had passed through his neck, another through his head; he was speechless and motionless, the blood was passing into his windpipe, but his dying eyes seemed to say he knew his own condition, as I believe he did. As his case was hopeless, I passed immediately on, only pausing a moment to gaze on the fearful mutilations of the human body lying around. There were crushed heads, mangled limbs, and torn up bodies, brains, hearts, lungs, and bowels released from their natural confines, eyes hanging out from their sockets, and all the lacerations and contusions that follow the use of fire-arms, the sabre, or the bayonet.

Brave officers, who had just participated actively in the fearful scene, told me they had enough of the horrors of war, and hoped never again to witness them.

I soon was earnestly engaged in my occupations, lopping off crushed limbs, and dressing wounds, snatching occasional moments to glance at the movements of the troops, as they moved along the causeways, by the aqueducts, to the city.

Along the direct road (Belen), for there are two from Chapultepec, passed Quitman's division, with Smith's brigade, of Twiggs', while by the other, or San Cosme road, Worth and Cadwalader advanced. Riley's brigade, of Twiggs' division, was engaged at the southern gates of the city, supporting Steptoe's and Taylor's batteries, which had been keeping up a ceaseless roar since Sunday morning.

One of the first persons who called my attention at Chapultepec, was a gallant lieutenant of engineers (Tower), who had rendered distinguished services on many occasions. He narrowly escaped with his life, as a ball cut the skin from the edge of his forehead. I put on a temporary dressing, and he started off to render new services, and run the gauntlet again. The wounded were brought

BATTLES of MEXICO

Survey of the

Map of operations of the Army under the command

of

MAJOR GENERAL WINFIELD SCOTT,

on the 19.th & 20.th of August & 8.th 12.th & 13.th Sept.t

1847

Made by

Major Turnbull, Captain M.c Clellan and
Lieut. Hardcastle Top.l Engineers.

Drawn by Lieut Hardcastle

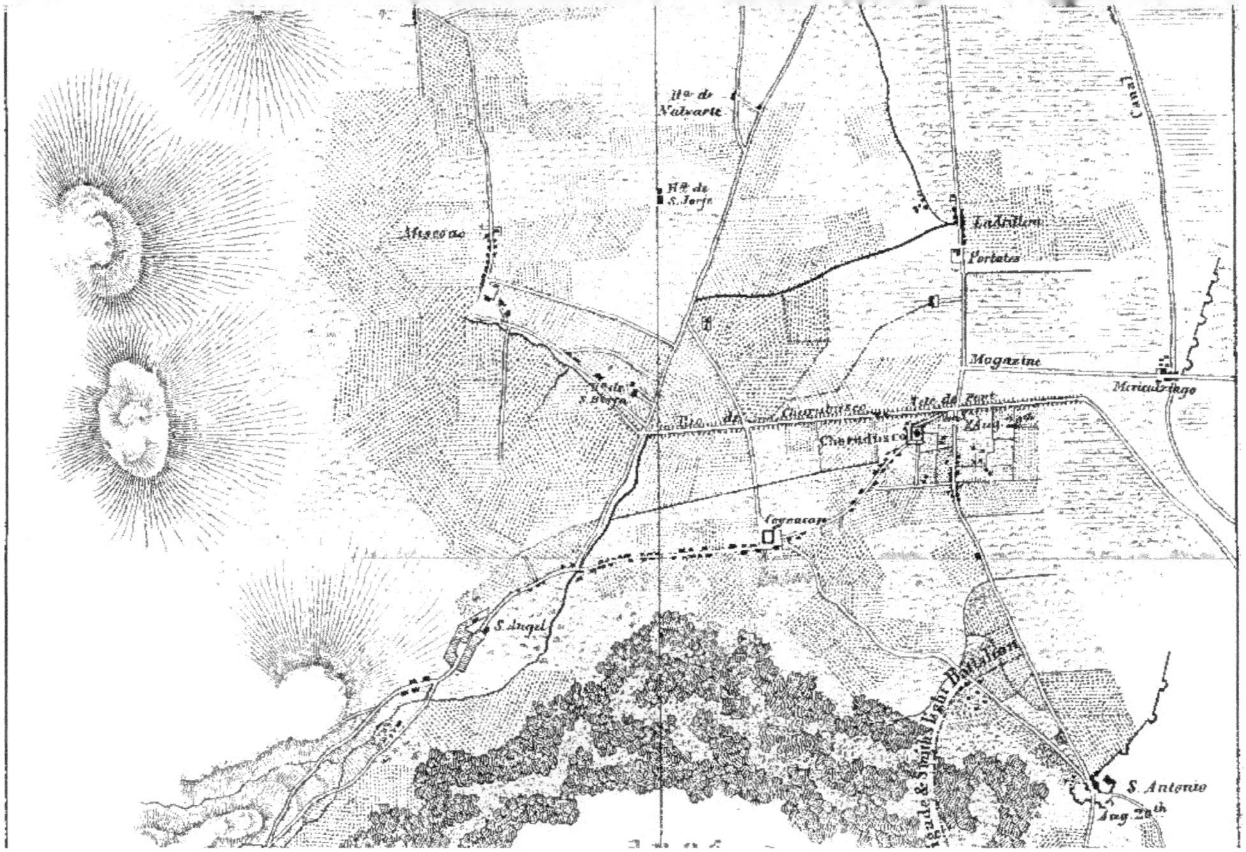

Hª de
Valvarte
Hª de
S. Jorge
Ladrillera
Portales
Magazine
Mexicalzingo
Churubusco
Coyoacan
S. Angel
S. Antonio
Aug. 20th
Canal

Pedregal
or
Field of Lava

S. Antonio

S. Juan de
Dios

S. Angel

San Mateo

in rapidly; the "labourers were few" but most diligent in their duties; yet the wounded suffered greatly for want of the most commonplace comforts. Such bedding as could be collected about the building was spread for them, but by far the greater part lay on the floor, or on the forms used by the scholars, for the castle was a military academy also, the West Point of Mexico.

I had been at work for some hours, had attended to all of my own regiment who came under my observation, and to as many others as I was able to assist, when I felt impelled to go in pursuit of the regiment, to render service on the spot.

As I passed up the causeway, it was strewed with dead; a temporary battery, half-way along the road, had been captured, and the head of the column was said to be at the city gate. I met many stragglers returning, who gave the most discordant accounts of progress. No one knew any thing in general, but only some little bit of detail that had passed under his own eye. All joined in one piece of advice that is, I was riding up the middle of the road, with my case of instruments under my arm, reminding myself of old Dr. Sitgreaves in *the Spy*, when they advised me to dismount, and slip along close into the arches of the aqueduct, borrowing protection from the jutting supports flanking the piers.

The devastating and raking cross-fires down the road had taught our people this precaution; and an oblique shot passing before me from the *Paseo*, decided me to follow their advice. I accordingly returned towards the castle to dispose of my horse, and trudge up with less pretension. When near there, how ever, I fell in with Surgeon-General Lawson, who was superintending his department with untiring zeal. He told me that the wounded from my regiment were all brought off as they fell, and that it was impossible for me to leave the castle.

I explained to him my wishes and intentions; and, after reflection, he concluded it would be advisable for me to follow up the regiment, and learn of the commanding officer whether any of his command wanted immediate attention. I returned then, and accompanied the surgeon-general to a house, converted into a temporary hospital, a mile from Chapultepec, where I left him, to pursue my solitary route. The ambulances were bringing back full freights, and wounded mules and horses were straggling on the road. I soon came up with the rear of the column, now sheltered partially under the arches, inquiring of all I saw to be directed to the regiment I was in search of. No man could answer, however, for any one but himself; and as the twilight began to hide objects, I almost despaired. Pushing on, however, I found myself at length facing a double arch, that could be nothing but the city gate. Such it was, indeed, the *garita* of Belen; and there, adjoining, across the ditch that flanked the right side of the causeway, I found our estimable commander, with a portion of his officers and men sitting and lying down around him, waiting for further action.

It was now dark, and the battle was quite suspended; but the night was to be spent in active preparations for an early attack on the citadel, about two hundred yards from the garita. So many were dead, so many were wounded; a considerable detachment was missing, headed by a gallant captain (Terrett), a man of iron nerve, who was either dead or doing good duty somewhere. His fate, and that of his officers and men, was entirely unknown. After a little conversation, finding the wounded had been carried back, I repaired once more to the great hospital at the castle.

The 15th Infantry had been left in charge, while the army pushed on to the city. That regiment, with the prisoners, the wounded, and the surgeons, were for the night the occupants of the fortress. I was fagged with labour, hungry, and sleepy; but there was no rest to be had there. I passed the night operating and assisting the operations of others. At times I threw my weary person down on one of the benches for a little sleep, to enable me to continue my labours; but sleep had fled far from me, and the groans and cries of the sufferers, the heavy tread of soldiers bringing in wounded, the flashing lights of the surgeons and attendants, dispelled the hope of a moment's repose. About midnight a considerate person boiled a little coffee for those who stood in need of it, or rather for such as saw it, for all were nearly famished; and I found half a tin-cupful, without milk or sugar, but accompanied by a little dry bread, refreshing and renovating.

GENERAL SHIELDS.

Although there was immense suffering among the wounded, they bore it generally with remarkable stoicism; men in their senses seemed to scorn to complain, but lay patiently awaiting the operation, or the change that was to decide the prospect of life or death. In one instance, while taking off the forearm of a rifleman, a sturdy son of the Emerald Isle, with a shattered wrist, he conversed calmly during the operation, uttering not a groan; and the arteries were scarcely tied, before he was smoking a pipe borrowed from a comrade. Men seemed to feel cut off from human sympathies, and certainly were not unnerved, as is so common in civil life, by the kind and gentle attentions of friends.

I must offer a passing tribute to the diligence and zeal of my colleagues; some of whom passed hour after hour, night and day, without pausing for a moment's rest; scarcely eating or sleeping for several successive days and nights. The medical corps of the army needs no eulogy, being equally distinguished for intelligence and high moral character; while among their temporary associates, there are many young men of superior acquirements, who are taking valuable lessons in this great school for practice.

CITY OF MEXICO, SEPTEMBER, 1847

During the night of the 13th, our troops were making the necessary preparations for bombarding the city. Worth's division was in occupation of the garita of San Cosine, and Quitman's of that at Belen. While anxiously waiting for the morning guns, that seemed now to be a matter of course, the news was passed that the Mexican army had vacated the city, and that the civil authorities had offered capitulation to the commander-in-chief. Quitman occupied the citadel immediately, leaving there in garrison the 2nd Pennsylvania volunteers; he then moved on to the grand *plaza*, and palace. Scott rejected all terms with the citizens, requiring an unconditional surrender, which could no longer be refused.

He entered the city triumphantly early on the morning of the 14th; the stars and stripes were already waving over the national palace of Mexico; and we thought all contest was for a time at an end; not so, how ever. Santa Anna had opened the doors of the prisons, and turned out thousands of felons, who, arms in hands, opened an unexpected fire in all quarters on our troops in the streets, while the assassins were half concealed on the house-tops, and sheltered by the parapets.

The fire was quite destructive, and the more exasperating, as foul, unexpected, and cowardly. The villains were as unsuccessful as their army had been. In a little while our troops were on the house tops; the unerring rifle was opposed to the murderous escopet. The Mexicans were worsted, as they always had been; they were driven from house to house, and from square to square, leaving their dead and wounded behind them.

Worth's division surprised them, as at Monterey, by perforating the walls of the houses, and ascending upon them from below. Mountain howitzers were placed in lofty towers, which dismayed, as they dispersed, the felon army. It was a day's work, however, and even on the 15th and 16th, there was occasional skirmishing, receding from the centre to the outskirts of the city.

General Scott issued a proclamation to the citizens, denouncing such warfare after the city had been fairly surrendered, and threatening the destruction of houses, and the execution of the occupants, wherever it was sanctioned or allowed. Holding in the other hand the olive branch, he expressed a most anxious wish to preserve the lives and property of citizens; he warned his own troops, at the same time, from any acts of injustice or unnecessary violence, under the severest penalties. The city authorities also published a proclamation, deprecating the attempts of the populace to oppose us. They declared that such warfare was only calculated to bring vengeance on peaceful and quiet citizens, and that the army having fled, such resistance was wholly unavailing. Between the proclamations, and our sharp-shooters, quiet was gradually restored, and the troops went into quarters. The gallant marines occupied the national palace, which they found infested by thieving *leperos*, who were ejected at the point of the bayonet.

My own time was occupied passing to and fro, between the city and Chapultepec, where a large portion of the wounded remained for some days after the fall of the former. A general appearance of gloom pervaded the ancient city; few persons were seen in the streets; the shops were all closed; grim artillery pieces stood as sentinels at the heads of the streets leading from the palace square; and the Mexican dead lay, for a time, where they fell, unburied. Waving flags, whether of truce or bearing the arms of neutral nations, flung out from every house, gave something of a holiday aspect to the silent mansions, and spoke of living tenants within.

In time, our missing friends who were not at Belen, came dropping in; they, in the heat of the pursuit, had taken the course of the 1st and 3rd divisions from Chapultepec, and were for a time with the gallant Cadwalader, doing brilliant service. Some from the other divisions, had taken our course in like manner. All had enough to do, and how they did it needs no comment. The troops found only temporary quarters until a distribution could be made in reference to garrisoning the city; ours moved, for instance, to the *Aduana* (custom-house); thence to the spacious Dominican convent at hand; and finally to a building used as a military college, in the street leading from the palace to the *garita* of San Antonio, near which was quartered the entire volunteer division.

The command of our brigade fell on Lieutenant-Colonel Watson of the Marines, as since its formation his seniors had all been removed from the line of duty, General Shields, by a most formidable wound of the arm, by which he was entirely disabled; Colonel Burnett, of the New Yorkers, by a desperate wound of the foot; Colonel Butler, of the Palmettos, by death on the battle-field, and Colonel Roberts, of the Pennsylvanians, by illness.[1] It may be added, too, as illustrating the scenes through which the brigade had passed, that nearly all the field-officers had been killed or wounded; thus, of the Lieutenant-

1. It is inaccurately stated that the Pennsylvanians belonged to Shields' brigade. The regiment formed part of Quitman's division, but was net brigaded.

Colonels, Dickinson, of the Palmettos, and Baxter of the New Yorkers, had given their lives to their country, and Geary, of the Pennsylvanians, received an honourable wound.

SCOTT'S VIEW OF CHAPULTEPEC

The admirable report of General Scott contains nearly everything in relation to the taking of Chapultepec and the city, in the way of exact knowledge, that would interest the general reader; the author, therefore, thinks he could not do better than to extract freely from it, drawing at the same time moderately from other sources of information.

The general opens by giving his reasons for striking at the city by Chapultepec, instead of by the southern entrances. The city is described as standing on "a slight swell of ground near the centre of an irregular basin, and is girdled by a ditch in its greater extent—a navigable canal of great breadth and depth—very difficult to bridge in the presence of an enemy, and serving at once for drainage, custom-house purposes, and military defence, leaving eight entrances, or gates over arches, each of which we found defended by a system of strong works, that seemed to require nothing but some men and guns to be impregnable.

Outside, and within the cross-fires of those gates, we found to the south other obstacles, but little less formidable. All the approaches near the city are over elevated causeways, cut in many places, (to oppose us,) and flanked on both sides by ditches, also of unusual dimensions. The numerous cross-roads are flanked in like manner, having bridges at the intersections, recently broken. The meadows thus chequered are moreover, in many places, under water, or marshy; for it will be remembered we were in the midst of the wet season, though with less rain than usual, and we could not wait for the fall of the neighbouring lakes, and the consequent drainage of the wet grounds at the edge of the city—the lowest in the whole basin.

The general having made a personal reconnaissance of the

southern entrances, under cover of Pillow's division and Riley's brigade, in presence of a fourfold number of the enemy, determined to seek less unfavourable approaches, but by a feint to keep him under the impression that the attack was to be made by those entrances, according to his anticipations. General Scott then—

.... ordered Quitman's division from Coyoacan to join Pillow, by daylight, before the southern gates, and then that the two major-generals, with their divisions, should, by night, proceed (two miles) to join me at Tacubaya, where I was quartered with Worth's division. Twiggs', with Riley's brigade, and Captains Taylor's and Steptoe's field batteries, the latter of twelve-pounders, was left in front of those gates, to manoeuvre, to threaten, or to make false attacks, in order to occupy and deceive the enemy. Twiggs' other brigade, Smith's, was left in supporting distance in the rear.

The stratagem against the south was admirably executed throughout the 12th, and down to the afternoon of the 13th, when it was too late for the enemy to recover from the effects of his delusion.

The first step in the new movement was to carry Chapultepec, a natural and isolated mound of great elevation, strongly fortified at its base, on its acclivities and heights. Besides a numerous garrison, here was the military college of the republic, with a large number of sub-lieutenants and other students. These works were in direct gunshot of the village of Tacubaya, and until carried we could not approach the city without making a circuit too wide and too hazardous. In the course of the same night (11th), heavy batteries within easy ranges were established. Numbers 1 and 2, commanded by Captain Drum, Lieutenant Andrews, temporarily, of the artillery, and Lieutenant Hagner of the ordnance, were supported by Quitman's division; and numbers 3 and 4 were commanded by Captain Brooks and Lieutenant Anderson, of the artillery, the latter alternately with Lieutenant Stone, ordnance, and supported by Pillow's division. Captains Huger of the ordnance, and Lee of engineers, traced and constructed the batteries, assisted by the younger officers attached to them. The batteries were intended to prepare the way for assault. Recent captures had not only trebled our siege-pieces, but also our ammunition; and we knew we should greatly augment both by carrying the place.

On the morning of the 15th, Pillow and Quitman had been in position since early on the night of the 11th. Worth was ordered to hold his division in reserve, near the foundry, to support Pillow; Smith's brigade was ordered to support Quitman. Riley's brigade continued actively engaged before the southern gates, with Taylor's and Steptoe's batteries, " holding there a great part of the Mexican army on the defensive.

Additional storming parties were furnished; from Worth's division, 250 men and officers, under Captain M. Huger, of 2nd Artillery, to Pillow; and from Smith's brigade, another, under Captain Casey, 2nd Infantry, to Quitman. Each of them was supplied with scaling ladders. At a concerted signal the columns advanced to the assault "with an alacrity that gave assurance of prompt success." General Pillow was struck down by a wound as he advanced on the west side, and his command devolved on Cadwalader. One brigade of Worth's division (Clarke's), was ordered to support Pillow at his call.

The broken acclivity was still to be ascended, and a strong redoubt, midway to be carried, before reaching the castle on the heights. The advance of our brave men, led by brave officers, was necessarily slow, though unwavering, over rocks, chasms, and mines, and under the hottest fire of cannon and musketry. The redoubt now yielded to resistless valour, and the shouts that followed announced to the castle the fate that impended. The enemy was steadily driven from shelter to shelter. The retreat allowed not time to fire a single mine without the certainty of blowing up friend and foe. Those, who at a distance attempted to apply matches to the long trains, were shot down by our men. There was death below as well as above ground. At length the ditch and wall of the main work were reached; the scaling ladders were brought up and planted by the storming parties; some of the daring spirits, first in the assault, were cast down, killed, or wounded; but a lodgement was soon made, streams of heroes followed; all opposition was overcome, and several of our regimental colours, flung out from the upper walls, amidst long-continued shouts and cheers, which sent dismay into the capital. No scene could have been more animating or glorious.

Major-General Quitman, nobly supported by Brigadier-Generals Shields and Smith, his other officers and men, was up with the part assigned him. Simultaneously with the movement on the west, he had gallantly approached the south-east of the same works over a causeway with cuts and batteries, and defended by an army strongly posted outside, to the east of the works. Those formidable obstacles Quitman had to face, with but little shelter for his troops or space for manoeuvring. Deep ditches, flanking the causeways made it difficult to cross on either side into the adjoining meadows, and these again were intersected by other ditches.

Smith's brigade was stretched out to the right to present a front to the enemy outside, and to support Quitman's storming parties, commanded, the one by Captain Casey, 2nd Infantry, until, when wounded, he was relieved by Captain Paul, and the other by the gallant Major Twiggs of the Marine corps, who fell at the head of his party, when he was succeeded by Captain Miller, of the 2nd Pennsylvanians. Paul's storming parties took two batteries, many prisoners, &c., while Miller's accompanied Shields' brigade and the Pennsylvania volunteers, crossing "the meadows in front under a heavy fire, and entering the outer enclosure of Chapultepec, just in time to join in the final assault from the west."

General Scott then compliments officers, regiments, &c.,

particularly distinguished; including all the general officers, the voltigeurs, the 9th and 15th Infantry; the storming parties; Colonel Clarke's brigade, &c.; and portions of the United States Marines, New York, South Carolina, and 2nd Pennsylvania volunteers, which, delayed with their division (Quitman's) by the hot engagement below, arrived just in time to participate in the assault of the heights, particularly a detachment, under Lieutenant Reed, New York volunteers, consisting of a company of the same, with one of marines;[2] and an other detachment, a portion of the storming party under Lieutenant Steele, 2nd Infantry, after the fall of Lieutenant Gantt, 7th Infantry."

In the meantime, the heavy batteries under the officers first mentioned, and superintended by Captain Huger, did faithful service; while practicable they kept up their fire over the heads of our troops, and thereby kept the force in the castle reduced to its minimum; a mountain howitzer, under Lieutenant Reno, of the ordnance, accompanied the Voltigeurs.

The operations of the troops heretofore mentioned, were on the west, south-east, and heights of Chapultepec. At the base of the mound, to the north, where it was inaccessible, the 11th Infantry, under Lieutenant-Colonel Hëbert, and the 14th, under Colonel Trousdale, with Captain Magruder's field battery of the 1st Artillery, "had some spirited affairs against superior numbers," drove off the enemy, captured a battery, &c.

When the castle was taken, the general-in-chief ascended to the top to get a full view of the field before him towards the city. The two roads, passing, one to the right, to the *garita* of Belen, the other to the left obliquely, to intersect the western or San Cosme road, are each—

> .... an elevated causeway, presenting a double roadway on the sides of an aqueduct of strong masonry and great height, resting on open arches and massive pillars, which, together, afford fine points both for attack and defence. The sideways of both aqueducts, moreover, are defended by strong breastworks at the gates, and before reaching them.

---

2. Under Lieutenant D. J. Sutherland, of that corps.

Worth and Quitman were prompt in pursuing the retreating enemy—the former by the San Cosme aqueduct, and the latter along that of Belen.

Clark's brigade and Cadwalader's were immediately ordered by General Scott to accompany Worth; while Pierce's brigade was ordered to join Quitman— the heavy artillery to follow each column as soon as practicable. The 15th Infantry, under Lieutenant-Colonel Howard, was left to garrison Chapultepec. General Scott accompanied Worth along the road to San Cosme, and found no obstacles prepared for the occasion, to repel him; at the first battery, or line of defence, there was not a single gun, which proved to him that the enemy expected us to fail at Chapultepec, or that if successful, the attack against the city would continue from the south, where Twiggs was still keeping up active, but delusory operations.

As Worth entered the suburbs of San Cosme, he was assailed from windows and house-tops. He ordered forward the mountain howitzers, "preceded by skirmishers and pioneers, with pickaxes and crowbars, to force windows and doors, or to burrow through walls. The assailants were soon put in an equality of position fatal to the enemy." By 8 o'clock in the evening, Worth had carried two batteries in this suburb. (At the taking of one of these "it became necessary, at all hazards, to advance a piece of artillery to the evacuated battery of the enemy, intermediate between us and the garita. Lieutenant Hunt was ordered to execute this duty, which he did in the highest possible style of gallantry, equally sustained by his veteran troops, with the loss of one killed and four wounded out of nine men, &c. Reaching the breastwork, he became muzzle to muzzle with the enemy. It has never been my fortune to witness a more brilliant exhibition of courage and conduct" Worth.) Between 8 and 9 o'clock, Riley joined Worth with his brigade of Twiggs' division; earlier in the evening, Steptoe's battery rejoined Quitman.

Scott, knowing that San Cosme afforded the easiest entrance to the capital, only intended Quitman to manoeuvre before, and threaten Belen, to favour the main attack by Worth; as Belen was directly under the guns of the strong fortress called the Citadel, and within convenient supporting distance from the southern gates. The largest force was assigned to Worth for the main attack. Quitman understood this distinctly:

> . . . . but being in hot pursuit, gallant himself, and ably supported by Brigadier-Generals Shields and Smith,—Shields badly wounded before Chapultepec, and refusing to retire,—as well as by all the officers and men of the column, Quitman continued to press forward under flank and direct fires; carrying an intermediate battery, and then the gate, before 2 o'clock in the afternoon, but not without proportionate loss, increased by his steady maintenance of that position.

Here fell the gallant Captain Drum and Lieutenant Benjamin of the 4th Artillery; Lieutenants Moragne and Canty, of the South Carolina volunteers, and many brave non-commissioned officers and men, besides many of all grades, wounded. Quitman, within the city gate, passed the night making preparations for taking the Citadel, &c., but meantime a deputation from the *ayuntamiento* (city council) offered the capitulation of the city; Santa Anna, the army, and the government, having fled under cover of the darkness. General Scott refused all terms except such as were imposed by himself and required by the dignity and honour of his country.

The city was taken possession of on the morning of the 14th, when the street fighting commenced, and continued until suppressed as mentioned in the letters.

Our total loss on the 12th, 13th, and 14th of September, amounted to, killed, 130, including ten officers; wounded, 703, including sixty-eight officers (many of the wounded have since died); missing, twenty-nine. Total 862.

Our grand total of losses in the valley of Mexico, amounted to 2703, including 383 officers.

On the other hand, this small force has beaten, on the same

occasions (all the battles of the valley), the whole Mexican army, at the beginning, of thirty odd thousand men, posted always in chosen positions, behind entrenchments, or more formidable defences of nature and art; killed or wounded of that number, more than 7000 officers and men; taken 3730 prisoners, one-seventh officers, including thirteen generals, of whom three had been presidents of this republic; captured more than twenty colours and standards, 75 pieces of ordnance, besides 67 wall-pieces, 20,000 small arms, an immense quantity of shots, shells, powder &c.

The remains of the Mexican army were dispersed in various small fragments "without magazines or a military chest, and living at free quarters upon their own people."

The author has made such copious extracts from General Scott's report, that neither time nor space will allow him to draw upon others as their interesting contents merit. He will, however, add a few more, drawn from the lucid report of General Quitman, and others, as illustrations of the course of events on the great occasions under notice.

Perceiving that all preliminary dispositions were made (for the assault at Chapultepec), Major Gladden, with his regiment (Palmetto), having passed the wall by breaching it, the New York and Pennsylvania regiments having entered over an abandoned battery on their left, and the battalion of Marines being posted to support the storming parties, I ordered the assault at all points.

The storming parties,[3] led by the gallant officers who had volunteered for this desperate service, rushed forward like a resist less tide. The Mexicans, behind their batteries and

---

3. Quitman's storming parties were thirteen officers and 250 men, of Twiggs' division, selected for the occasion from the Rifles, 1st and 4th Artillery, and 2nd, 3rd, and 7th Infantry, under command of Captain Casey, 2nd Infantry; and another of 120 officers and men, of the volunteer division, under command of Major Twiggs, of the Marines. A pioneer storming party of choice men, also selected from the volunteer division, and under command of Captain Reynolds, of the Marines, was provided with ladders, pickaxes, and crows, to accompany Twiggs' stormers.

breastworks, stood with more than usual firmness. For a short time the contest was hand to hand; swords and bayonets were crossed, and rifles clubbed. Resistance, however, was vain against the desperate valour of our brave troops. The batteries and strong works were carried, and the ascent of Chapultepec on that side, laid open to an easy conquest.

Captain Casey was disabled by a severe wound, and his command devolved on Captain Paul, 7th Infantry, who distinguished himself greatly.

In like manner, the command of the storming party from the volunteer division devolved on Captain James Miller of the 2nd Pennsylvania Regiment, by the death of its chief, the brave and lamented Major Twiggs, of the Marine corps, who fell on the first advance at the head of his command.

Simultaneously with these movements on our right, the volunteer regiments, with equal alacrity and intrepidity, animated by a generous emulation, commenced the ascent of the hill on the south side. Surmounting every obstacle, and fighting their way, they fell in and mingled with their brave brethren in arms, who formed the advance of Major-General Pillow's column. Side by side, amid the storm of battle, the rival colours of the two commands struggled up the steep ascent, entered the fortress, and reached the buildings.

General Bravo, the commander of the Mexican forces, was taken prisoner by an officer of the New York volunteers.

As large bodies of the enemy, were on the direct road to the city—(the road, it must be remembered, is "a broad avenue, flanked by deep ditches and marshy grounds on either side," the aqueduct, or its series of arches, passing along the centre)—General Quitman ordered his command forward as soon as supplied with ammunition, drove back the enemy, took a strong battery thrown across the road about a mile from Chapultepec, which resisted obstinately, but was carried by assault by the Rifles, who we're in advance, with the aid of an eight-inch howitzer under

Captain Drum. The column was here reorganized for an attack on the batteries at the city gate (Belen). The Rifles and Palmettos were placed in advance, "three rifles and three bayonets under each arch," supported by Shields' brigade, Marines and New Yorkers, the Pennsylvania regiment, and Smith's brigade—

.... with a part of the 6th Infantry, under Major Bonneville, who had fallen into this road. In this order the column resolutely advanced from arch to arch of the aqueduct, under a tremendous fire of artillery and small-arms from the batteries at the garita, the Paseo, and a large body of the enemy on the Piedad road to the right, extending from the left of the *garita*.

A destructive enfilading fire from that road was stopped by a few rounds of canister from a piece under Captain Drum, and Lieutenants Benjamin and Porter. At twenty minutes past one, the *garita* was carried, and the city entered from that point." General Santa Anna commanded in person at the *garita*, until he no longer hoped to save it, when he repaired to that at San Cosme, "there to try his fortune against General Worth."

On our approach to the *garita*, a body of the enemy, who were seen on a cross-road threatening our left, were dispersed by a brisk fire of artillery, from the direction of the San Cosme road. I take pleasure in acknowledging that this seasonable aid came from Lieutenant-Colonel Duncan's battery, which had been kindly advanced from the San Cosme road in that direction, by General Worth's orders.

The capture of the *garita* by no means stopped the fight. Our heavy ammunition was soon expended; the enemy, perceiving which—

.... redoubled their exertions to drive us out of the lodgement we had effected. A terrible fire of artillery and small-arms was opened from the citadel, three hundred yards distant, from the batteries on the Paseo, and the buildings on our right, in front. Amid this iron shower, which swept the road on both sides of the aqueduct, it was impossible to bring forward ammunition for our large guns. While awaiting the darkness to bring up our great guns and place them in battery, the enemy, under cover of their guns, attempted several sallies from the citadel and the buildings on the right, but were readily repulsed by the skirmishing parties of rifles and infantry. To prevent our flank from being enfiladed by musketry from the Paseo, Captains Naylor and Loeser, 2nd Pennsylvania regiment, were ordered with their companies to a low sand-bag defence, about one hundred yards in that direction. They gallantly took this position, and held it in the face of a severe fire, until the object was attained. At night the fire of the enemy ceased.

At dawn of day a white flag was brought General Quitman, surrendering to him that for tress, while "Captain Steptoe was preparing his heavy missiles," &c.

A single extract from the report of Captain Magruder, of the 3rd Artillery, showing the spirit of the enemy with whom we had to contend, may be allowed to close the excerpts, perhaps too freely used, in the preceding pages. It is to record what he calls—

. . . . a miserable trick, which, upon this occasion, might have created much inconvenience to my battery. Soon after the re-entrance of the cavalry (driven back to their entrenchments by the battery), a Mexican was seen running from the forts to us, and shouting. The officers and men naturally crowded into the open space to receive him, or hear what he had to say, when one of our officers, who had been at Monterey, came up, and recognising the trick, explained it in a moment, the object of the enemy being that we should crowd forward, attracted by this appeal to our sympathy on the part of a deserter, and when a sufficient number should be collected thus together, without formation or order, in a spot of which he had measured his range, to explode his shells in rapid succession and to destroy us. The troops, however, were forthwith ordered to their posts; and I had barely time to have the caissons and limbers removed further to the rear, when three or four shells burst, very rapidly, in the centre of the section, fortunately without any material injury to it—wounding, however, in two places, an officer of the 15th, who was temporarily on duty with it.

Like the mines at Chapultepec, the trick, without hurting our people, only served to show the low resources to which the great army of Mexico was driven by a mere handful of brave men, led on by skilful and scientific officers.

CITY OF MEXICO, OCTOBER, 1847

A fortnight after getting into quarters, the dangers and hard ships of the battle-field were rarely recurred to, and all the great and stirring events that occurred since we reached this valley seemed to be gliding, among the actors, into the realms of oblivion. But we know that a great reacting swell will one day return here from our country and the world, and that the details so familiar, and trite even, on the field of action, will resound through the regions of all civilized nations. Few, however, I believe, think much, either of the past or future; the temptations of a great capital are daily unfolding themselves, and young and old join in the pursuit of pleasure.

The hospitals alone show that we came here on no holiday excursion; and many a good fellow, whose heart is panting for out door enjoyment, has to lie patiently on his rough couch, waiting for time and the doctor to repair his "shivered tim-bers." A good number of wounded died after reaching the hos-pitals, as much from previous exposure and frequent changes of place, as from the violence of their wounds. The fatality, indeed, caused many of the men to believe that the Mexicans had used poisoned weapons, but without sufficient reason, as the deaths bore no unusual proportion to the injuries inflicted, allowing for the circumstances.

It was extensively circulated and believed that the Mexicans used copper balls, with what truth I know not; but a canister shot I picked up at Chapultepec, and supposed to be copper, was in fact bell-metal, and was probably converted into its present use from motives of expediency or necessity on the part of the enemy, and not with the barbarous intent of inflicting poisonous wounds.

When not engaged in professional duties, which are still quite onerous, I have generally passed my time in search of a quiet abode, where, domesticated with a respectable family, I could cultivate the language, and gain an insight into the manners and customs of the people, as shown in private life. The search has been useless, however no resident family, of moderate respectability, appears to be willing to admit inmates upon anything like the footing of boarders.

I had at length to take to the *dernier ressort,* of "mine inn," where, with some friends, we enjoy a very pleasant, though somewhat expensive, mess, under the supervision of a taut and tidy French woman. We are living in hired quarters, near the barracks, and at some distance from the *fonda*; which last has not only the recommendation of a rosy-cheeked, bright-eyed landlady, balancing about on the meridian of eight-and-twenty, but it is remarkable for its cleanliness and the excellence of the table. If ever you come to Mexico, that you may find it without difficulty, proceed to Holy Ghost Street (*Calle del Espiritu Santo*), and look out for the *Bazaar de Grandes Muebles*; enter the clean and spacious court thereat, and ascend the broad stairway, at the head of which you will be met by Madame, all smiles, who, for the moderate sum of seven dollars a week, will give you daily breakfast and dinner, and a splendid one too, but you must pay as much more for lodgings, and trifling extras will triple the first charge. You cannot miss the place, as every shop almost in the street belongs to *El Espiritu Santo;* thus we have the Holy Spirit's Tailor Shop, (*Sastreria del Espiritu Santo ,*) The Holy Spirit's Shoemaker Shop, (*Zapateria del Espiritu Santo,*) &c., all in one vicinity.

Our people were much startled one fine morning not long since, by the occurrence of an earthquake of some violence, though by no means a first-rate specimen. Yet it was enough; many of us, including myself, were made deadly sea-sick, before we had time to imagine the cause of it. I did not believe my own senses, that the massive walls before me were in motion, but thought the apparent motion was owing to some unaccountable dizziness that had seized me, and that I was reeling, as was probably the case. But shouts of "Earthquake!" from the men, and the sight of hundreds of prostrate and kneeling Mexicans in the streets, soon explained the case.

The heaving of the earth made on me exactly such impression as is made by a heavy ground swell at sea; and many complained that it left upon them a *quasi* sea-sickness for several days. The city would probably have been levelled to the ground long before this, but that it stands on a soggy soil, that checks the vibrations of the earth, like the deadening of elasticity by a pith ball, suspended between those of ivory. I was told that upon the first shock, while the Mexicans ran out to pray, many of our troops ran instinctively to their arms.

General Quitman, the able and gallant commander of the volunteer division, was appointed by the commander-in-chief, civil and military governor of the city, very soon after our possession. Martial law prevails, and plunder and pillage, that some thought the lawful right of the victorious army, are most strictly forbidden. The regulation appears to me equally just and wise; just, because the city surrendered promptly and unconditionally, as soon as freed of the army that enslaved it; wise, because we have every reason to believe that had the troops been allowed to load themselves with plunder, it would have led to a great increase of immorality in the army, to the subversion of discipline, and probably enough to utter destruction.

The courage and bearing of the army are above all question; it has achieved more than wonders. During the late actions it caused a loss to the enemy, in killed, wounded, and prisoners taken, equal to its own complement at its fullest, that is, of between ten and eleven thousand persons, besides dispersing many times that number, in addition. Upon entering this city, of near 200,000 inhabitants, it probably numbered but little over 5000 duty men, for we had an immense number of sick, besides the killed, wounded, and missing. Wisdom and moderation were therefore eminently necessary, and both demanded that we should not exasperate the citizens by robbing them, on the one hand, nor receive among us the certain seeds of destruction on the other.

The conquering Spaniards, who preceded us here, three hundred years ago, were nearly brought to annihilation by their ill-gotten wealth; Hannibal lost Rome by the corruption sown in his army while revelling in the spoils of Italy; the wary Alexander led his Greeks to endless conquest by making a bonfire of their riches gained in war, first throwing in his own.

General Scott allowed no plunder, but he demanded of the authorities a moderate contribution of $150,000, to be paid in four instalments, of which sum he made the following humane distribution: "Seventy thousand dollars shall be appropriated to the purchase of extra comforts for the sick and wounded in hospitals; ninety thousand dollars to the purchase of blankets and shoes for gratuitous distribution among the rank and file of the army; and forty thousand dollars reserved for other necessary military purposes."

CITY OF MEXICO, OCTOBER, 1847

My rooms are now in the *Catte del Puente de Jesus* (Street of the Bridge of Jesus), and are comparatively very comfortable. We occupied hitherto, officers and men, quarters at the *Escuela Militar*, a recently evacuated military college, held, however, by regular troops during our approach to the city; we found it, like all other Mexican barracks, filthy in the extreme, and swarming with vermin. As the officers had not sufficient room, we left there, a portion of us, rejoicing, hiring our present rooms through the quartermaster. It is *malum prohibitum*, to occupy private quarters except by permission of the occupants or owners, who receive a fair rent.

This street, as many others, is called of the bridge, because, in former days, bridges and boats were required in nearly all parts of the city, and the name is retained, though the bridge has long since given way to a low, substantial pavement. Its sacred designation, which sounds so irreverent in our ears, is less so apparently, according to the Spanish pronunciation, *Haisoos*. The city was formerly very subject to inundations during the overflow of the neighbouring lakes; the immense drain, however, one of the most remarkable works of the kind in the world, now saves it from such inflictions; still, it stands on but a crust of made soil, and a hole dug anywhere to the depth of three or four feet, finds brackish water.

The drinking water is brought from a distance, (the nearest from Chapultepec,) by the aqueducts so often mentioned, that enter by Belen and San Cosme. There are abundant fountains in various parts of the city, supplied by the aqueducts; and a set of men (*aguadores*), water-carriers by profession, furnish families with the precious fluid, which they carry in huge earthen jars, suspended from the head by straps, and balanced, the larger one in front by the lesser between the shoulders. Two or three *clacos*, (eight *clacos* to the *real*, or 12½ cents,) will procure a day's supply.

Amusements are abundant now; more abundant, to my taste, than attractive. The city has five theatres,—the *Nacional*, for instance (lately *de Santa Anna*, but judiciously rechristened as his star was sinking), is among the first in the world, and only surpassed perhaps in size and magnificence by the Scala, at Milan, the San Carlos, at Naples, the Tacon, at Havana, and one or two others. There are now engaged fragments of various companies, Italian Opera, French, Spanish, and American actors, whose principal business is to amuse our army. I attended once or twice, but finding only a military audience, familiar faces, I determined to wait until the good people of the city chose to display there their handsome features.

Sunday is the great day for amusements; the theatre, circus (a company came with the army from the States), bull-fights, and other diversions, are in full operation. The Paseo, a beautiful drive, like an ancient race-course, straight for nearly a mile, shaded with young trees on both sides, with side-walks and stone seats, its bubbling fountains adorned with sculptured figures, is frequented daily by the wealthy residents, in coaches and on horseback. On Sunday, however, when the sun is disappearing in the western horizon, it is absolutely crowded, and is the best place for seeing the fair and fashionable of Mexico.

The Alameda, a beautiful park near the Paseo, is laid out in smooth walks diverging in rays from equidistant fountains; noble old trees shade the walks, and the intervening plots are of bright green grass, enamelled with shrubs and flowers. But walking is not fashionable in Mexico; so the Alameda is generally relinquished to the French *modistas* (dressmakers, &c.), and others, who are too poor to breathe the aristocratic dust of the Paseo from their coach windows.

From my engagements, I did not immediately look up my friends from San Augustin, but latterly have spent several pleasant evenings with them. The old gentleman is an oracle of Spanish and Mexican history. His favourite topic is, of course, the Peninsular war, in which he played a part in his fourth act of the seven ages. He is a widower, but his two sons with their families live in adjoining houses; they are very polite and gentlemanly, and their wives, no longer strangers, are refined and handsome women. Mexican ladies appear to live on *dulces* (sweetmeats), and this appears not only in the sweetness of their dispositions, but always on their evening tables. The mode is, to dine about five o'clock, then to drive to the Paseo, and upon the return, when it is quite dark, to take a course of *dulces* and chocolate. I was invited to one of these repasts a few evenings ago; there was a beautiful display of cut glass and silver, and sweetmeats enough for a regiment of Americans. There was a variety of fine wines and liqueurs, some sandwiches, imported cheese, bread, cakes, and the unfailing chocolate. I certainly never saw more beautiful sweetmeats, nor tasted finer; but my Virginia taste dwelt on the few substantiate present, and I punished most the Gralicia ham and the rich, fragrant *Xeres* (sherry) that flanked it. I knew my bearings with them. *La Señora* graced the head of the table.

Mexico has undergone somewhat the same external revolution as the other cities through which our army has passed. Thus, all public and prominent places are frequented by crowds of our country men; tavern and store signs announce American occupation; so that a stranger, let down among us without a knowledge of recent events, would be sadly puzzled to know into whose kingdom he had fallen.

The republican flag of the stars and stripes waves over the (once) vice-regal palace; the Anglo-Saxon tongue prevails therein; but without is a medley, in which a modified idiom of the Castilian predominates. Besides, the houses are all Spanish; the iron-grated windows are a sufficient proof of that; and a mongrel, motley race, swarming in the streets, make it plain that the town is not what we call American. These are the *leperos* (or *lazzaroni*, in Italy), a half-naked set of *mestizos*, with brown hides, blackened by dirt and sun, whose profession consists, sometimes, of a little honest labour, enough to eke out their gains by begging and robbery. They are probably the lowest people in the civilized world, with no ideas of decency or morality. Marriage is rarely practised among them, except *fuera de la iglesia,* or behind the church.

I have been told by an intelligent citizen, that for one couple married, a hundred live together without the ceremony. It is in sheer contempt of morals, for while considerable fees are paid to the church for the marriage of people in high life, the poor have but little to pay, and the very poor nothing. The marriages are truly *de convenance*; a man hires himself to a gentleman as porter, or other servant, marries one of the maids, and remains her faithful and attached husband until he changes his abode, and generally no longer. These worthy people, known as greasers among the Americans, constitute a large proportion of the citizens of this fair metropolis.

City of Mexico, November, 1847

On the 1st inst. (*Fiesta de todos los Santos*), a considerable train left here for the great depot at Vera Cruz, and with it many distinguished officers (including Major-General Quitman), who returned to the United States on account of impaired health, wounds, or for private reasons. When the numerous wagons, ambulances, travellers, soldiers, horse and foot, music, &c., were assembled in the grand *plaza*, and the line was seen forming, and extending, and slowly receding from the sight, and we bid *adieu* to the homeward bound, many a stout heart had to acknowledge the sinking that marks nostalgia, a disease that has no pathology, and yet that has proved so often fatal.

After a "last fond look," I turned to walk around the now half deserted, but never lonely *plaza*. It is a noble square, presenting perhaps a thousand feet on every side. On the north is the immense cathedral, with its walls highly ornamented with figures in stucco, carving, and gilding; its pilasters and towers, its domes and turrets, and its deep, rich, musical bells, whose full tones first rouse the drowsy citizens from their slumbers in the early watches of the morning, cheer at intervals their daily labours, and warn them of the hours of rest in the stillness of the night.

On the east is the palace, a long, unpretending edifice, much more republican in appearance than name; it occupies a square, fronting only on the *plaza*, and embraces at once the executive mansion, the halls of the legislature, the supreme court of justice, and, in rear, the mint. On the south and west are long portales, giving shelter to numerous small vendors, who plant their tables and stalls against the columns, while the rooms in rear, on the ground floor, rejoice generally in the gaudy ornaments of fancy stores.

The upper apartments are private dwellings. In the centre of the *plaza* stands the pedestal of what is to be a great triumphal column, which, when completed (if ever), will be unsurpassed in America. The design is to be seen in the print-shops. To complete the beauty of the *plaza*, four large fountains, throwing up lofty *jets d'eau,* are to be placed intermediate between the column and the angles.

On All Souls' Day, the tables in the portales were more than usually laden with toys for the children, but of an unusual kind, and commemorative of the occasion. Thus, the little ones were regaled with deaths' heads, and cross-bones, of sugar, tombs, monuments, urns, and other mementos of the destroyer that knows no mercy.

We find this climate somewhat overrated; we have had many days of raw, damp, cheerless weather, more disagreeable, and more injurious too, than a much greater degree of dry cold. During a spell of the former, in October, there was great mortality among chronic cases of disease; and wounds that had been doing well previously, broke out afresh, and in some cases proved fatal. Yet the general uniformity of the climate is so great, that, from all I can learn, that terrible scourge of the more varying regions of the North, tubercular phthisis, is here almost unknown.[1] The mean annual temperature of the *tierras frias*, upon which we stand, is given at 63° F., but there is considerable variation, as in winter there is sometimes frost, though rarely. There is no provision whatever made against cold, except in the thickness of the walls; fire-places and chimneys are unknown; but during a cold spell the *brasero* is introduced with a glowing fire of charcoal.

I took passage a few days ago, with some friends, in a *diligencia*, to the renowned village of Guadalupe, a place of no small note in Mexico, as the seat of the miraculous appearance of *Nuestra Señora* to a poor Indian, who was pursuing his lonely way over the rugged mountain. Every writer on Mexico gives the details as an item of the national history, so I shall only trouble you with the following outline, as currently stated in the country. *Nuestra Señora* showed herself to the Indian, gave him some instructions, and directed him to report what he saw and heard to the metropolitan bishop. In obedience to his instructions, he repaired to the bishop, who paid no attention to the account he gave; a second appearance and a second message met with the same incredulity and indifference. Our lady appeared a third time to the Indian, and directed him to gather some of the flowers at his feet (on a rugged rock, where not

---

1. There is perhaps no part of the world more free from tubercular consumption than the interior of Mexico.

GENERAL TWIGGS

even a blade of grass had ever been seen before), to wrap them in his coarse apron of ayate, and carry them to the bishop, with instructions as before.

The man obeyed faithfully, told the bishop what had occurred, and mentioned the wonderful growth of the flowers; when the bishop asked for them, the Indian unfolded his apron, when, instead of flowers, a painting of the blessed donor, of surpassing loveliness, was found on this rough canvass.

The bishop immediately erected a chapel in commemoration on the rock where the flowers were found. The first chapel, though not small, was soon found not capacious enough for the thousands of devout pilgrims who thronged to the shrine, so a magnificent cathedral and a spacious convent rose at the foot of the hill; and the obscure Guadalupe was elevated to the dignity of an episcopal see.

The cathedral church is among the handsomest I have ever seen; its proportions are vast, without being colossal, and though highly adorned, the ornaments are all in good taste, and well arranged. The church is extremely rich and abounds in the precious metals. A large balustrade, three feet high, of pure silver, encloses the grand altar, and extends on either side of a passage-way in the body of the church to the choir, a distance of perhaps forty feet. The wonderful painting is suspended over the grand altar. There are many paintings and models on the walls, deposited by pious persons, commemorating miraculous cures obtained (they say) through the intercession of *Nuestra Señora*.

On the hillside is a stone wall, built to resemble the sails of a ship, erected there by a Spaniard, in acknowledgement of her assistance in rescuing him from shipwreck. At the foot of the hill is a sacred fountain, muddy to the sight and disagreeable to the taste, but it has some medicinal properties, perhaps from containing salts of iron, and all pilgrims drink of it. A kind publican took us to his house; we ordered refreshments pretty freely, and we were not a little surprised when he refused all compensation. He was by birth a Corsican, but having resided in Philadelphia, he looked upon the United States as his adopted country. The bishop is said to be "an humble, simple-hearted old man, whose only pride and pleasure appeared to be that he was the familiar servant of *Nuestra Señora de Guadalupe*."

Having taken leave of our kind host, we hired a *coche*, and the driver, mounted as usual on the near mule, feeling elated perhaps at the prospect of an extra real from the lively *Americanos*, drove, or rode like mad, to the city, offering no chance to the gentle men of the road, who so often delay travellers outside of the city gates.

When General Quitman retired from the command, his division, which reflected honour on him as it received it from him, was distributed. The sturdy sons of Pennsylvania and New York were assigned to General Worth; the chivalrous Palmettos and the gallant Marines to General Twiggs.

CITY OF MEXICO, NOVEMBER, 1847

On Sunday I attended *misa mayor* (high mass), at the Cathedral, where one may generally hear some good music. This immense edifice is full of costly ornaments, though its riches are probably overrated. It is true, that before our arrival, many precious articles were removed for fear of pillage; and that the government has from time to time levied heavy contributions on the sacred ornaments of gold, silver, and precious stones, to fill the empty treasury (or the pockets of the *empleados*), so that former accounts, which were truthful in their day, perhaps, are not so now. The much-vaunted balustrade of gold alloyed with silver, does not contain one particle of either; or it belies its looks and smell, which savours more of the brazen serpent than of the golden calf. On the grand altar is an immense tabernacle of silver; but gilding, carving, and bronze, are much more abundant.

The first object presenting itself on entering the building is an enclosure for the musicians, between two immense organs, in the body of the church, each of which exceeds thirty feet in height. The next object is the high altar, surrounded by the famed balustrade, which, leaving a passage-way enclosed by it, connects the choir and sanctuary. There are between twenty and thirty altars in the church, ten, I think, on each side of the nave, shut out from it by handsome gilt open-work, so that they may be all seen, in succession, each altar being in a separate apartment or chapel. Withal, the Cathedral[1] is not attractive generally, because it lacks the air of neatness, tidiness, or comfort; there are no pews, and the rough wooden floor is neglected and dirty. Things are different at the church of the Profesa, where cleanliness and taste are conspicuous. That, and the church at the Convent of St. Francis, are the most frequented by the *ton* of Mexico; the cathedral is generally abandoned to the humbler classes, except on great occasions.

I may remark that the *padres* of the Profesa and San Francisco bear the best private characters of any of the regular clergy of this city; the former, I am inclined to believe, are allied to the Jesuits; who, though banished from Mexico, were perhaps the most exemplary labourers ever employed in this vineyard. It was for that reason, probably, that they were expelled. The Franciscans contested the palm with them especially upon the missionary field. Other orders were less successful.

The first missions of old California were formed in 1698, by the Jesuits. Under the management of these fathers, the savages had abandoned their wandering life. In the midst of arid rocks, of brushwood and bramble, they had cultivated little spots of ground, had built houses and erected chapels, when a decree banished them from Spanish dominions.

The governor who was to carry out the decree, expected to meet an army of their proselytes armed to defend them.

Far from this being the case, however, he beheld only venerable priests, with silver white hair, coming humbly forward to meet him. The Jesuits were accompanied to the place of their embarkation by the whole body of their parishioners, in the midst of sobs and exclamations of sorrow.

---

1. An exterior ornament of the cathedral, the great calendar stone of the Aztecs, attracts always the attention of the antiquary. The Aztecs, it is generally known, calculated time with more accuracy than the most enlightened nations among the ancients; this huge stone is therefore a relic of great interest.

The Franciscans succeeded them with success, but the Dominicans, who obtained the government of a portion of the missions—

.... either neglected, or managed them unskilfully" "The Franciscans, on the contrary, constitute the happiness of the Indians. Their simple dwellings have a most picturesque appearance. There are many of them concealed in the interior of the country, far from military posts; their safety is insured by the universal respect and love with which they are treated.—*Malte Brun.*

It would, perhaps, be difficult to explain why, when the Jesuits were expelled, many others were allowed to remain in quiet possession, who, without the energy, zeal, or learning of that famous order, were not free from their imputed faults. Common rumour has a great deal to say against the clergy of the present day, who are condemned indiscriminately by most travellers, and even their own countrymen speak of their faults and follies without reserve, though they say there are many good and exemplary men among them.

There is a well-known order here, once distinguished for practical charities, whose lives were spent in such duties as ransoming captives, traversing for this object the distant and hostile soil of the infidel and heathen; now, alas, unless belied, their lives, in this country, are as scandalous as once creditable to Christendom. In thus holding up the character of these *frailes*, it is with no intention of reflecting on the religion they profess, but do not practise. I do not propose to discuss the national faith of Mexico, but the national customs as they appear to me. The general character of the clergy, is a sufficient proof of what, to the American requires no proof that is, that the connexion of church and state is reciprocally detrimental. A church glutted with temporal riches, naturally attracts its host of office-seekers, whose hearts would be far from it, were not the treasure there.

One remark must, in justice, be made of the Mexican clergy—a remark made to me by an intelligent resident—the idle and bad are always most prominent to strangers; while the virtuous and conscientious quietly pursue their course unseen. The author of the *Year in Spain*, gives the following lively sketch of friars he had seen:

> Like the other hermits the hermano mayor wore a large garment of coarse brown cloth, girded round the middle with a rope, and having a hood for the head. The only covering of his feet consisted of a coarse shoe of half-tanned leather.

The dress, or a similar one, is common to many friars, but, "as he now stood before me, in addition to the effect of his apostolic garment, his complexion and his eye had a clearness that no one can conceive, who is not familiar with the aspect of those who have practised a long and rigid abstinence from animal food, and every exciting aliment. It gives a lustre, a spiritual intelligence, to the countenance that has something saint-like and divine; and the adventurous artist who would essay to trace the lineaments of his Saviour should seek a model in some convent of Trappists or Carthusians, or in the ethereal region of the desert of Cordova."—(*A Year in Spain.*) The author gives a most interesting account of a visit to a brotherhood at the place just mentioned, where the brethren, under the superior he describes, earn an humble and simple livelihood by faithful manual labour. I fear that worthy fraternity has no counterpart in Mexico.

CITY OF MEXICO, DECEMBER, 1847

On the 18th ultimo, we had the pleasure of receiving, for the first time, a mail, bringing letters from home. The dates were old, but having had no tidings whatever, since leaving Camp Vergara, on the beach, they were highly acceptable. You may conceive the happiness, and misery too, perhaps, diffused by the arrival of a large mail among such a number of people, so long from home; but after the first glow of pleasurable excitement, when the letters have been read and re-read until every little item of detail is familiar, there succeeds a melancholy reaction, because one feels his loneliness and desolation the more, as the home-scenes are now brought more vividly to his memory. Never in my wanderings do I feel a sadness more oppressive than that which follows even the most cheerful letters from the family circle.

I have lately been reading Madame Calderon's *Life in Mexico* a charming work, a little too highly coloured perhaps; but she was here under the most favourable circumstances, and if everything appeared to her "*couleur de rose*," it was the more pleasant for her self, and the more entertaining for her readers. I know an excellent couple here, who first met at the grand English ball mentioned in the work; the lady says Mrs. Calderon does great injustice to the fair sex of Mexico, and that such is the general sentiment, but my opinion is, that she has drawn a very fair picture indeed.

As I write, I have to stop my ears to shut out the stentorian bawling of a lusty beggar, who, planted across the way opposite my window, has kept up a ceaseless fire on the passers-by the entire morning; he invokes alms in the name of *Nuestra Señora de Guadalupe, por el nombre santissimo de Jesus,* and of all the saints in the calendar; and though his words are pious and respectful, his manner indicates that he has the will to take vengeance, *vi et armis,* on all who neglect to drop their mite into his ever-extended palm. His song is never the more agreeable for preserving always the same high pitch, without cadence or inflection.

This is the land where beggars and robbers are in the ascendant, par excellence. Madame Calderon says, and I have no doubt justly, that the *leperos* consider begging more reputable than service; the free prowling wolf, before the well-fed mastiff, with his chain and collar. As to robberies, great and small, they are perpetual; and most householders, upon retiring, have their loaded fire-arms at the head of the bed. Murder and robbery go frequently hand in hand, and this blighted country groans in the depths of social misery.

Wealthy proprietors, lords of immense estates, have told me they would sell all for enough to secure a most moderate income in other lands; but who will buy? They are, like the veriest serfs, chained to the soil; the rich man is doomed; now a prey to a rapacious government, now the victim of ferocious robbers, against whom the government gives him no protection. So great is the misery of the better classes, that many families are preparing to leave for ever a land, where, tantalized by the gifts of fortune, they have found nothing but dregs of bitterness. If you speak to a wealthy Mexican of peace, he shrugs his shoulders, and sighs. "In your happy country" he says, "you know and enjoy peace; here, alas! we know it not, nor can we hope to know it. Even now, overrun by a conquering army, we enjoy more tranquillity than under the government of our own factious rulers, when free from foreign war."

A friend and myself rode out some days ago to Chapultepec: it is a beautiful drive of three miles, and a favourite resort of the Mexicans when making a *fête champêtre*, or *dia de campo*. I have given you some accounts of the castle, which is remarkable, among other things, for offering from its roof one of the finest views in the world; but not to the building do the picnic parties repair; there is, at the base of the hill, a grove of surpassing magnificence; carpeted with luxuriant grass, and well provided with rustic benches. A venerable cypress, known to be at least four hundred years old, and that is still flourishing, attracts great attention; Montezuma himself has reposed in the shade (*sub tegmine-cupressi*) of its wide spread branches, and it now bears his name, "The Cypress of Montezuma."

> The trunk is forty-one feet in circumference, yet the height is so majestic, as to make even this enormous mass appear slender.—(Ward)

The castle was built by the Viceroy, *El Conde de Galves* (who gave name to Galveston), for a summer palace, but its site and strength drew upon him the suspicion of the Spanish government; and his palace was easily converted, by the latter, into a fortress. No despot could have wished a more elegant, or a more safe retreat.

Returning, in the evening, I had the pleasure of attending a *tertulia*, given by an English lady. It was a very agreeable little reunion, and gave the few Americans, who had the *entrée*, an opportunity of meeting *las Mexicanas* in company. The entertainment was very like ours, in the United States; we had music, dancing, and cards; the señoritas waltzed to perfection, and flirted their fans with the peculiar grace of the daughters of Spain. We had fine music, amateur and professional, songs in French, Spanish, and Italian, with piano accompaniment. It seems to be the custom for a performer to play for the singe; the lady rarely sits down at the piano to play her own accompaniments. The advantage of this is manifest, as it allows the freedom of attitude, and expansion of chest, necessary for a full development of the vocal powers.

The mammas chaperoned the daughters, and watched them, with the tender anxiety to be seen in all countries; while the more callous papas retired to an adjoining room, to enjoy, in peace, their cards and segars. They stuck to these like the sages immortalized by Mustapha in Salmagundi; heedless of gay music and the giddy waltz, they raised not their eyes from the hieroglyphic papers before them, until stimulated into a consciousness of animal life, by the diffused fragrance of generous wines. Then for a moment, they were very cheerful, until the talisman departed, when they relapsed gravely into the depths of their devotions.

Some of the girls were quite pretty, though there was less beauty than may be always seen among the same number at home. The mammas will pass, if they incline to corpulency, but otherwise the elderly, or middle-aged women of Mexico are far from handsome. When the dark brunette, charming perhaps in youth, has subsided into a dull yellow, and the once full face has become wrinkled and skinny, the last traces of beauty are more than effaced. But fair, fat, and forty, are not uncommon in Mexico; indeed, some of the fairest women I have ever seen are Mexicans, with eyes as bright, and as blue, as any from the north of the Rhine. Such beauties abound in Spain, among the fair daughters of the Goths, in provinces that remained free from Moorish dominion.

A *tertulia* in these days is not to be neglected, as the company assembles, if not reluctantly, at least in fear and trembling. The gentle *Mexicanas* fear equally the *ladrones* of their own country, and the American soldiery; and while they could find it in their hearts, doubtless, to smile a little upon the gallant invaders, prudential reasons keep them generally within a wall of reserve that our warrior beaux find harder to penetrate than were the massive stone walls of their mansions.

On the way home, in the small hours, I met a party of policemen having in charge the body of a man just murdered; a matter of small note in Mexico.

MEXICO, DECEMBER, 1847

I met in company, a few evenings since, a young Miss of pure Indian blood, who was reputed wealthy and accomplished. Her father, herself, and a boy, said to be a lineal descendant of Montezuma, are the only representatives of the aboriginal race I have met with, or heard of, in society. The Aztec features are far from handsome, at least when compared with the Caucasian, but the young lady, I have no doubt, would pass for a beauty in the celestial empire, except that her feet could not now be compressed into "golden lilies." Her cast of face was decidedly Chinese. A common origin may account for this, as in all probability the Aztecs; as well as other Indians of this continent, draw their descent from some branch or branches of the great Mongol race. As their origin, however, is a bone of contention among the philosophic inquirers into the history of the human race, I will venture no further remarks on that subject. The Indians, who come daily under observation, may be more properly discussed. Once lords of the soil, their highest offices now, as a general rule, are the menial tasks imposed by their present masters. They are not slaves, it is true, by law, and yet in condition and appearance, they appear inferior to the negroes of the Northern Republic. Throughout the United States, even in those where slavery is most unmitigated, every man of the coloured race has his stamp of individuality, and not a few, respectable consideration; while among these freemen, it is hard to estimate any one among them as other than an animal from the herd—rare, indeed, is it to see one, to whom you can attach the idea of an identity, that may raise him above, or distinguish him from, the lowliest of his unhappy brethren.

Humboldt estimated the number of Indian residents in the city at 33,000; which number has probably increased considerably, though a large proportion of those who may be seen daily in the streets are from the surrounding country. They come in in files, more than half naked, men and women, carrying heavy burdens on their backs, like so many pack-mules. The poor women carry, besides, in most cases, miserable little pledges, strapped to their shoulders, whose young faces have the gravity of premature age, looking as if conscious of their race's degradation. The Indians have continued to increase in population in spite of many inflictions of the three great scourges, war, pestilence, and famine. They have been visited at various times by the small-pox; and by a much more formidable disease, known among them as *matlazahuatl*, said to bear some resemblance to the black vomit, to which malady, however, they are but little subject. Humboldt quotes from Torquemada, that in 1545, the *matlazahuatl* carried off 800,000, and in 1576, the immense number of 2,000,000. He thinks, however, the fatality was overrated. The hard labour of the mines, for which their slight forms were little fitted, carried off a great many in the earlier days of Spanish rule; but a wiser policy corrected the evil by moderating and subdividing the labours.

Famine has, at times, proved very desolating, as the Indians—

.... naturally indolent, contented with the smallest quantity of food on which life can be supported, and living in a fine climate, merely cultivate as much maize, potatoes, or wheat, as is necessary for their own maintenance, or at most for the additional consumption of the adjacent towns and mines. The inhabitants of Mexico have increased in a greater ratio than the means of subsistence, and accordingly, whenever the crops fall short of the demand, or are damaged by drought, or other local causes, famine ensues.

With want of food comes disease, and these visitations, which are of not unfrequent occurrence, are very destructive.—(*Humboldt's Travels and Researches.*)

The same author remarks of the character of the Indians.

The men are grave, melancholy, and taciturn; forming a striking contrast to the negroes, who for this reason are preferred by the Indian women. Long habituated to slavery, they patiently suffer the privations to which they are frequently subjected; opposing to them only a degree of cunning, veiled under the appearance of apathy and stupidity. Although destitute of imagination, they are remarkable for the facility with which they acquire a knowledge of languages; and notwithstanding their usual taciturnity, they become loquacious and eloquent when excited by important occurrences.

It is by no means rare, now-a-days, to see them "excited" into loquaciousness, by nothing more important than *mescal* or pulque; whether eloquent, or not, is more than I am able to testify. The Indians generally are a peaceful and harmless class, without, apparently, any wish or hope to improve their condition. They regularly attend divine service, where their manner indicates genuine devotion; yet is said they have not entirely forgotten the gods of their fore fathers.

Mr. Bullock, in 1823, obtained leave to disinter the image of the goddess *Teoyaniqui*, of which he took casts, exciting the laughter or contempt of the whites, while the Indians looked on with feelings of reverential interest. They may have regarded it with a superstition transmitted from their ancestors, through a concealed traditionary current, or merely as a memento of the days of their national pride and glory.[1] Many of the remoter tribes from the city yet retain their native freedom, their fierceness, and their worship. Our army had even been threatened with the *Indios Bravos,* that is, the Apaches,

---

1. With the fall of their national pride fell their national crime of human sacrifices, a depravity, sufficient of itself to justify the conquest, even according to the views of this age.

CITY OF MEXICO, FROM THE CONVENT OF SAN COSME.

Lipans, and others, who, we were told, were to fall upon us in connexion with the regular troops of Mexico.

The broken-spirited sons of the soil in this vicinity, are measurably free from vices towards their white neighbours, but the ungainly descendants of the two races, the mestizos, combine the evil qualities of both, with little comparative improvement from the admixture of European blood. They constitute about one-fourth part of the population of the city; from them are taken generally domestic servants, &c., while they furnish too, the worthy fraternity of begging and robbing leperos. Mr. Brantz Mayer, of Baltimore, has given of these charming characters a most correct and lively picture in his entertaining work on Mexico, to which I can add nothing; but I have thought a quotation from Cervantes, in the *Year in Spain,* would apply to them admirably, by substituting for gipsies, *leperos,* thus:

> It would seem that the *leperos* were solely born into this world to fill the station of thieves. They are brought up among thieves; they study the profession of thieves; and finally end by becoming thieves, the most current and thorough-paced on the face of the earth.

Note.—The suspension of the onerous *alcabala,* or excise law, by order of the American authorities, was hailed with delight by the Indians who traffic with the city. The nature of the law is probably known to the reader. It is an odious tax on every species of barter and sale, from the transfer of a great estate down to the commonest necessaries of life sold in the markets. The poor Indians, who in some cases bring on their backs heavy loads of humble produce, from a distance of twenty or forty miles, or even more, are arrested at the city gates, obliged to deposit their burdens until they get a certificate at the custom-house of having paid the *alcabala.* Their patience is often abused both at the gates and the custom-house, they are rebuffed and delayed by the officials, and sometimes lose a whole day in buying permission to sell a few *reals* worth of marketing.

The *alcabala* is a legacy of old Spain; it was introduced there to defray the expenses of wars against the Moors; after the wars, how ever, it was found so very convenient in filling the royal coffers, that it obtained the honour of perpetuity. It was introduced in due time into Spanish America, and fell heaviest of course on the humblest classes. The Indians, who had suffered so long under the infliction, could scarcely believe their senses when they found "free trade" allowed them, *"Vivan los Americanos!"* they cried with enthusiasm *"Vivan los Americanos!"*

They seem to be out of the pale of the law, and are the terror of all good citizens. Yet they are not utterly intractable. Under the old Spanish *régime*, when the laws were sometimes well administered, even the leperos were brought into subjection; as, for instance, during the term of the Viceroy Revillagigedo, who, by a system of rigid justice, little tempered with mercy, conducted the ship of state better than was ever done before or since, either under monarchical or republican rule.

CITY OF MEXICO, DECEMBER, 1847

One evening last month, we had an entertainment at the *Teatro Nacional*, far surpassing the average there. It was on the occasion of Cañete's benefit; she is the presiding genius of the Spanish company in this city, and is really a most gifted woman. She has the versatility of Mrs. Fitzwilliam, who has afforded us so much amusement, but she is of a higher order of talent. On that night she took the leading parts in the *Gamin de Paris*, and *Loan of a Lover* (both in Spanish), and, without knowing a word of English, she had the tact to make the plays intelligible, by her inimitable manner.

The congregated thousands there (for the immense house was full to overflowing), gave long and loud shouts of approbation, and at the end, she came forth with a set speech of "tanks," in the prettiest English that was ever heard, though it was harder to be understood, I must say, than her pure Castilian. The Mexicans have no actors worthy the name; Italy, France, and Spain, however, make up the deficiency. Between the acts we were favoured with fine music by the orchestra; dancing by Gozze, a Spanish Celeste; and a variety in the diversion by the introduction of a troupe of Sable Harmonists, whose familiar songs were received with roars of applause. A few resident ladies appeared in the boxes, for the first time since our arrival. The theatre was highly adorned and brilliantly illuminated. On entering, the lofty pillars of the vestibule were seen dressed with lights and flowers, and beautiful transparencies, while two of the best bands of our army lent their attractions, giving forth rich strains to the open air.

We hear reports, every now and then, of insurrection, and no doubt such projects have been, and perhaps are still on foot; the annihilation of our army is, of course, the object intended: this we do not fear; but we have to beware of the midnight assassination of individuals or small parties; many stragglers have been already cut off, but commonly from their own reckless imprudence.

On Sunday, I heard a sermon at the convent church of San Augustin: it was a very good one; the padre recommended earnestly the practical virtues, and in his discourse, there was nothing to which the most thorough Protestant could object, except occasional appeals to *Nuestra Señora Santisima*. His manner was frank and sincere, utterly free from clap-trap, and that striving after effect which so often destroys the merit of the best composed sermons.

You want a general description of the city, which I cannot well give, formally, though I will try to throw into my letters, without much regard to system, such facts as I can gather, either from observation or books, where the latter do not run counter to the former. The learned and diligent Humboldt is the pioneer, in general science, of this country, and his immortal works the source from which most succeeding travellers have drawn their data. Nature has changed not at all, since his visit; and society, less, perhaps, than in any other country on the continent of America. Scientific knowledge was so limited in this country, and so little was known, that it remained for him even to settle the latitude and longitude of the capital; the maps were so inaccurate—

> . . . . that the inhabitants were thrown into consternation by the occurrence of a total eclipse of the sun, on the 21st of February, 1803; the almanacs, calculating from a false indication of the meridian, having announced it as scarcely visible.—(*Humboldt's Travels, &c.; Harper's F. L.*)

The city takes its name from the ancient war god *Mexitli* (alias *Huitzlipochtli*), though it was more commonly called, before the conquest, *Tenochtitlan*. It stands about in the centre of the remarkable valley, or basin, so often mentioned as formed by a mountain circle, which springs from the lofty plains of *Anahuac* (the great plateau, or table-land of the summit of the Cordillera). Looking in any direction from a point of elevation above the house-tops, this chain presents itself at a distance of from twenty to thirty miles, like a barrier cutting off communication with the surrounding world. Towards the southward and eastward, we have in perpetual view, forming part of the ridge, the ever snow-crowned Popocatapetl and Istaccihuatl, whose grandeur, like that of the boundless ocean, seems to preach of eternity. The eyes are never weary of resting on them, as they are ever sublime and ever beautiful.

The streets of the city are perfectly level, and as rectangular as those of Philadelphia. The houses are built of hewn stone of two kinds, a "porous amygdaloid, and a glassy felspar porphyry;" they are plastered, or painted, in light colours, and are uniform in their terraced roofs and iron balconies. Over the latter, when the sun is pouring down his ardent rays, are flung white or fancy-coloured awnings, screened behind which the fair *señoritas*, partially or entirely concealed, make their observations on the living current below. The effect of a long line of awnings, as down Plateros Street, &c., to the Alameda, half a dozen squares, is picturesque and beautiful. One of the peculiarities of the capital is, that the name of a street continues only with a square, to the annoyance and confusion of strangers. Suppose, for instance, Chestnut Street, in Philadelphia, were to be named after the Mexican style, we would have as many streets as squares, thus there would be State House Street, Hotel Street, &c., and enough throughout the city to confound even her own keen lawyers and sharp-scented police.

The ancient Mexico stood upon an island communicating by dikes with the main land. You remember the legend of its origin: that a few poor adventurers were directed by their oracle to locate a city where they should find an eagle resting on a nopal, and that the spot was found amidst the waters of Lake Tescoco. Here, in 1325, they fixed their residence, founding their humble city in the waves, like the Venetians, rather for protection from strong and hostile neighbours, than from deference to the oracle. When it grew to greatness, and fell into the power of the Spanish conquerors, they destroyed it, to build another on the same site. The waters of the lake, however, have receded, leaving the city on a crust of dry land. So infirm, however, are the foundations, that the cathedral has sunk, as have other buildings, as much as six feet. This, indeed, is not perceptible to the general observer. Lake Tescoco is now not less than seven or eight miles from the city, though during the season of rains the extensive inundations of the surrounding low grounds present still something of the appearance of former days. All the lakes of the valley are diminishing in size, and the surface of the soil once occupied by them, is whitened by a deposition of the salts of potash and lime, which form rapidly and unaccountably. Muriate of soda (common salt) is present in limited quantities, but in too impure a state to be introduced into use. The saline efflorescences cover, sometimes, large tracts, like a frost, hindering or destroying cultivation.

Mexico has, if not its "leaning tower," a church so inclined from the perpendicular, that it can no longer be used. It is a large and handsome edifice, *La Iglesia de Nuestra Señora de Loreto*, probably built upon piles, as the public buildings generally, but, shortly after completed, it was subjected to the trial of a severe earthquake, which left it in its present condition. It reminds one, for all the world, of a stout ship at sea, heeling to the breeze.

City of Mexico

When early in the night, before the hours of repose, you hear the gentle tinkling of a little bell approaching, you may go to your window to see the passage of the *viaticum*, or the host, on its way to be administered, for the last time, to some poor mortal about to pass into the realms of the hidden world. All the good people, on both sides of the street, light up their windows and fall on their knees until the *cortége* has passed; the throngs in the streets, removing their hats, fall on their knees and remain bowed to the earth while the host is passing. Not a sound is heard but the silvery tinkling of the warning bell, and a low, monotonous musical chant by the attendant train, singing mournful psalms, or the litany for the dying. The consecrated element is carried by a priest in an illuminated carriage; the attendants, dressed in white surplices, precede and follow the coach, bearing aloft lighted torches. The effect is very striking; from a general commotion, the buzz of many voices and the trampling of many feet, such as is always heard when night first begins to spread her mantle over a great city, the first notes of the bell are followed by a deathlike stillness, then all is hushed, the world scarcely seems to breathe, the approaching music falls on unbroken silence, and not a motion is made by the crowd until the last notes are flung back, echo-like, from the receding singers. Then a simultaneous rise takes place in the kneeling multitude, and the outdoor world resumes it tumultuous courses.

There are many beautiful church ceremonies in use in Mexico, but in many cases they are carried too far for American taste, particularly where (as is generally the case) we do not understand them. Sweeping charges are constantly brought against the clergy of the country, of overdoing the forms of religion, while neglecting its intrinsic essentials, and great abuses are said to exist, some of which are obvious.

An instance that I have noticed may be introduced here. In the cathedral, near one of the principal altars, are two tablets, informing the people, that by certain conditions, of assisting at masses, reciting prayers, or giving alms, they may redeem so many souls from purgatory: thus, one condition observed will relieve three souls, another six, another ten, &c.; making definite rates, not authorized, so far as I know, by the doctrines of the Catholic Church.

A greater abuse is, that though there are between forty and fifty convents in and about the city, of monks and nuns, that the education of the lower classes is so much neglected. Surely these brethren could not be better engaged than in diffusing freely the blessings of education. The convents are generally rich, and able to sustain free schools out of their revenues; the friars must be competent to teach; if not, so much greater is the shame for them. As it is, their influence is said to be constantly decreasing, as might naturally be supposed. The people of Mexico are thoroughly attached to their religion, although they speak freely of existing abuses. In this utilitarian age every man is called on to play an active part in life, in accordance with the spirit of the times. The wealth of the convents at this day must be much diminished by the constant demand on them from the government, which, by all accounts, is as plundering as the knights of the highway. With all the apparent influence of churchmen in this country, they have been constantly buffeted by revolutionary partisans, and plundered by *empleados*, until, under the general disorganization, they have become less free to act, either for good or evil, than in almost any Christian country in the world. Such at least is a statement made to me by one of the clergy.

The parish priests lead different lives from those in convents; the nature of their duties keeps them in more active occupation, and their general appearance is less forbidding. You know them by their costume: they do not wear cowls, or expose their tonsured crowns, but they wear broad-brimmed beavers, standing straight out, fore and aft, and curled up at the sides; a long black gown (cassock), and commonly shorts, knee and shoe-buckles, complete their ordinary dress.

It may not be interesting to recur so often to the clergy, but it can scarcely be avoided on account of the great space they occupy in the community; they number thousands in the city and its immediate vicinity.

On the 12th inst., I accompanied a party to Guadalupe. The anniversary of the appearance there of *Nuestra Señora,* was celebrated on that day with the most gorgeous ceremonies. The church is certainly the handsomest I ever saw, and the decorations for the occasion are beyond description. The principal altar was in a blaze of lights and jewels, and the vestments of the priests sparkled with gold and precious stones. The music corresponded with the ceremonies. The crowd was immense, to be numbered by tens of thousands; armies of Indians came on their annual pilgrimage to the shrine, and perhaps one-half of the citizens of the capital repair there during the day. At night, in town, many of the devotees of "Our Lady of Guadalupe" had her portrait at their balconies, surrounded by lights, while their houses were also illuminated.

I have paid several visits to the National Museum, which, by a liberal policy, is open every afternoon to the public, free of charge. It occupies a portion of the University, within a square of the palace, and contains some objects of general interest.

The first that strikes the eye upon entering the court, is the colossal equestrian statue of the unlucky Carlos IV., in bronze. It is the work of a native sculptor, Tolsa, who, it is said, died of mortification, when a radical defect was pointed out to him, that most observers pass unnoticed; that is, the absence of the excrescences, or figs, on the legs. The horse is about the size of a full-grown elephant the rider in proportion; and Humboldt says of the work, that in beauty and purity of style, it exceeds anything in Europe, except the Marcus Aurelius, at Rome. Another object of leading interest in the court, is a supposed sacrificial stone, used by the Aztecs, a large cylindrical stone, flat, or slightly rounded on top, with a groove from the centre to the circumference, which is considered a channel for the blood of the victims. The sides are deeply carved with hieroglyphic figures.

The conservator of the Museum, who is an antiquarian and a very intelligent man, says that it is not a sacrificial stone, but a calendar; that the Spaniards destroyed all but one of the former ever found, which was sent to Spain, where it remains. There is, however, a stone urn preserved, into which the Aztec priests threw the yet palpitating hearts of their human victims. There are numerous idols, utensils, instruments of music, &c., in good preservation, mementos of the age before the conquest. I took less interest in them, however, than in specimens of vegetable, mineralogical, and other natural products from various parts of this extensive republic. There are some models of mines, which are very interesting; the whole process of mining is shown in miniature. Sections of mines are shown where the puppet workmen are pursuing all their various duties, deep in the dark recesses of their subterranean world.

There are many specimens of stuffed birds, some beasts and reptiles; besides those of Mexican art, ancient and modern. The Indians (or *leperos*) excel in making wax figures, and at the Museum may be seen Lilliputian men and women, of all ranks and grades, from high *bon ton* down to squalid beggary. The figures are perfectly natural, and each appears in his proper costume and character,

CITY OF MEXICO, DECEMBER, 1847

A resident friend informed me a few days ago that his father-in-law had just sustained a loss of thirty thousand dollars' worth of effects, by robbery, on the highroad between Orizaba and Puebla. He had made purchases to that amount in Europe, and put them, on their arrival in this country, under charge of a hired escort. The latter fled at the first charge of the robbers;—whether in collusion with them, or not, is a matter of no small doubt. I have had my losses, too, in a small way; eleven of my twelve pocket-handkerchiefs, some of them handsome and costly, have mysteriously passed from my possession into the domains of greaserdom. I think, were it my misfortune to be a citizen of Mexico, I could almost- find it in my heart to colleague with the veteran *administrador* mentioned by Madame Calderon, who notified the government he would have to join the robbers in self-defence, as no other class of citizens obtained protection in their avocations.

Goods and produce from the country are generally brought in on the backs of mules and donkeys, wheeled vehicles being comparatively little used. The *arrieros*, or muleteers, on the highroad, are generally a jaunty set of chaps, decked out in tight-fitting short-jackets, pantaloons open from the knee down, the external seam made to open the whole length, and fastened down the sides by numerous close-set silver buttons; the boots of untanned leather, and the heels armed with massive and jingling iron spurs. The *sombrero* is a cone of felt or straw, with a broad brim, covered for the road with glazed canvass. A band of glittering tinsel encircles the hat; and near the crown, on either side, is a projecting ornament of silver. If mounted, the accoutrements are whip, sword, pistols; and carbine; an extra pair of leathern leggings, tanned with the hair on, hang from each side of the saddle-bow. The saddle and bridle are both profusely adorned with silver. These gentry are either Criollos, or the better class of half-breeds.

They offer a strong contrast to the poor Indians, bringing in their supplies from the surrounding country; these wear no ornaments, frequently not even the serape, or blanket, which is the daily mantle and nightly covering of the *leperos*; but they trudge after their laden donkeys, carrying no other weapon than a staff, which they use as a goad, while very commonly on their own shoulders is strapped a weighty pannier, which may contain, and often does, the third of a donkey's load.

Countrywomen, who enjoy a few rays of the sunshine of prosperity, come mounted on donkeys, their nether limbs either within, or hanging down in front of the panniers; they wear the broad-brimmed *sombrero* of the *arrieros*. Speaking of costume, I may here remark, that of each class is distinctive; the low women of the city have no other tog for every-day wear than a chemise, and a petticoat of the shortest; a *rebozo* on the head (a long, coloured scarf), with which they conceal their full bronze busts when convenient—for they throw them open without ceremony—and a pair of slippers on their feet. The very poorest dispense with all but the petticoat; none wear bonnets, high or low. The ladies wear on their heads rich silk shawls, fastened under the chin when in the street, though in most other respects they dress *à la Française*. The gentlemen dress as we do, except that in the saddle it is *de règle* to wear a short jacket and broad-brimmed hat.

Some disorderly Mexicans were sentenced, not long since, by an American military commission, in perpetual session, to the whole some old-time correction recommended by the wisest of men for unruly children,—great was the indignation in greaserdom, and a forcible rescue was threatened, if the Americans would dare to carry this sentence into execution. When the time came, some thousands of the motley tribe collected about the grand *plaza*, for a rescue, if their hearts failed them not; or at least, to offer groans and tears of sympathy. As the work commenced, showers of stones fell on the American guards, who charged on the valiant assailants, took some of the leaders, who now get their deserts in weekly instalments of the very currency they were trying to put out of circulation. The better citizens are delighted; they say nothing short of hanging could have subdued the whole legion of evil-doers so promptly.

This month, like our April, has been blowing hot, and blowing cold, alternately; it has, however, been unusually cold for the climate. Roses generally bloom the year round, and early in the month, they were plenty; not so now:—in open grounds there are none, though the weather is of that genial warmth described by travellers as perennial in Mexico. I went some days ago to the botanical garden in rear of the palace. It is small, and not very attractive,—a single rose, the last of winter, was "all blooming alone" which the gardener gave me. He said that the *leperos* had broken in and destroyed many fine flowers, vases, &c., when the city was surrendered. A lofty summer-house, overgrown with dense foliage, stands over a bubbling fountain surrounded with rare flowers; it must be a delicious retreat during the heats of summer, as the rays of the sun find no entrance there.

Respectable Mexican families are opening their houses slowly and cautiously, to American officers; acquaintance is extended by a process of induction,—thus, having the *entrée* at one house, the friends and relations invite you to theirs, and sometimes, are even polite enough to call for you in their coaches. They do not venture upon this, however, during the broad light of day; an execrable system of espionage, equal to that of Fouché, but entirely destitute of legitimate aim, keeps a check on all social movement in Mexico, not only towards strangers, but among each other. General society, from all I can learn, is scarcely known—a few families, related or connected, form their little circle which they rarely leave, unless for some formal visit of etiquette.

General Scott has got out of the good graces of the fair sex, by rejecting the petition of numerous ladies in favour of the *San Patricio* prisoners (deserters from our army). Reasoning after the fashion of women, from the heart, they think it very cruel indeed to keep the *pobres* in irons, &c., now that our arms are so completely triumphant. They want to draw a parallel between General Tyler and General Escott (as they call them); they think the former, who, they say, is beloved by the whole Mexican nation, would not have been deaf to their prayers.

On Christmas day, I went first to the Cathedral, where a full orchestra lent its aid to the immense organs and the singers; finding myself rather late there, I repaired to the beautiful church of *La Profesa*, where I found a scenic representation of the stable at Bethlehem. The divine child lay in his manger, and besides his parents, the humble apartment was shared between the admiring shepherds and dumb brutes gazing listlessly at their unwonted company. The spectacle presented nothing trivial far from it, indeed—it was an impressive lesson for the learned and the unlearned. I had intended witnessing the *Misa de Gallo,* or midnight mass, at the Cathedral, but a social evening with a brother in arms (scalpels and catlings), at the custom-house, drove it from my mind.

Christmas night I ate *dulces*, sipped chocolate, and drank bumpers in pure old *Xeres*, with a pleasant Mexican family, on my proposition, to the fair *Mexicanas*, on theirs, to *las Americanas* (God bless them!), and then, perhaps, to ourselves. The gentry of this country are very temperate, rarely exceeding the bounds of moderation. The evening passed off pleasantly with music, conversation, and segars.

CITY OF MEXICO, JANUARY, 1848

There are a great many blind beggars in this city, and deformed ones too, high authority to the contrary notwithstanding. We hear frequently of artificial deformity, induced permanently, or temporarily, by the beggars themselves; and terrible stories of mothers destroying the eyes of their children to insure their claims on public sympathy. Putting out their eyes is merely furnishing the youngsters with a sufficient amount of capital to drive a successful business in their future career. I know not how far to believe these accounts, but the multitude of beggars show that the profession is in favour; they seem to understand that the world owes them a living, which they are determined to have. Their name is legion they must, therefore, be a heavy burden on the productive classes.

Fortunately, (?) the necessaries of life are cheap; *tortillas* (corn-cakes) and *frijoles* (beans) cost almost nothing, and these, with a little Chilli pepper and a glass of strong pulque, are luxuries enough for a beggar's palate. At nearly every street corner, some dirty old woman has her table and her *brasero*, from which she will furnish an ample meal, including even a stew of beef and Chilli, piping hot, for half a dozen *clacoes* (nine cents). Furnishing their garments does not enrich the tailors much; an excuse for a pair of breeches, reaching to the knees, and a serape worn gracefully over the shoulders, make a fair average of costume— sometimes additional gear is worn, and just as often, the serape, or the breeches, dispensed with. Warm clothes are little needed, but some primitive garment, an improvement on the fig-leaf, is always preserved for decency's sake.

There was great commotion among the rabble when our army was approaching the city. Santa Anna had his recruiting parties out, who, asking no questions, pressed every young fellow they caught from home, who had no protecting influence. People could not even send their servants out of their houses. At the house of one of my friends, it was indispensable to send to the post-office, and the expedient hit on, was to send a man disguised in women's clothes, at dusk. He took his letter safely, and was returning, when some vagrant pursued with no good designs the unprotected woman.

he, of course, was coy in the extreme, admitted no familiarities, but virtuously took to flight. Her unaccustomed garments, however, impeded her motions, so she was soon in the possession of the amorous assailant. Great was his surprise when he found a lusty man in his arms—but here was a mystery, the police was called, and the doubtful character committed to prison. The poor fellow was scared out of his wits, and his life was threatened, because it was clear to everybody, without further evidence, that a person so disguised, must be an American spy. He protested, but in vain; his mistress was a foreigner, his master also (a distinguished French architect, an accomplished and hospitable gentleman), who was absent from the city, and there was no one able or willing to save him from punishment. Next morning he made his condition known to his mistress, who with great difficulty obtained his release.

Balls and parties are got up nightly for the special benefit of the army. Gay music may be heard in various sections of the city, and dashing couples may be seen through the open windows, whirling gracefully in the giddy waltz. That the ladies are all of the first respectability may be learned from the newspaper advertisements, which announce, very decidedly, that no others will be admitted. But they have queer ways for real ladies. The most pretending and exclusive of the public balls, are given at an ex-convent in Belemitas Street, where the French *modistas* enjoy undivided sway. Every Sunday evening they congregate there with their beaux, who, like themselves, escape from the trammels of the shop to figure upon this field of social elegance. Now the ladies, with more taste than discretion, began to despise their familiar faces, when *Messieurs les jeunes officiers Americains* appeared on the boards, and being aware of the great prowess and daring gallantry of the latter, surrendered to them unconditionally, after a very trifling resistance indeed. This was right enough, to be sure, but their devoted knights of times past were not pleased; so they made a renewed attack on the fair deserters, not with martial arms, nor even with the arrows of Cupid, but with ill-natured soubriquets, which have fallen among the ladies like so many hand-grenades. A tall slender lady, for instance, will live and die, Palo Alto; a short, thickset lady, her dearest friend, Cerro Gordo; and others, Contreras, Churubusco, and so forth, from some real or fancied analogy between their characters or appearance, and the fields of American victories.

Being desirous of learning the art of making money (an art that has always been a sealed book to me), I repaired some days ago to the mint, with a friend, where we were politely shown the whole process—though I have not yet reaped any practical advantage from my information. However, we saw everything, from the massive shapeless ingots of silver, down to the bright, finished dollar. The silver, a little alloyed with copper, is first run through a furnace, then passed through a machine for making strips of proper breadth and thickness; a circular punch takes out the size of the dollar, and the round, black-looking piece is then submitted to an instrument for marking the edges. A polishing process follows, then the last act is completed by the stamp. The dollars are turned out with great rapidity, though the entire machinery is worked by hand. The pieces are often weighed during the progress, to see that they preserve the standard. In another apartment, they were coining gold from black sheets that might readily have passed unnoticed for so much copper.

The mint is under the same roof as the palace; but the work is carried on by private enterprise. We were informed that improved machinery had been ordered from England which has not yet arrived.

We have had considerable reinforcements in the last few weeks under Generals Butler, Patterson, and Gushing—the famous Colonel Hays, with his Texas Rangers, accompanied General Patterson. Some troops have been assigned to towns further in the interior; our own battalion remains with General Persifer P. Smith, governor of the city, since the departure of General Quitman. Governor Smith, in wisdom, equals General Smith in valour, which is saying a great deal.

There is extensive sickness throughout the troops quartered in the city; fevers abound, and they assume a low typhoid type, difficult to manage, except in good constitutions. We have our vicissitudes of weather; some three weeks of summer, and one of winter during the month, when the raw, keen winds descend upon us from the mountains. The men are, besides, considerably crowded in their apartments, which is particularly trying to those who have spent their lives at home in open fields, in the pursuits of agriculture.

General Smith has established a military police of 400 select men from the army; that he has established at the palace, and in four different sections of the city. My two messmates have been assigned to the command of two of the companies, thus breaking up my domestic arrangements, for the good of the service. The arrangement is admirable: small parties, well armed, patrol all parts of the city every nigh; and marauders, Mexican or American, are seized and committed for trial, so promptly, that we begin to hope for a change equal to that effected by Tacon, in Havana.

CITY OF MEXICO, JANUARY, 1848

I spend, perhaps, on an average, two evenings a week in social intercourse with resident families. Every polite head of a family puts his house at your disposal, and everything therein; his house is the *casa de usted,* but that is a mere form, and not to be understood as an invitation, unless accompanied by a manner of undoubted earnestness. When you make an informal call, a cup of chocolate may be handed, with a bit of bread or cake, after which mama takes out her little case of paper segars, hands it to you and the elders around her, and then commences a round of smoking little interrupted until the time comes for taking leave.

The *Niñas* (as the daughters are affectionately styled in the family circle), do not join the smokers, so that the fashion, for ladies, appears to be going out with the rising generation. Some little games of fortune-telling, &c., are introduced for the young folks, while the old look on with approbation. The manners of the children towards their parents are free, yet respectful, and neither seem to impose restraint on the other. The family circle, for a stranger, is rather dull, generally, except where music is introduced, as, by the way, it very commonly is. The *muchachos* and *muchachas* (boys and girls), are both better instructed in accomplishments than in practical knowledge; the education of the girls is particularly defective. Music, in many families, is highly cultivated by both sexes; drawing and painting among the boys, and embroidery among the girls, have also many proficients; but, when it comes to waltzing and dancing, there is no limitation; young and old, grave and gay, seem to waltz by intuition; and the American, with his utilitarian views, who has devoted his life to filling his head with such stuff as grammar, geography, and arithmetic, to putting steam in traces, and writing his letters in lightning, all at the expense of his heels, is a *sujeto mui mal instruido*, indeed.

The ladies have a very limited fund of conversation, when the topic of music is exhausted; they do ask numerous questions concerning the manners, customs, and appearance of their sex in the United States, giving, at times, some very slight hints of their own superiority. They have generally very small feet and hands, of which they are exceedingly proud, and, with something of a triumphant air, they mention having heard that our ladies are not remarkable in this particular. I declare that ours are so many Cinderellas, at which they look very incredulous. Nothing from the States amuses them so much as the accounts of Tom Thumb; an *hombre tan chiquitito*, as to be compared with the *dedo pulgar*, (thumb,) and yet so well made and rational, and a general too! The idea is enchanting. I have described him a hundred times (without ever having seen him), and the interest he excites is universal. The ladies have all heard of him; and if Mr. Polk wants to send a lion here as commissioner, Tom Thumb would be the man, as better known than any statesman in America. Then the señoritas are so crazy to see him!

When a sufficient company is in the house for a little dance, the couples are on the floor immediately; the piano is put in requisition, and off they go. The old folks probably sit down to a game of *tresillo*, which finds the favour here that whist does in English society, while it appears to exercise equally the memory and judgement. At times the betting is pretty free, and *pesos* (dollars), change hands with some rapidity. This is the smallest scale of Mexican gaming. The youngsters are much more innocently engaged in music and dancing. Now and then some fair damsel is called to the piano for a song, and you are surprised with a beautiful piece of music from an Italian opera, in which even the original language is preserved. Other voices, male and female, are generally ready to strike in at the chorus. If any laughing, bright-eyed Andalusian is present, she will favour the company with some of the lively *chansonnettes* of her native land; a portion of Spain where an almost French vivacity predominates greatly over the proverbial gravity of Spaniards.

Spanish residents consider themselves generally far superior to the Mexicans, and with this much reason, that they have had the advantage of a residence in two worlds. The Mexicans yet look upon Spain with a reverence she has long ceased to obtain from any other part of the world; at the same time, between the two classes, there is little love lost. The Spaniards hold the Mexicans in contempt, while the latter regard the former with feelings of jealousy and distrust. They are known in Mexico by the soubriquet of *Gachupines*. The feeling, which was once very bitter, is now, however, little more than a reminiscence, or a theory; the parties visit, and intermarry freely.

I was quite entertained a few evenings since by a conversation between an old lady, who had never been out of hearing of the cathedral bells, and an American officer; she was curious to be in formed of his travels, and her questions made a very sufficient expose of her attainments in geography. Among other things, she wished to know what was the principal town of New Orleans; and whether he had ever been in Spain or France.

"I have never been in Europe" he said.

"Yes, but in France?" said the old lady, inquiringly, when he repeated his remark, and she her question. The gentleman looked considerably puzzled—must he explain to her that France is in Europe? However, the husband came to the rescue—he saw his wife was asking very foolish questions, and abruptly turned the conversation. I do not think the old lady could have misunderstood him; more likely, in her mind fair

España, with the great nations of Andalusia, Castilla, Gralicia, &c., was a convertible term with Europe. This was an extreme case, doubtless, but probably not a solitary one.

Per contra, I may mention having met with a young married lady, Mexican born, whose acquaintance with the affairs of modern Europe was very accurate and extensive; she was versed in the better kind of French literature, and was withal highly educated. I was very much surprised, but learned on inquiry, that her parents, who are of the *ricos hombres*, millionaires, of Mexico, had spared neither pains nor expense to procure for their children the first masters. This, then, is another extreme case. I have been much gratified, in the social circles of Mexico, in observing the filial respect of children to their parents—the fond attachment of the elders is rewarded by the devotion of the juniors—a trait that is sure to enlist respect and good-will wherever seen.

A Mexican gentleman never completes his education in Mexico; he travels on the continent of Europe, and occasionally in England or the United States, after a collegiate course, partial or complete, in Spain or France. Such persons consequently have much more liberal and enlightened views than the mass of their countrymen. The study of the French and English languages is becoming much attended to by the rising generation of both sexes; accomplished French teachers are not scarce, females particularly, though there are perhaps not two competent teachers of English in Mexico.

Now and then, I drop in at some of the shops kept by women, and make a small purchase the pretext for a long talk. 'they are habitually shrewd, and frequently intelligent. Some of them, indeed, read much more than their superiors in the social scale. I found one reading a French *Télémaque*, without instruction. I assisted her a little, which gave her an exalted idea of my scholarship, and led her to express her views pretty freely on history, politics, languages, Mexican character, religion, &c. She repelled indignantly a remark I quoted from a Spaniard, that the *ladrones* made offerings to their patron saints to give them success in their unlawful excursions; she said, they were bad enough for anything, but not such fools as that implied. Her religious toleration far exceeded my expectations; she thought God alone could judge for the fate of Catholic or Protestant, Jew or Gentile; and that men are only responsible according to the lights given to them.

City of Mexico, February, 1848

I have made a valuable acquaintance in the person of a gentleman of the city, who completed his education in England. Being an exceedingly well-informed man, his society is particularly desirable. He expressed an anxiety to keep up his acquaintance with our language, while I am equally desirous of mastering his; so we resolved to lend each other a hand, and the result is highly gratifying. For some time back my attention had been captivated by large street bills, announcing for sale *"Historia de la Conquista de Mejico, por Don Guillermo Prescott,"* which I had determined to read; and I was much pleased upon learning that Don R. had a copy in his possession, translated by his personal friend, Don Lucas Alaman. We went to work with a right good will; I read the portion for the evening to Don R. (in his parlour), who corrects my pronunciation, after which he takes the book, and renders the Spanish into good English; then in comes a hissing tea-kettle, and my friend, who learned other things in England beside the idiom, brews a hot gin toddy, and offers wine, cordial, chocolate, or other beverage, according to circumstances.

La Señorita (young married ladies in Mexico, scarcely old ones indeed, like the more formal *Señora*, Mrs., or Madam) gives us her company and conversation for half an hour, smokes a paper segar or two, while Don R. and myself demolish each a *puro*; then she leaves the field for us to resume our duties. Don R. gives me some well-written book of simple style from his library, as *Chesterfield's Letters*, which I render into Spanish, after a fashion, though he is polite enough to say I do it remarkably well.

These sessions we have on stated evenings; between ten and eleven, I buckle on my armour for the long, lonely walk homeward. The same precautions are always reiterated, "Beware of the *ladrones*; keep in the middle of the streets; give a wide berth to the corners" &c.; all of which goes to show the miserable state of this great city, where honest people dare not walk at night, without the fear of being sprung upon by robbers from behind every dark recess or corner. With a sword and revolver, however, an American may pursue his way in peace. I always carry them at night, but have never had occasion to use either. These valiant assassins, who are so familiar with "cold iron," have the most holy horror of firearms, which few of them know how to use. They suppose all American officers provided with, and ready to use them, which is probably the reason we pass unmolested.

This *Señor* Prescott's work is one of intense interest, read in any country; you may suppose how much it is enhanced here, where one may look out from his windows upon hills and valleys immortalized by the scenes our gifted countryman describes so vividly. I this day read his thrilling account of the *noche triste*, when Cortes and his adventurous little band made their retreat to Tacuba (which I visited a few days ago). They pushed on rapidly, but mournfully, for the friendly soil of their Tlaxcalan allies, taking some slight repose at a temple, a few miles beyond Tacuba, on an elevation where now stands (plainly visible from my position) the church of *Nuestra Señora de los Remedios*. Cortes' victory over the Aztecs at Otumba is an instance of truth surpassing fiction. Brave and adventurous was this warrior always; wonderful in prosperity, but in adversity superhuman.

Tacuba is now a miserable hamlet, distinguished only for its history; a very antique church, said to have been founded by the conqueror, is the most noticeable object to a stranger. The route we took (a small party of officers) led us by Alvarado's Leap and the causeway, through a region so densely populated, for the first four miles, after passing through the *garita* (of San Cosme), as to appear a continuation of the city. On either side were low, rich fields, covered by the lake in the days of the conquest, now reclaimed, and in a high state of cultivation.

From Tacuba we proceeded to the Carmelite convent of San Joaquin (pronounced *walk in*), where we were politely received by the friars, and shown around their ample grounds and gardens. We took a roundabout course homeward, riding over a desert to Molino del Rey, having passed for several miles but a single mansion (*Hacienda de los Morales*), which was surrounded by its vineyards (*maguey* plant). We then returned by Chapultepec to the city. Comparing my own observations with Mr. Prescott's descriptions, I cannot but be astonished at the accuracy of the latter, the more wonderful when we remember they are from the pen of a, student, who, thousands of miles distant from the scenes he paints so truly, cannot even enjoy the sight of those around him. His is a striking instance of genius prevailing over misfortune. Intelligent Mexicans hold his name in sincere and hearty veneration.

Living in this city, in high life, appears to be an expensive business, averaging in families addicted to style, from ten to twenty thousand dollars *per annum*. This great expenditure does not reach as far as with us, on account of the high prices paid here for all luxuries. My informant, a Spanish resident merchant, told me that, in some cases, four or five thousand dollars are consumed annually in keeping up coaches, horses, mules, and servants. It is a matter of pride and rivalry to keep a variety of elegant coaches, which are bought at an enormous price, kept in repair at rates unknown among our mechanics, and taxed beyond credence. Mexican horses are never driven; either mules, that bring some five hundred dollars a pair when well broken, or *frisones*, northern horses that sometimes bring a thousand dollars each, are used by the gentry.

The horde of servants retained in wealthy families should scarcely be reckoned among luxuries; they might be better classed as necessary nuisances. Rents, taxes, furniture, dress, theatre, &c., run up the remaining expenses. The hotels are very expensive, and not the most comfortable; a number of the officers have associated themselves into a very pleasant society, under the title of the Aztec Club, where good cheer may be had by members at moderate rates, and good company for nothing. There is perhaps as much comfort at the club as in the princely mansions of the wealthiest Mexicans.

By invitation, I rode some days ago with a Spanish resident to visit a cotton factory belonging to an English manufacturer, on the banks of the river Contreras, beyond San Angel. The proprietor, who married in this country, entertained us with true English hospitality. In the fastnesses of Mexico he adheres to his ale, and his old port, that he brought out in profusion, and though we were too early for dinner, about two o'clock, he had a collation set consisting of various dishes, piping hot from the kitchen; among others some boiled ham, of his own curing, very like ours of Virginia. He gave us, in fact, little time, to look at the works, which are plied by native operatives. The machinery was, for the most part, from the United States (Patterson, New Jersey); some of the looms, &c., however, were English and French. He informed me that he obtains his raw cotton from New Orleans, which stands him, at his factory, about five times the original cost. While we were at his house a number of Mexicans passed, carrying loads of fire-arms, which they had found and concealed after the battles. It gave our host great uneasiness, as he said numerous murders were committed in the neighbourhood every Sunday and feast-day. We accompanied him to the nearest *alcalde*, or judge, a slip-shod half-breed, who had courage enough to arrest the party carrying arms, of which he relieved them.

Our English friend told us he did this at the risk of his life, and that he himself had incurred a great risk in giving information. The judge kept a small shop, and offered us some mescal, the alcoholic product of the maguey. It resembles Irish whiskey. Taking leave, we returned through San Angel and the antique Coyoacan, where Cortes desired his remains should repose, thence through a most picturesque country, to the city.

CITY OF MEXICO, MARCH, 1848

Upon a single occasion, I was led by curiosity to the *Plaza de Toros*, where a grand *funcion* (every diversion here is a *funcion*) was announced for the opening of the season. I cannot say that I was disappointed, inasmuch as my tastes were not likely to be gratified there; I went to see a national diversion, once called the "gentlest pastime" of Spain, and which has for so many centuries maintained unrivalled popularity among the people of that country, and the wide-spread nations acknowledging that origin. We had a poor entertainment; half a dozen bulls were successively let in, worried unwillingly to combat, and soon despatched by the hands of the *Matador*. My sympathies, little roused, inclined to the bulls.

The building for the purpose is a large amphitheatre; the vast open space of the centre is enclosed by a circle of sheds, of two or three tiers, for the spectators. The division of seats is for the "sunny-side" and the "shady side;" the latter, of course, belonging to the aristocracy. A full band of music amused the spectators, until everything was in readiness; when, at a proper signal, the first bull was let into the arena, whose ferocity was confined to attempts to clear the barrier, and make his escape. Worried, however, by the *banderilleros*, a set of attendants armed with sharp arrow-like goads, ornamented with rosettes and streamers of ribands, which they discharged upon his neck and shoulders, where they hung suspended, floating in the air, he turned on his tormentors, rushed at a *picador* (one of the mounted assailants), and lifting horse and rider on his horns, threw them over a low barrier into a smaller ring, intended for circus feats; the horse would have been killed, but that the points of the enraged animal's horns had been sawed off (to the indignation of the spectators), so as to prevent his goring.

The attendants, or functionaries, wore rich, tight-fitting dresses, highly adorned, and on their shoulders light scarlet mantles, for the purpose of enraging the bull. The dress of the *matador* was of rich silk, splendidly embroidered with gold and silver. This gentleman is a character of no small importance in his own estimation, and that of numerous admirers. There were no ladies present—but few women, and they of the lowest.

The circus company that came with the army, has not been

very well supported. I made one call there for the purpose of seeing the theatre occupied by them, which before the building of the *Nacional,* was considered a fine establishment. It is now deserted, for its more showy rival, except by inferior companies of native artists, and those who look for cheap entertainments.

I have had no gratification in the way of sight-seeing in Mexico, equal to the panoramic view from the lofty towers of the cathedral. Ascending, you pass through the ample apartments of the bell-ringer's family above the roof, and immediately under the belfry. The eye, from the latter, ranges over the proud city, looking down upon its domes and terraced roofs, over the beautiful valley, dotted with its lakes and mountains, fields, chapels, villages, and castles. On the plain, beyond the gate of San Lazaro, may be seen at times, a body of troops going through their division drill, with the accompaniments of dragoons and flying artillery, resembling, in the distance, a puppet show; crowds of pygmy people, pygmy coaches, horses, *padres,* soldiers, water-carriers, women, children, Indians, donkeys, fill the streets and *plaza,* reminding you by their motions, of the shifting machinery used by artists, to serve up precisely similar scenes.

On the 8th inst., I was reminded that Lent had set in, by seeing crowds of persons, generally females, returning to their homes with the cross, of ashes, on their foreheads. It was Ash Wednesday. For a week previous, the city had been enjoying the carnival, with less display, however, than under other circumstances. There were some masquerades, public and low, and private and respectable. From my windows, I witnessed a private one across the way; the masks wore a great variety of costumes, and the scene, with the gay music and dancing, was quite attractive. The shops were perfect museums of *disfraces;* full-rigged figures, like actors representing various ages, stood arrayed, ready to give up their spoils to players, not, like themselves, dummies. *Vive la bagetelle!*

I have two Spanish works on my table of great interest; one, a poem of the first order, *El Moro exposito, o Cordoba y Burgos,* by Don Angel de Saavedra, which is highly recommended to me as containing lofty sentiment, in pure language, without any of the bombast in which Spanish poets indulge so freely; the other, *El Liceo Mejicano* a spirited literary periodical, that enjoyed a few years of existence in this city. I borrowed it for the purpose of reading the histories of the viceroys, published in a series of articles embracing a great portion of the Mexican history of their times.

The first viceroy, Mendoza, introduced copper coin for general circulation, which the Indians of his day resolutely refused to receive for their commodities. They scorned so base a circulating medium. By rigid laws, however, they were forced to receive it, which they appeared to do cheerfully. All of a sudden it was observed that not a coin of that metal was to be found. The Indians, by concert, had collected all that was to be had, and thrown it into the lakes. A small silver coin (*cuartillo*), equal to two copper *clacos*, or three cents of our currency, was introduced, which followed the fate of the copper. The objection to them was their small size and liability to be lost. At this day, the poor Indians rarely touch any more precious pieces than the lowly *clacos* their fathers treated with so much scorn.

Without continuing the lives of the viceroys, the bold stand taken by the second, Velasco, in favour of the weak against the strong, the oppressed against the oppressor, deserves commemoration. He devoted himself to rescuing from a most cruel slavery the unhappy children of the nations of Anahuac; they were worked to death in the mines, and when his efforts were bitterly opposed by the proprietors and the king's officers, saying, that their emancipation would leave no workmen for the mines, his reply was, "That the liberty of the Indians was of more importance than all the mines in the world, and as to the rents of the crown from this source, they could not justify the trampling under foot of all human and divine laws."

At this season (Lent), the fashionable afternoon drive shifts from the Paseo to LaViga, a beautiful avenue, ornamented on both sides with luxuriant shade-trees and flanked its entire length, on the eastern side, by the canal to Chalco. Double lines of coaches, public and private, the former generally very rusty, and the latter very elegant equipages, pass gaily up one side and down the other, freighted with the wealthy and the fair of Mexico. Papa and mamma (*padre*, father, and madre, mother, are terms not used in domestic life, they are considered too stiff for household use,) throw themselves back in state, not deigning to see the dashing cavaliers who gallop by on their fiery *frisones*; but the bright-eyed *señoritas* are more observant, and are not so wanting in charity as to throw themselves back where their fair faces would be hidden from the admiring gaze of the gallant invaders.

The canal is covered with boats as various in their fashions as the coaches; they are occupied by Indians, who enjoy themselves singing and dancing, and playing on rude instruments of music. Each boat is a floating flower-garden, from which the occupants of the coaches buy wreaths to crown their children. The coaches have their halting-places at semicircular expansions of the road, where they turn in and face to front, resting long enough to allow the compliments of the day between friends, and to make a few observations on the gay throng in motion. Then the bucks run the gauntlet! As the dews of evening begin to fall, first goes one coach, then another, then a section of horsemen, then other coaches and other horsemen, until the last lingering group leave the ground to find themselves bringing up the rear of a great procession, until the parties diverge to their respective homes.

City of Mexico, March, 1848

A company of about a hundred prisoners in a chain-gang, (reminding one of the worthy party released by the valiant knight of La Mancha,) have been passing my quarters daily, of late, carrying picks, shovels, spades, and other utensils for cleaning and repairing the streets. This important duty falls principally on them, for though the *Ayuntamiento* levies annually heavy taxes for that very purpose, many of the citizens think the sums collected tend rather to soil the hands of certain of the functionaries, than to sweeten the highways and by-ways of the city. The keeping the last clean, and in order, is difficult in the extreme, as may be read-

GENERAL PILLOW.

ily understood when it is remembered the city is in the bottom of the basin, and that efficient drainage is impossible.

The citizens know that large sums are collected for the purpose, and expended—how collected they know full well; but how expended, is altogether another question. The work done is effected principally by the convicts, who are sent out in gangs under charge of an armed escort of soldiers, mounted and on foot. The convicts are chained in couples—an iron girdle around the middle connects by a chain six feet long with another girdle around another prisoner; thus making an unwilling pair of Siamese twins, to spend years together, if not a lifetime. The chains go clinking over the stones, sounding, when the company is large, like many little tinkling bells; a most grating music, no doubt, to those who wear them. The poor wretches, vile and criminal as they undoubtedly are, enjoy a little human sympathy, for by many a one trudges the poor wife, or *querida*,[1] more faithful, perhaps, in adversity than she ever was in prosperity.

The Mexican commonalty think our ideas of marriage as loose as their own. A sprightly dame of the middle class, asked me if it was not the custom in the United States for couples to marry for a term of years, according to special agreement. I told her no, that people were married for life, like the respectable classes of her own country. She contradicted me promptly, saying that an English resident, who had passed some time in the United States, had made her acquainted with our customs, and that she knew the temporary marriages were among them. I said, rather roughly, that the Englishman had been imposing on her; that, in short, he was a gross liar.

"Oh! don't be angry," she said, "I know it is a custom of your country, but I did not think of finding fault with you for it; I am sure the blame is not yours."

I laughed at her misconception, but she looked upon it as an admission, and added I might as well have admitted the truth from the first, as she had American as well as English authority

1. *Querida*, mistress. They assume the fidelity of the wife for the time being. The Spanish language has no word proper for wife. *La Señora* is only Don Fulano's *mujer*, woman.

for her information. I could only suppose that some unworthy countryman of ours had been him self in pursuit of a better half in a connexion, tied by a slip-knot, that should only last "during the war."

Certain orders in this country retain privileges the most anti-republican in their nature, unworthy remains of the days of monarchical rule. A case has just come under my notice. Don R. has a claim against a Mexican army officer, which is incontestably good, and not even disputed by the latter, but he throws himself on his *fueros*, (privileges referred to,) by which a military man is put above the civil law. The debt cannot be collected except judgement be given by a military court, so that at present, in the disorganized state of the Mexican army, which will continue indefinitely, the claim is almost worthless. These *fueros* are more extensive in certain corps of the army, as in the *facultativos*, or scientific arms of artillery, engineering, &c., than in others less favoured. The clergy, too, have their fueros, which are ample, as may be supposed.

We have *lionizing* here, Herr Alexander, the German magician; he does many wonderful things to amuse and astonish us, but the most remarkable is, that he draws full houses at the *Nacional*, including a fair proportion of the gentler sex. The theatre is the nightly resort of the ladies of the *beau monde* in times of peace; but they have avoided it hitherto, by general consent, since our occupation. It requires a disciple, or a master of the black art, to draw them out. There are some fine-looking women to be met in such places, but few or none of a high order of beauty. Black eyes and dark tresses predominate, but the beauties of Mexico are by no means exclusively of the dark order. Blue eyes and fair hair are not uncommon, and are much admired.

I have not yet written to you of the "*Hospital de Jesus*," a venerable institution to which I paid a second visit some days ago. It was founded and endowed by the immortal Cortes, and contains many memorials of himself and his times. I had the pleasure to meet there Don Lucas Alaman, one of the most reputable gentle men, and distinguished literary characters of Mexico. Mr. Alaman is the *apoderado*, or attorney, of the heirs of the conqueror, and is by virtue of his office governor of the hospital. His countenance expresses a high degree of benevolence and intelligence, both of which he exercised in furnishing our gifted Prescott with most interesting details of the conquest, taken from the archives in his possession. Among the curiosities of the Hospital I saw historical documents, in manuscript, that have been kept there for upwards of three hundred years; the original signatures of the conqueror, of *La Marquesa* his wife, and of the Emperor Charles V., signed to an illuminated manuscript document, (patent of nobility to "*El Marques*") according to the fashion of the Spanish sovereigns

"*Yo, El Key.*" We (I met there accidentally, Colonel Childs, the distinguished governor of Puebla, escorted by Captain N——, 2nd Pennsylvania Volunteers, a competent cicerone in the antiquities of Mexico) were politely shown through the various apartments of the hospital, as in the wards, where there are at present forty patients comfortably provided for, by the bountiful charity of the founder; into the original chapel where he worshipped, now used as a laboratory for the service of the hospital; into a sacristy, adjoining the modern chapel, with a rich ceiling in arabesque, the only specimen in Mexico, and rarely seen in Europe, except in temples and palaces reared by the Moors during their domination. In one of the rooms is a splendid full-length portrait of the conqueror, taken during his lifetime. It is a striking picture, and looks *vraisemblable*; according to it, the hero was rather a slight man, of graceful figure, and fine countenance; a fiery devil lurks in his eye, yet every feature of his face is winning.

Public amusements are less attended during Lent, than at other seasons; but, in my visits, I have found music, dancing, and cards quite current in the domestic circle. You would be struck by the Christian names of the women and children; thus, half the boys seem to rejoice in the *nombre* (given name) of José-Maria, and as many of the gentler sex in that of Jesus (call it always, Hai-soos). The female names are more prominent, as they are addressed by them, by everybody, as among the friends, for life. It sounds strange enough, at first, to hear a young girl call a venerable matron, old enough to be her grandam, Maria, Antonia, or Anita, but it is by no means irreverent, and soon passes unnoticed. Affectionate diminutives are in universal use; thus, Jesus is most commonly turned into Jesusita (Hai-su-se-ta), Ana, Anita, &c. A great strapping beggar implores your aid, not for a *pobre* (poor man), but for a *pobrecito*, that is, a poor, dear, sweet creature. Such a person appealed lately to me as a *caballarito* (a sweet little caballero), making, at the same time, a piteous statement about his *madrecita*, his dear little mother. The houses of this country show the devotional tendencies of the people; within, are pious pictures; with out, very commonly, are painted, or moulded on the walls, crosses, sacred hearts, and pious ejaculations, as to the *Santisimo nombre de Jesus*.

City of Mexico, March, 1848

The Court of Inquiry involving the cases of Generals Scott and Pillow and Lieutenant-Colonel Duncan, is now in session at the palace, and is the focus of attraction for the army. Generals Towson, Gushing, and Colonel Belknap, constitute the court; Captain S. C. Ridgely is the judge advocate. I frequently look in, not only to hear the developments brought out by the examination of witnesses, but also to see the numerous distinguished officers of the army who daily assemble there.

General Scott frequently addresses the court, and always with visible emotion; it is evident that he is deeply hurt and mortified, at being stricken down from his high command, where he rendered such eminent services to his country, to be arraigned as if his course had been questionable and unsatisfactory. If his country prove ungrateful, which I do not believe, he will have the melancholy satisfaction of knowing that his case has had many illustrious precedents. He is a man of large proportions, about six feet five inches in height, without being unduly tall; time and care have traced their lines on his ample brow; and, advanced in years as he is, his appearance is at once venerable and majestic. Pillow, his antagonist, is a young man, apparently little over forty, and may be called handsome. He is no doubt a man of some talent, and I would suppose him an acute and shrewd lawyer, but a first-rate in no respect. He has no reputation in the army as a general, but is too ambitious a person to keep back during the dangers of the combat, so that his personal courage, so far as I know, is unquestioned. Gushing is the most *distingué*-looking man in the court, but he looks more the pale student than the doughty general.

Several officers and myself rode a few days ago to *Peñon de los Baños* (rock of the baths), a place of note a league from the city. From the base of an isolated rocky knob arises a fountain of hot water, over which is erected a large stone building divided into various apartments for bathing and other purposes. The baths are said to be valuable in rheumatic cases, and are resorted to, as are the springs elsewhere, with this difference, that in this case, the visitors have to carry bag and baggage, provisions and bedding. Empty rooms, with kitchen ranges adjoining, and the baths, are all that money will obtain from the keepers.

We ascended to the mountain top, partly on horseback and partly on foot; we enjoyed a hasty view of Lake Tescuco and the many beauties of this wonderful valley, but we did not venture to lose sight long of our horses; several Americans, who have left theirs but for a moment in this vicinity, have been under the necessity of returning to the city on foot, without ever learning the fate of their animals and equipments. Solitary horsemen have more than once been dismounted; have lost their horses, and barely saved their lives. This kind of robbery is so common, that few Mexicans are to be found who will venture out of the city gates alone. Our road led us by the *garita de San Lazaro*, near which is a leper hospital, which is always pretty well filled. The leprosy of Mexico is the result, direct or indirect, of filthy vices and abandoned debauchery.

In the sketches of the lives of the viceroys, which I am yet reading, are many interesting historical details, interwoven with endless petty quarrels between the viceroys and the bishops; feuds among different orders of the clergy; the mal-administration and perverseness of the royal *audiencias*; the revolts of Indians, and so forth, all tending to mar the welfare of the suffering people. General inundations and fearful earthquakes caused, at times, great desolation, but were scarcely more disastrous to the masses than the factious contests of their local rulers. During some of the inundations, the waters rose to the height of eight or ten feet in the streets of the city, drowning thousands, of Indians especially, destroying their habitations, and bringing, secondarily, pestilence and famine.

Widespread disease followed the slow drying up on the surrounding *potreros*, or low grounds, while famine followed the extensive loss of provisions caused by the floods. It became, of course, a matter of the first importance to protect the community from such disastrous visitations, and even in the days of Montezuma, dikes and drains were made at great labour and expense. They were, however, quite ineffectual, so much so, that after the Spaniards had devoted many years of scientific labour to the same object, as late as from 1629 to 1634, the streets of the city were under water, and intercourse had to be carried on in boats.

Many expedients were devised for directing the superabundant water of the lakes out of the valley, which, after many delays, was at length effected. Of the five lakes in the valley, the surface of three is higher than the level of the city; of the three to the north of it, that of Tescuco, the nearest, is some three feet below that level; that of San Cristobal, a mile beyond Tescuco, is eight feet above it, and that of Zumpango, a league to the north ward and westward, is about twenty feet above the level of San Cristobal. Into Zumpango emptied the river Guautillan; and as the former had no outlet, during a long prevalence of northerly winds, its waters passed to San Cristobal, where, uniting in one, the two, rushing into Tescuco, spread rapidly over the low shores upon which stands the city. By immense labour, the Guautillan has been turned from Zumpango to the river Tula, or Montezuma, by which it passes, through the Rio

Tampico, to the ocean. Drains from San Cristobal and Tescuco connect with the great river channel, called the Rio del Desagüe; and thus the city remains free from the dangers of deluge. This diversion of waters, while it saves the city, has been the cause of robbing the valley of a great part of its fertility. The floating gardens we read so much of, have long since disappeared; there are now to be seen in place of them, slips of land reclaimed from the marshes, intersected by numerous ditches, and which can only be approached in boats. These, then, represent the floating gardens, and contribute to supply the city market with fruits, flowers, and vegetables.

The great work of the Desagüe, or drain through the mountains, was effected, as everything else in Mexico in the way of great internal improvement, under Spanish dominion. The Mexicans are beset with the *laisser aller* spirit of old Cuffee, who would not leave his chimney-corner to repair his leaky roof during the rain, and as to repairing it during dry weather that was useless, as the old roof answered as well then as a new one.

The Mexican government sits like an incubus on the people, doing nothing for their welfare, and the old people look back with regret to the old *régime*. They say it is a mockery to speak of the Mexican republic; that they have the burdens of monarchy without its stability. That abuses abounded during the time of the vice-regal sway is admitted, yet in those days it appears there was greater security for life and property. The scientific establishments planted and fostered then, have now dwindled into insignificance; the great highways and bridges are in the state in which the republic found them, except for the ravages of time.

It matters little what a government is called, the spirit of a republic exists not here. The old nobility retain their titles (by custom); high functionaries affect princely style, and the humbler empleados practise more than courtly servility. Mexico, to become a republic, wants regeneration, wants a People, for there is nothing in the land deserving that appellation. The middle classes (that body politic that gives strength and stability to states) are but fragmentary; great landholders and princely merchants represent the aristocracy; the army, the church, shopkeepers, artisans, &c., and adventurers, and place-seekers of all kinds, fill up the space between the *ricos hombres*; and the peons of the soil. Your honoured profession (law) is in the hands of unworthy members generally, who, besides a character worse than indifferent for integrity, have neither the reputation for learning or talents, so common to the bar throughout the civilized world. The faculty of physic embraces some clever men, but generally, they are either foreigners, or indebted to other lands for their education.

Mexico, April, 1848

Much to my surprise, a Mexican gentleman called on me not long since, inviting me to take up my residence in his household. As his house is distant from my hospital, beyond, but near the palace, I hesitated to accept his kind offer, but his urgency, coupled with my own desire to cultivate acquaintance among the citizens, overruled all objections, and I am now comfortably established in one of the most elegant mansions in this city. The gentleman has travelled in Europe and in the United States; the lady too, which is more rare, has also visited the continent. The house is an elegant one, richly furnished, combining the commodities of wealth and taste, and preserving eminently the neatness, cleanliness, and order that are usually found here in the habitations of the wealthy. The Mexican gentry are cleanly in their houses and in their habits; they are much addicted to bathing, holding it, properly, advantageous, if not indispensable, to health.

The family in this case consists of Don S——, a gentleman of about five-and-thirty, his lady, *la señorita*, some five years younger, and two or three little children. Don S.,—— speaks English, and the lady French, which she sometimes uses to explain a word, or phrase of Spanish, a little beyond my scholarship. She has a cultivated taste in the fine arts, and is herself not unskilful in the use of the pencil, but being in a certain condition (*embarazada*, as it is here termed), she keeps much in the background, leaving her lord and myself *tête-à-tête* many times when her society would be a very agreeable relief.

Speaking of her condition, I may say here, once for all, that custom neither requires nor admits any mincing of terms in such cases. I have always thought a refinement, too subtle to be commendable, pervades society at home, in common conversation between gentlemen and ladies; such is not the case in this country; one may say anything, not absolutely indecent, that comes up naturally in his discourse. It would alter the case, no doubt, for a man to be trying how far he might go.

You would like to know, probably, the style of living of a genteel family, so let me introduce you for a moment to Mr's daily dinner table. I had taken breakfast, supper, and *dulces*, in other families before coming here, but dinner was something new, and I hoped to be allowed to have some two articles on my plate at once, contrary to the custom I had seen everywhere observed. My taste was to a certain extent gratified. Now for the dinner. In the first place comes soup (*caldo*), say plain chicken soup, such as you find at our hotels where French cookery is adopted; then, one or more *sopas* of rice, *fidéos* (vermicelli), or bread, in a semi-fluid state, then El Puchero,[1] a mixed dish of homely ingredients, of exceeding popularity among all classes of Spaniards. It is composed of *bouilli*, bacon, a little cabbage, bananas, garbanzos (chick-peas, a coarse but valuable vegetable), and other variable ingredients, to which may be added a little tomato sauce. It makes a good standard dish, in my opinion, though perhaps I am unduly partial, as it allows me to indulge a vulgar taste for bacon and greens, to say nothing of the other staples, without taking, according to the prevalent fashion, first a plate of bacon, and then another of greens. El Puchero weathers the fashion. When that is disposed

---

1. The glazed earthen vessel in which the contents are served, and from which they take the name.
2. Segars entirely of tobacco, so called to distinguish them from those in common use, wrapped in paper, or corn-shuck.

of, meats roasted, stewed, and boiled, and vegetables have their turn; then a salad; then a course of fruits, and lastly, before the turn on the *Paseo* or *La Viga*, a round of *dulces*. Whenever you rest a moment from your labours, ah attentive servant whips off plate, knife, and fork, and supplies the place with others.

My host is a man of delicate stamina, eats nothing gross, and has his meals prepared with a precision that men in high health would consider over nice. The old world contributes to his well-supplied table; thus, his hams come from Spain, as well as his wines, some of the choicest of which are sent from the vineyard of a relative near Cadiz. When the lady retires, and sometimes sooner, Mr.—— brings forth his *puros*[2] from Havana, and by the time we finish them, a servant announces that my horse is waiting in the court to take me to the hospital before going to the *Paseo*, and as I mount, Mr.——'s fine northern horses are prancing in one of his three coaches, ready to whirl his family to the gay resort of fashion.

I am about as indifferent to creature comforts as any other man, though always enjoying them when they come in my way; what gratifies me most in my new position, is the opportunity afforded of seeing familiarly, private life among this reserved people, for I take more interest in the manners and customs of a people than in the grave accounts of the bickering and contentions of their Solons and Lycurguses.

My invitation into this family was in part complimentary, but burglary and other crimes are so rife (involving in some instances the characters of certain Americans, who should be above suspicion), that many families now prefer to have a friendly American domesticated with them, feeling it to be something of a protection. The obligations between the entertainer and the entertained, are there fore somewhat mutual.

This city enjoys a fine market,[3] so that you may see on the table, every day in the year, the fruits and vegetables of temperate and tropical climates; the former the product of the *tierras*

---

3. I have not seen the Mexican *caviare* called *ahuanhtli*, a famous dish made of the eggs of the insect called axayacatl.

mas, or the table-land; the latter, of the tierras calientes, or low-lands of the coast. Tropical fruits may be seen growing abundantly in this valley, but they rarely reach perfection. The only vegetable that I find wanting, that we use in the United States, is the *okra* (*Hisbiscus esculentus*); there may be others, but if so, I have not missed them. The vegetables of the valley are, however, very inferior to ours, of the same kind, in flavour; they are beautiful to the eye, but comparatively insipid. This may be owing to the fact that they are so commonly produced in beds more of water than of soil.

I must give you a sketch of Holy Week, which has just expired, lasting from Palm to Easter Sunday. On the former day, "Birnam Wood" appeared to be moving through the city, in the form of lofty palms, cut into fanciful figures, and dressed with bouquets and wreaths of flowers. About the Cathedral stood a forest of these palms. On Wednesday evening, Mr.—— took me in his coach to visit the Rev. Dr. R—— , a *canonigo* of the cathedral, who was to officiate on the following day (Holy Thursday), and to request him to procure me, as a stranger, an eligible position for witnessing the ceremonies. The *canonigo* is an old gentleman, of venerable aspect and pleasing manners; he has the reputation of being a learned and good man, which he appears to deserve. Mr.—— told me that he is the *padre confesor* of half the high-bred *señoritas* of the city, among whom he is a great favourite.

On the following morning, notwithstanding the press of his duties, he was kind enough to get me a seat in the choir, from which I had a full view of the proceedings. At a certain stage of the service, the host was carried in procession through the aisles of the church, accompanied by a large train of clergy in gorgeous vestments, and distinguished civil officers, wearing showy insignia. A full and powerful band preceded the procession, alternating its music with the chanting of the priests.

A sermon was preached in the usual earnest and emphatic manner of the Mexican preachers; it is heard by the congregation standing, as there are no pews in the churches of Catholic countries; but from time to time, the assembled thousands fall on their knees to make some short special prayer, as recommended by the preacher; when they rise, he resumes his discourse.

After service at the Cathedral, I made a tour to numerous churches, following the crowds, "Visiting the Sepulchres." At every church was a representation of the Last Supper, either on canvass, over the altar, or in figures of the size of life, seated at the table in front of it. All the churches were ornamented with branches, fruits, flowers, and wax figures. Some of the churches were adorned with fantastic ornaments, in violation of the principles of good taste; others, however, offered to the eye, not only nothing offensive, but very touching emblems of that period of the Redeemer's suffering.

In the squares and streets, fanciful tents and booths, almost concealed by flowers, are erected for the sale of *aguas frescas,* fruits and other refreshments for the Easter holidays. On Good Friday, the throngs in the streets and churches were immense; in all the principal thoroughfares, the people were jammed as far as the eye could reach. Not a carriage is allowed to make its appearance, and all the fair dames and their lovely *ninas*, who rarely put their fairy feet on the vulgar pavements, make on this day an humble pilgrimage on foot to numerous churches. In the latter the paintings and ornaments are all veiled; the prominent figure is a full length of the Saviour, in wax, laid out for interment. There is no music, and for one day all the bells of the city are hushed in silence. In the churches, *matracas* (rattles) designate the stages of the service; and without, thousands of them, as toys, are rattling in the hands of all the children, and of half of the grown folks.

On Saturday, the bells all broke forth in loud and musical peals; the coaches and other vehicles appeared in the streets, and things returned to their usual course, and thus ended Lent, with its real and supposed mortifications.

MEXICO, APRIL, 1848

During this month, I have visited most of the neighbouring villages, which at this season are highly attractive. On one occasion I accompanied Colonel Riley, of 2nd Infantry, a gallant veteran and thorough old school soldier, a worthy son of the Maryland pilgrims, to the beautiful village of Tacubaya. Several regiments of our troops are quartered there, occupying the charming *casas de campo* of wealthy townspeople, who, for the present, have to content themselves in their city quarters.

The gardens and grounds attached to each house are spacious, clean and tasty; beautiful gravel walks, overhung by fruit and shade trees, are adorned at their intersections with arbours and fountains, while borders of flowers hide the less showy but more useful growths of the kitchen-garden. Tacubaya is on a swell of ground considerably above the adjoining plains and the level of the city; it is high and dry, and therefore much more healthy than the latter, as the experience of the troops now stationed there proves.

There are two objects of attraction in the city to which I have not yet paid my respects, *viz.*: the Academy of Arts, and the *Mineria*, or school of mines. The former I am told is quite decayed, though once so highly esteemed and patronised; the latter, a magnificent building, is occupied, or has been, I should say, by the gallant regiment of voltigeurs. It is a school of mathematics, mineralogy, and I believe, of natural philosophy generally, but though in operation, it is not considered flourishing.

The two commissioners from the United States, Hon. Messrs. Clifford and Sevier, reached here lately within a few days of each other on their mission of peace. They were received with the high est military honours by the army; and we trust an enlightened spirit of compromise will make their duties light, and enable us to return at an early day to our homes.

I have been amusing myself for the last few days translating an account of a survey of the Isthmus of Tehuantepec, by Mr. Mora, an eminent Italian engineer. The survey was made at the expense of Mr. Garay, who had made some arrangement with the government of Mexico for the rights and privileges of a canal for ships connecting the two oceans. Mr. Mora estimates the whole expense of the canal at not less than twelve, nor more than seventeen millions of dollars. He draws a comparison between that line and others proposed (Nicaragua and Panama), and by his showing, which is apparently very fair, the advantages offered by the Tehuantepec line are quite decided. The paper is an interesting one, accompanied by geological maps. It has been published, I am told, in English, but there are no copies to be had here. I sent my condensed translation to our friend D——, of Baltimore.

The better classes of this city are by no means very desirous of peace, and with reason. They dread the day of the evacuation by the American troops; they expect the worst, without knowing what it may be, some even apprehending the horrors now enacting in Yucatan. They would gladly pay the expenses of our army to keep it among them. They have no respect for their own government, declaring they only know it by its extortions, and not by any protection it gives them. The rulers are but too commonly unprincipled adventurers, pushing their own fortunes at the expense of the honour and welfare of the nation. Many of the best citizens decline all connexion with the government, rather than sanction evils they could not control. Demagogues fill the high places, and fatten on the suffering state. To drive them off is to invite another swarm, yet more hungry.

"We all know and feel this," said an intelligent gentleman to me, "and we devise remedies simple enough in design, but difficult of execution. Like the rats who agreed unanimously to protect themselves from the stealthy incursions of puss by putting a bell around her neck, the plans are unexceptionable, but *quien va poner el cascabel al gato?*—who is going to put the bell on the cat's neck?"

There is the difficulty. The army belongs to the government or the factions in power; the people can do nothing but bear the fleece for the shearers. Thus, industry is paralysed, and honest labour contemned; for who will go to the pains to accumulate to be marked for plunder by professional robbers, or robbers by virtue of their government commissions? Misrule enjoys a perennial ascendency, with rare exceptions, from the highest to the lowest functionaries. Walk in the streets at night, and you will find half the watch asleep, their lanterns, which they always carry, burning away beside them. And they are perfectly justifiable. When some of them were questioned lately on their remissness in their duties by an American editor of the city, they replied that they never received their pay proper, and rarely, indeed, paltry fractions of it; not enough to keep their wives and children from starving, begging, or stealing. It is actually to their interest to wink at crime, for while they receive no compensation for doing their duty, they are certain of punishment, perhaps assassination, if they venture to take an active part against the *ladrones*.

The most respectable citizens are influenced by the same feelings. An individual would avert his face from robbery or murder rather than give information, for the following reasons, which I give literally, as has been stated to me. A disinterested person sees an assassin, or assassins, fall upon a wayfarer, murder, and rob him. He gives information, when the accused parties, if caught, are committed for trial. This comes on, the informant is dragged before court after court, badgered by the lawyers, frowned at by scowling faces, friends of the accused, and when he has given evidence and truth to the best of his ability, some flaw in the indictment, or negligence, or bribery, saves from the *garote* the accused, who, perhaps, after a trifling imprisonment, are turned loose again upon society to pursue their evil courses. The informant is probably the first victim.

By a singular perversion of law, it is almost impossible for a landlord to eject a bad tenant from his premises, provided the tenant have a quantum of influence. One case has come to my knowledge, where a judge of the Supreme Court occupies a fine house for which he has paid no rent for years, yet he holds possession in spite of the owner. In another case a landed proprietor let his hacienda, which, under an *administrador*, or overseer, brought him an annual income of fourteen thousand dollars. The tenant now in possession has influence enough to keep it without paying rent, nor can the owner eject him without ruinous costs.

Other illustrations of misrule may be taken from the conduct of the army. A regiment of cavalry on the march, may quarter on an estate, supply themselves with provender for man and horse, press the owner's mules and horses, according to their necessities, paying sometimes nothing, or at best government bonds, which are but little better.

I have spoken of the espionage, under which society is ever trembling. I give a special instance. Two American officers are quartered in the house of a respectable family. Their gentlemanly demeanour recommended them to the residents, who extended to them considerable civility, inviting their visits, &c. The officers were much gratified, and took occasion to introduce some of their friends to the family. This was spoken of among some Mexicans, when one of their officers present, inquired particularly what family was thus intimate with Americans. When told, he made a record of the fact in his memorandum-book, intimating that he would one day bring vengeance on the household. And this probably was some coward knave, who, unable to protect, was just brave enough to persecute his peaceful fellow-citizens.

Many good, nay, the best citizens, desire annexation, or connexion with our government, on any terms. They declare they see no prospect, near or remote, of peace, law, and order, under their own rulers. The instances I have given in this letter of bad laws, and the worse administration of them, are precisely as I have them from the most reliable sources among this unhappy people.

ALVARADO, MEXICO, MAY, 1848

My fair prospects of a thorough acquaintance with "Life in Mexico," were suddenly demolished, like an airy castle, by an urgent order for the Marine battalion to escort a specie train to the port of Vera Cruz. I was not allowed time even to leave a farewell card with the various families who had offered me friendly attentions for the time I enjoyed their acquaintance; for there were few Americans, as a Spaniard said to me, so well *relacionado* in the city as myself. Although the circumstances were most unfavourable, I had cultivated society with some success;

197

and was called away just at the time when my acquaintance "behind the scenes" was becoming most agreeable and familiar.

To go to the coast was, with us, very different from going home, as we were only to assume new relations; and unwelcome whisperings hinted at a tour of duty on a projected survey, in a tropical region, under a summer's sun, between the two great oceans.

On the 28th of April, we received our orders; on the night of the 29th we were, in camp and quarters, at the village of Ayotla, seven leagues from the renowned city. We came over a fine natural road, flanked by ditches, through an open, arid, desert country, formerly the bed of a lake,—now perfectly dry, except for occasional saline marshes. We passed quietly by the great *Peñon del Marques*, out of respect to which we had made so circuitous a route to the capital. At Ayotla, when the diligence came in, I was called on to dress the wounds of a passenger, inflicted by robbers. An American rifleman (whose body we found the next day) had been killed by his side. The diligence is attacked everyday, whether in time of peace or war. Numerous wayside crosses indicate to the traveller where foul murder has left its victims; speaking with silent eloquence of the depravity and weakness, the sorrow and shame of Mexico.

At *Rio Frio* we found a garrison of Ohio volunteers. We met a party of them on the road, in search of the robbers of the day before. Strange to say, we met a gang of the latter tribe, escorting a merchant with his train to Mexico: they are more reliable when under pay, than Mexican regulars. Through all the mountain passes, we found heavy pines cut down, and turned from the road, though they had lain on it. They were cut after the army passed up, to prevent retreat; after our defeat near the city, when the scattered remains were to be hastening back pell-mell to the coast, they were to be annihilated, as arrested by these obstructions. The intention was good, no doubt, not to leave "one man to tell the story."

As we approached Puebla, we found the wheat harvest half accomplished. The crops appeared very abundant. About ten miles beyond the city, the great pyramid of Cholula, a remarkable monument of the Toltecs, is distinctly seen. It was measured by Humboldt, who says:

> .... it has a much larger base than any edifice of the kind in the old continent, its horizontal breadth being not less than 1440 feet; but its present height is only fifty-nine yards, while the platform on its summit has a surface of 45,210 feet.

It is built of sun-dried bricks, alternating with clay. A small chapel now surmounts its summit.

We passed one night in quarters in the clean and beautiful Puebla, and there, I may remark, was the only place where any attempt was made to do me wanton personal injury. Walking with two officers across a bridge, a large stone passed by our heads, thrown with such force as to be crushed against the parapet. We looked in vain for the assailant. We encamped for the two successive nights at Pinal and Ojo del Agua, passing through Nopaluca, a small village, garrisoned by Indiana volunteers. The next night found us in quarters in the gloomy town of Perote. I paid another visit to the great castle of San Carlos, which, though among the strongest on the continent, fell without striking a blow. We had close at hand again, the famous *Cofre*, likened by Humboldt to an ancient sarcophagus, surmounted by a pyramid.

Before reaching the pass of La Hoya, we were warned to expect a brush for our specie train; that a body of guerrilleros, stronger by half than our battalion, was lying in wait for us. This seemed probable enough—we had two and a half millions of specie, under a very small escort. It was hurried off from the city, as many other similar trains had been, to avoid the heavy export duty under the Mexican laws. We prepared for an encounter, but met, at the pass, some troops of the 6th and 8th Infantry, under Captain S——, of the latter, returning from the execution of similar duty to our own. Whether we had been deceived, or the guerrilleros thought the two parties too strong for them, I cannot say—certain it is, we passed without obstruction.

We met almost uninterrupted merchant trains passing up to the city, laden with merchandise; pack-mules by thousands, and great lumbering wagons, drawn in some cases by nine pairs of mules. These great supplies are also intended to evade the duties, levied on goods going inward.

We rested one day near the most picturesque town of Jalapa, which I visited twice. Around it, are many tasty country-seats, such as you see on Long Island; the town is a great place of resort for wealthy merchants from Vera Cruz, who repair to it during the season of vomito. It is garrisoned by volunteers from Maryland and District of Columbia; at present, large general hospitals are established here for the army, in anticipation of a general evacuation of the country. The peak of Orizaba looms up from this point of view, like a great silvery liberty cap suspended in the air. It was well termed among the aboriginal inhabitants *Citlaltepetl*, or the starry mountain. It took this name from the luminous exhalations that formerly played over its snow-crowned summit. In times of peace the inhabitants of Jalapa are distinguished for politeness and sociability.

Our next night was passed at the base of Cerro Gordo, on the Plan del Rio, where Pierce' s brigade was detained all of one day, going inward, to make a road down the steep bank of the river, because the Mexicans had, by great exertion and some loss of life, destroyed a noble bridge to arrest American progress. At the National Bridge we found a garrison of Tennesseeans. The influence of the *tierras calientes* began to creep over us the place was very sickly, and numerous low sand mounds, in each of which reposed half a score of silent tenants, whispered to us a mournful story. Another night found us at San Juan, the mud-hole of the inward march. We found there also a garrison of Tennesseeans, and shops with refreshments; the place that we once found so solitary and dismal, looked now almost like a thriving Yankee village.

An early march the following morning brought us to our old camp at Vergara, on the sea-beach. Vera Cruz looked as lively as ever, and much cleaner. We spent a few days on the beach, and then steamed it to this place, the hottest and dullest in Mexico. The first thing I saw was the funeral of a child; it was laid on a board, dressed in its best clothes and enveloped in flowers. A man was carrying it on his head with the same nonchalance as if it were a plaster cast; no train of mourners followed; but, after some time, I observed an afflicted-looking family slowly proceeding towards the cemetery.

Our battalion, brought here under command of Major D——, is associated with a larger one of the same corps under Major H———. Time is to develop our destination; meantime we are to swelter here until otherwise disposed of. We are already plunged in war with mosquitoes and sand-flies, and expect soon to be attacked by their ally the *comito*. That has not yet visited Alvarado, however, for this season, and the inhabitants declare the place is very healthy.

B S. M.

Su Casa de Usted, May, 1849

Mui Señor Mio,

I send you my last with a genuine Mexican heading, avoiding a blunder I once made with a gentleman of the city, by addressing him as *Señor*, Sir, which, it seems, is only admissible in an address to the king, or the King of kings. The B. S. M. informs you that I kiss your hands; the *su casa de usted*, that my house is yours. Our plain English admits of some romancing of the same kind in signing one's self your obedient humble servant, from which it will not be inferred that the writer means to be considered literally what he styles himself. I have hastily rewritten for you my old letters, such as they are, with their original defects, little corrected. No *importa*, what cannot be learned from them, may be from the works of Baron Humboldt, Mr. Prescott, and Madame Calderon de la Barca, who have covered the whole ground of Mexican geography, and natural science, history, and society, as it exists, or did exist, a few years ago.

Besides these, the highly interesting books of Mr. Waddy Thompson, Mr. Brantz Mayer, and other American and English travellers, would have left me little to say but for the changes resulting from invasion. The humble Puchero is offered to the world with perhaps a few new ingredients, or at all events, with some old ones served in a new style. Those who relish the fare may partake of it; those who do not, may readily find some thing better. A few rashers served up in extracts, will complete my poor dish, which you are kind enough to say is not altogether without a relish of its own. The extracts agree with my own observations, or are particularly worthy of note, from the information they convey.

Subjoined, finally, is a list of all officers, now or then in the service, who were engaged in the battles of the valley, with a special note attached to the names of the killed and wounded. The brevets conferred on all officers engaged therein are also added. The list is quite authentic, being taken from that prepared by General Scott's order in the city of Mexico, shortly after the battles.

To give some idea of the general capacity and products of Mexico, I draw from the deep fountain of the immortal German traveller, the Baron de Humboldt. After speaking of the well-known divisions of the country, according to elevation, the *tierras calientes*, of a mean annual temperature of 78 F.; the *tierras templadas*, of a mean annual temperature of 68 F.; and of the *tierras frias,* averaging below 62 F., all in the same latitude, he says:

> The physical condition of that kingdom (the present republic) confers inestimable advantages upon it in a commercial point of view. Under careful cultivation, it is capable of producing all that commerce brings together from every part of the globe; sugar, cochineal, cacao, cotton, coffee, wheat, hemp, flax, silk, oil, and wine. It furnishes every metal, not even excepting mercury, and is supplied with the finest timber; but the coasts oppose obstacles.
>
> The western part (of the State of Vera Cruz) forms the declivity of the Cordilleras of Anahuac, from whence, amid the regions of perpetual snow, the inhabitants descend in a day to the burning plains of the coast. In this district are displayed in a remarkable manner the gradations of vegetation, from the level of the sea to those elevated summits

which are visited with perennial frost; In ascending, the traveller sees the physiognomy of the country, the aspect of the sky, the form of the plants, the figures of animals, the manners of the inhabitants, and the kind of cultivation followed by them, assuming a different appearance at every step. Leaving the lower districts, covered with a beautiful and luxuriant vegetation, he first enters that into which the oak appears, where he has no longer cause to dread the yellow fever, so fatal on the coasts. Forests of liquidambar, near Jalapa, announce by their freshness, the elevation at which the strata of clouds, suspended over the ocean, come in contact with the basaltic summits of the Cordilleras. A little higher the banana ceases to yield fruit. At the height of San Miguel, pines begin to mingle with the oaks, which continue as far as the plains of Perote, where the cereal vegetation of Europe is seen. Beyond this, the former alone cover the rocks, the tops of which enter the region of perpetual frigidity.

Under the head of agriculture, this author says:

The banana, manioc, maize, wheat, and potatoes, constitute the principal food of the people. The maguey, or agave, may be considered the Indian vine. Sugar, cotton, vanilla, cocoa, wax, and cochineal, are plentifully produced.

Under the head of manufactories, "Cotton and woollen cloths, cigars, soda, soap, gunpowder, and leather, are the principal articles manufactured." Since that day, paper-mills, breweries, &c., have been established by foreign enterprise.

He says of the banana, that it is to the inhabitants of the torrid zone, what the cereal grasses, wheat, barley, and rye, are to Western Asia and Europe; and that probably there is no other plant on the globe capable of producing so much nutriment on as small a space of ground. He estimates the produce of the banana to that of wheat as 133 to 1, and to that of potatoes as 44 to 1.

It is calculated that the same extent of ground in Mexico on which the banana is raised, is capable of maintaining fifty individuals, whereas in Europe, under wheat, it would not furnish subsistence for two.—(*Humboldt's Travels, &c.,* by M'Gillavray.)

The *manioc,* or *fecula* of the Jatropha, is converted into a bread known as *Pan de tierra caliente.* It is very nutritious; and although the original product of the bitter Jatropha contains a highly poisonous juice (prussic, or hydrocyanic acid), the latter is evaporated in drying, which leaves the cassava, or flour, sweet and wholesome.

With the other vegetable products you are perfectly familiar; I will not therefore dwell on them.

My task is ended. I bid a long *adieu* to Mexico. Although I have suffered many hardships on her soil, I have nothing to look back to with any feelings of disaffection. In my intercourse with the people I have experienced a great deal of kindness, and I have found among them, wherever it could be properly expected, much refinement and intelligence. They have their faults, "as which of us has not?" yet I must add, that their vices are best known to me by hearsay.

Our days at Alvarado, "though evil, were few;" and we soon had the happiness to relinquish the *fandangos* and fevers that were spreading among us, of that pestilential region, for our own favoured land, to enjoy for a season its peace and prosperity, amid the smiles and endearments of happy homes.

The Siege of Vera Cruz

The battles fought by our gallant army under General Scott in Mexico, from the capture of Vera Cruz and the strong castle which defended it, to the capture of the capital city, present almost every variety of military conflict. The campaign began by a successful descent upon an exposed coast, by an army of all arms, in boats, followed by the regular investment of a fortified city, protected by one of the strongest military fortresses in the world, both of which were taken chiefly through the agency of the heavy artillery, and skilful bombardment from the batteries on shore, and the ships at the anchorage.

Cerro Gordo followed, where the scene of action was among the mountains, ravines, and gorges of that strong pass; and the leading characteristic of that well-stricken field, was the bold and successful storm of an almost inaccessible height, crowned with cannon and bristling with musketry. Contreras was fought and won, without cavalry or artillery; but, before the capital city was entered, cavalry, artillery, and infantry, all had their appropriate work to do, and all did it manfully and successfully. Whether breasting the northers on the sea-coast, scaling the hills at Cerro Gordo, wading through the swamps around the lake, or fighting inch by inch, along the exposed causeway, there seemed to be the same unconquerable spirit in the hearts of these gallant soldiers, and the same military genius and experience to direct them in their arduous duties.

But we question if the veteran officer whose high merit it is to have directed every battle of this memorable campaign, gave in any one of these battles higher proof of skill and true military merit, than in the first blow, struck at Vera Cruz. It is a vulgar saying, that "the first blow is half the battle' There is some truth in the saying, applicable as well to the great, complex, important movements of large masses of men, involving the multifarious considerations of feeding and clothing, arming and protecting, as well as fighting them, as it is to a fisticuffs fight on a court-green. If you don't give the first blow, and plant it well, you may receive it your self; if you don't stun your adversary, and daunt him by the vigour of your onset, you may never retrieve your ill-fortune. It was especially and imperatively necessary at Vera Cruz. Waddy Thompson, Esq. says in his clever recollections of Mexico:

> The fortress of San Juan de Ulloa has always been looked upon as one of the strongest in the world. With a proper armament and competent engineers, I should regard it as almost impregnable, if indeed that term can now with truth be applied to any place, after the recent inventions and improvements in this department of military science. When it was blown up in 1839, by the French, the armament was in a most wretched condition; and as to scientific engineers and artillerists, there were none. Even then it would not have been so much of a holiday affair, had it not been for the accidental explosion of the magazine. Any future assailant must not expect so easy a victory, if it is tolerably defended.

Mr. Thompson may have added that, according to all accounts which we had when the whole country "held its breath for a time," awaiting the result of Scott's attack, this very defect in the arrangements of the fort, which was said to have caused the accident, was provided against by magazines absolutely fire-proof, by which the ammunition of the fortress was secured in dry reservoirs, perfectly covered over; and, besides, that water-batteries had been constructed, stretching around upon the shoals, so as to command every approach, and all other needful additions to the defences, as well as a thorough repair, had been made; so that it was termed the "Gibraltar of America." It was the great defence of their seaport, a fortified gate, commanding the entrance to the country and the great national road, leading to the capital city. It was the armed sentinel, guarding the only important place of assault upon the coast of Mexico. Besides this, the Mexicans well knew, and calculated upon what Mr. Thompson calls a more effectual protection than all these fortifications, "the northers and the *vomito*" the first a tremendous north wind, which blows like a tornado, without warning or regularity, driving before it the loose and shifting soil of the coast,

Like clouds of sand,
That far in Afric's desert land,
Obey the Siroc's force.

rendering the anchorage of the open bay or roadstead of Vera Cruz (for it cannot be called a harbour) unsafe to every vessel, from a canoe to a ship of war; the second, the yellow fever, having its home in Vera Cruz, more to be dreaded in the warm months than the missile "that flieth by day," for it is the dreaded pestilence that "walketh in darkness," as well as "the destruction that wasteth at noonday." Against both of these General Scott had to guard. His knowledge that the northers prevailed most in the winter and early spring, made it imperative upon him to encounter these, that he might complete his undertaking against the city and castle, and march into the interior, before the period for the yellow fever. This necessity alone added greatly to his labours, and perilled his enter prise. Not being appointed to the command of the expedition (in fact, the same not having been decided on by the government) before November, 1846, he was forced to hurry his preparations, withdraw troops from General Taylor's command, pass the winter months on the northern coast of Mexico, in incessant labours to organize his invading force, and at last make the attack at least a month later than he had intended.

It was on the 9th of March, that the landing of his troops was effected. Before twenty days, the city and the strong castle were garrisoned by American troops, under the flag of their country, which floated from the walls of Vera Cruz, and the battlements of the castle. For several days and nights, the investing batteries of cannon and mortars sent a storm of balls and bombs upon the devoted city, and its massy, protecting castle; even at times, as many as 180 discharges in the hour, from the shore; while 400 cannon mounted on the enemy's defences, returned the fire.

From the ships of our gallant squadron (at first, under Captain Conner, who was relieved by Commodore Perry early in the siege), the same service was manfully performed by our sailors and marines; and yet, when the storm of battle ceased, and 5000 prisoners, 400 pieces of ordnance, 5000 stand of arms, and the fortified city, and mighty fortress, were taken General Scott had to report but two commissioned officers killed, and not a dozen private men. Neither was the strife carried on, with heavy guns and mortars alone; for clouds of skirmishers hovered around the city on the sand-hills and in the dense *chaparral*.

Along the lines of investment, extending for five or six miles, the enemy had to be driven off at various points by our gallant volunteers and cavalry; still, this great victory may be regarded as almost a bloodless one. Who does not remember the feelings of surprise as well as of joy, which spread over the land when the news reached the United States? The friends of Scott, felt proud of their General of science. The friends of humanity rejoiced, that while the enemy, disregarding the summons to surrender, had to lament the loss of many of his unresisting citizens, as well as combatants; yet, such was the skill and judgement of the commander, such the harmonious cooperation of our gallant naval officers and tars with the land troops, that we at home, had but few widows and orphans to lament over the result of the Siege of Vera Cruz. Indeed it was almost amusing, to find some of those who had been in the habit so long of underrating and reviling Scott, actually attempting to disparage his great achievement, because he did not have more killed.

It is a disgraceful truth, that some of our own citizens were at first disposed to unite in the sneers of an English traveller, George F. Ruxton, Esq., of Munchausen memory a gentleman who passed through Mexico the summer previous; whose hunting feats, when he was alone, sometimes in deep snows, and sometimes in the fiery prairies especially when shooting a wolf by holding a rifle across his knees, charged with his hickory ramrod which ignited as it flew into the wolf, who darted into the prairie with it sticking in him like a fiery comet; and many other marvels of the like kind, render his severe criticism upon Scott less formidable than they might be from a more veracious, but less amusing voyageur. We quote from Mr. Ruxton's book his opinion of the Siege of Vera Cruz:

> Since my visit, it has also felt the force of American ire and withstood a bombardment for several days, with what object it is impossible to divine, since a couple of thousand men might have at any time taken it by assault. The castle was not attacked, and was concluded in the capitulation without being asked for *Cosa de Mexico*. The town was attacked by the American troops under General Scott within ten months after my visit. It suffered a bombardment, as is well known, of several days, an unnecessary act of cruelty in my opinion, since to my knowledge there were no defences round the city which could not have been carried, including the city itself, by a couple of battalions of Missouri volunteers. I certainly left Vera Cruz under the impression that it was not a fortified place, with exception of the paltry wall I have mentioned, which, if my memory serves me, was not even loopholed for musketry. However, temporary defences may have been thrown up in the interval between my visit and the American attack; still, I can not but think that the bombardment was cruel and unnecessary. The castle could have been carried by & frigate's boarders, having but seven hundred naked Indians to defend it.

In endeavouring to mitigate the severity of this military gentleman of the ramrod (as famous for his horse Panchito, as the renowned Sancho for his Dapple), we find that he lays it down as a clear proposition, page 176, "The American never can be made a soldier." Knowing this, he should have been less severe upon us; for if we had no soldiers, even the seven hundred naked Indians might have held San Juan against us; and how were we to get these very Missouri battalions from California in time? They were the very men, by the way, under Colonel Doniphan, that the unsparing Mr. Ruxton was speaking of, when he pronounces the oracular military maxim above named, (though in the previous sentence he admits that they defeated "four times their number of Mexicans at the Sacramento.") But while the opinions of Mr. Ruxton defeat themselves by their very inconsistencies and manifest absurdities on their face, yet something like this charge of inhumanity on the part of Scott has come from more respectable authority.

We allege that it is utterly unwarranted. If there be one trait in the character of General Scott, proven and palpable, it is his humanity his willingness always to spare the effusion of blood his love of, and efforts for, peace, though a man of war from his youth. The adjustment of the border troubles on the Canada frontier; his dignified prudence in South Carolina; his humane and wise treaties with the north-western Indians, after the Black Hawk war; all carry with them the negation of such an imputation. But let us look to the facts of the Vera Cruz siege, to disprove the charge.

General Scott's troops landed on the 9th of March; no bombardment was commenced until the 22nd, in the afternoon, as appears from the Report of Colonel Bankhead, the chief of the artillery. As early as the 13th, General Scott, in answer to a note from the Spanish consul, sent safeguards for all the foreign consuls, their families, &c. Late on the 24th, two days after the bombardment began, these consuls requested of Scott to suspend hostilities, to permit the women and children to leave Vera Cruz. Scott, in his answer, refers them to the fact, that before he fired a gun, he made an appeal, by a formal and respectful summons to the Governor of the city, telling him that he had invested the city, and anxious to spare their beautiful town, its defenders, and its peaceful inhabitants, women and children inclusive, he proposes a surrender; nay more, he went so far as to pledge himself, if the Governor would surrender the city, that no gun should be fired from the city, its bastions or walls on the castle, so as to draw its fire upon Vera Cruz, unless the castle fired first. The Governor chooses to defy Scott, takes no notice of this last humane and generous proposition, and tells him to commence his operations in any way he thinks best. General Scott further tells the consuls, in his answer to them of the 5th, that he had purposely, up to the 23rd, to allow the escape of the neutrals, (in which term he manifestly includes the women and children,) left open the communication between the city and the neutral ships lying off Sacrificios; that having done all he could to spare these defenceless persons, he is still willing to spare them, if the Governor is willing to surrender.

War has its evils, and among the most lamentable is the suffering of the innocent and helpless, who are oftentimes involved in the fate of their sterner protectors; at the same time, war is no child's play, and has its duties too; and when the assailant has done what humanity dictates, and he proposes to the besieged to spare these victims of war by a timely surrender, or on fair terms, of arrangement for their safety, the responsibility is shifted to the beleaguered party. What more could General Scott do? Was he to relinquish the enterprise, because bombshells would burst and cannon-balls demolish? Whose fault was it that those stern, iron visitors fell upon the hearth-stones, and shattered the household gods? Not General Scott's, we say again. The Governor could have averted it by a surrender: he could have yielded to Scott's humane proposition to give up the city alone, and make it safe from the cannon; he could have done this, at any hour from the evening of the 22nd of March, when the first gun was fired, up to the 26th, when he did do it at last. We blame him not, he may have done his duty to his country, but neither should our General be blamed for wanton or useless blood-shedding.

We shall be brief in our details of this memorable siege. The leading facts are known to the world. The brave men who participated in it, as well of the navy as the army, deserve all to be known and named. We hear of none who did not do their duty and let it be remembered, that the navy deserves more credit than it has received, for its services in the war of Mexico. The whole of a sailor's duty is not comprised in fighting his ship. Here had our gallant tars been, on this coast, for months before, taking the towns, watching the ports cutting off the commerce of the enemy no safe harbour to run into, under the storm of the sudden and violent north winds and during the siege they did their full share of the land duty.

It is said to have been one of the most exciting spectacles ever witnessed, the landing of our army, in the surf-boats. The white-washed houses and tall steeples of Vera Cruz shining in the sun the frowning fortress of San Juan de Ulloa the graceful ships in the offing sixty-seven large boats, each commanded by a naval officer, and rowed by seamen, filled with soldiers, first General Worth's brigade of regulars, then the volunteers under General Patterson, then Twiggs' reserve of regulars were successively landed upon the shore below the city, as quietly and as safely, as if they had been ferried over a river at home.

Four gun-boats from our squadron had at daybreak left Antonio Lizardo under Lieutenants Sterret, Benham, Biddle, and Shaw, and an choring within a pistol-shot of the shore, fired upon some videttes of cavalry, or squadrons of lancers, who took the hint and retired and by the way, these same valuable little vessels, with the addition of the *Spitfire* under Tatnall, the *Vixen*, under Sands, with another schooner, the *Falcon*, on the 24th, run almost within a mile of the city, and fired away most daringly, until Commodore Perry actually had to recall them from a position most hazardous, if the enemy had not been too busy, or too awkward to sink them. Tatnall and his coadjutors, however, did yeomen's service with this part of the fleet.

The experienced Colonel Bankhead was the chief of artillery, and he makes four reports during the siege, to head-quarters, in one of which he speaks of the lamented death of Captain Vinton, commanding battery No. 3. And eleven days before, during the investment, a gallant officer, young in years but old in service, Captain William Alburtis of Virginia, who had been brevetted for his gallantry in the Florida war, was killed by a distant shot from the city or castle, which at the same time killed a private and wounded two others. Vinton and Alburtis were the only two commissioned officers killed. The writer may be pardoned for a pause of sad regret at this untimely catastrophe. That fatal ball, how ever, only deprived him of a valued friend; while an aged mother, his young widow, and an only son, felt the heavier bereavement of a dutiful son, an affectionate husband, and devoted father. Strange to say, he had a presentiment, a distinct premonition of the event his last letters, written upon landing, contained his will, with minute directions as to the education of his child. Peace to his ashes! He died as a soldier wishes to die, in the ranks of his country, in the discharge of his duty his sword in his hand and his face to the foe!

The investment of Vera Cruz was no parade duty. It was arduous and perilous. The infantry, under Patterson and Twiggs General Pillow commanding the volunteers from Pennsylvania and Tennessee drove the enemy through the dense thickets of chaparral. General Quitman, who commanded the men of the South, the gallant South Carolina regiment, (called the Palmetto,) the Georgia, and companies of the Alabama regiment, cleared the outskirts of the city of skirmishers and lancers. Shields, with the New Yorkers, aided in the preliminary duty; while the bold Colonel Harney and the gallant Sumner, with their dragoons of the second regiment of that arm, assisted by the brave Colonel Campbell of the first Tennessee volunteers, routed the enemy at the fortified post of Puente del Morena, and drove them six or eight miles from the scene of action.

The engineers under Totten, with such aids as Colonel Smith, Captain R. E. Lee, Saunders, and the gallant subalterns of this valuable corps, had their day of work at this time. Batteries were to be placed, trenches were to be dug, the science of the West Point alumnus was now to be tested, in actual service, under fire. The artillerists, under Bankhead, such men as Brooks and Vinton and M'Kenzie and Anderson, were to show their skill and prowess, and stand to their cannon, day and night. The ordnance officer, Huger, was to give his time and care and provident attention to the supply of these instruments of death and destruction. All were at work faithfully, constantly, unremittingly, and cheerfully.

On the evening of the 22nd, the hurricane of iron missiles began its ravages upon the devoted town; northers blew the clouds of sand into the faces of the besiegers, and over their works, filling up the trenches; water and food had to be carried sometimes five miles; the soldier lived in the trenches, and if he slept, slumbered to the sound of cannon and the burst of the bomb-shell; half a million of pounds weight of iron balls and shells were from the 22nd to the 26th of March, hurled through the troubled air, besides those fired from the city and castle. The houses are shattered, the churches are on fire; the devoted city, like the "cities of the plain" is under a shower of destruction. The Governor, Landero, yielding at last to the calls of human- ity, proposes a capitulation, and after a brief negotiation as to the terms, articles of capitulation and surrender are signed by the commissioners of our army and navy, Generals Worth and Pillow, and Colonel Totten and Captain Aulick, on behalf of the navy, and Colonels Villaneuva, Roblis, and Herrera, on the part of Mexico. The Castle and city are surrendered, with all forts, armaments, and munitions of war the garrison as prisoners of war. The officers and soldiers are discharged on parole, (and the wisdom of the step was proved by the fact, that they were not found at Cerro Gordo, a month afterwards,) the flag of the United States was raised over the city and the far-famed fortress of San Juan de Ulloa, on the 29th of March.

Thus was this great work done. Let the reader of military an- nals furnish a parallel, if he can, to this exploit; let him point out in the wars of the Peninsula, or Napoleon's campaigns, where he can find such a work performed in twenty days from the deck of the transport, to the planting of our flag on the highest bat- tlement of the water-girt fortress.

The reflections which naturally suggest themselves to the mind on reading the accounts of this siege, are in part already referred to. Another is, that the capture was effected strictly according to plans carefully made and written out by General Scott, before he left the seat of government for the seat of war.

The ancients regarded the favour of the goddess "Fortune" as the highest recommendation of a leader in war. General Scott, it is very manifest, is rather disposed always to trust to his own judgement and foresight than to the smiles of the fickle goddess.

He said to the Secretary of War, on the 27th of October, 1846:

> To take the Castle of San Juan d' Ulloa, would no doubt be a virtual and prompt capture of the city lying under its guns. The reverse of the proposition would probably not be equally certain I mean in any short time. The castle, after the loss of the city, might still hold out for many weeks, perhaps months, until compelled to surrender from the want of subsistence and water, unless earlier reduced by land and water batteries, escalade, &c.
>
> It is believed that the castle, with a proper garrison, cannot be taken with water batteries alone, or by the latter and an escalade, without a very heavy and disproportionate loss of life on the part of the assailants, besides a loss of time, which by running into the season of the *vomito*, might quadruple the waste of life, and cause the invading army to lose a campaign.
>
> For these reasons, it seems decidedly preferable to capture the city first, and by its means (shelter and guns), to attack the castle by land and water, including joint escalades, unless it should be found probable that the want of food and drinking water would lead to an early surrender.

He goes on to point out even the very place proper to land our troops, to suggest the plan of surf-boats, to propose additional bomb-ketches; and on the 12th of November he again proposes to take the castle through the capture of the city, and suggests that he shall have an ample force to press the war into the interior 1, because it would shorten the war, and thus economize life; 2, because a little war is a greater evil than a big war. He looks at the under taking in every point of view, and under every probable result; and in this instance, as in almost every other during the war, his sagacity and military foresight, to the mere civilian, seem wonderful. The ablest generals have had their reverses, and have made mistakes. The art of war has been compared to the game of chess. Where will you find the most skilful commander who has never made a false move, and has never been checkmated, especially when he must play out the game with the lack of many of his pieces? And yet, when we contemplate the history of Scott's campaign, from March to September, 1847, in Mexico, where do we find any one serious reverse to his arms?

On the 20th of August, the memorable day of Contreras and Churubuseo, he fought in one day five battles. He was gallantly supported by his brave officers and indomitable soldiers; still, his was the hand that made the moves upon the military chess-board; his was the eye that overlooked and planned the game; his the commanding and lofty bearing through the various conflicts, that inspired the poorest soldier with the spirit of a hero, and gave him assurance of success.

He fought yet again, and again; still victory perched upon his banner. He flung out the stars and stripes from the national palace of the capital, and as they waved over the conquered land, they shone bright and untarnished by a single defeat. Cortez, hundreds of years before, was forced to lament over the "night of despair" that followed his defeat upon the causeway Scott's gallant band crossed it at the pas de charge, and greeted, with loud cheers, on the *plaza* of the capital, a leader who seemed to carry in his right hand the prestige of victory.

APPENDIX 2

Cerro Gordo

About ten miles from the National Bridge, the road from Vera Cruz to the capital reaches a small hamlet, on a comparatively level piece of ground, in a basin surrounded with mountains: this place is one of the Mexican *ventas*, or stopping-places for the traveller, situated on the north side of the small river called Rio del Plan, giving name to this Mexican *caravanserai*, which is called Plan del Rio. The National Road here crosses two branches of the river Chacalacas, which unite a short distance below the venta or inn; and on this spot the American camp was pitched, about the middle of April, 1847.

At this place the *tierras calientes*, or tropical country, may be said to end; here begins the slope of the *tierras templadas*, the temperate regions, extending up to the region of the pine forests, opposite the lofty Coffer, or volcanic peak of Perote.

From Plan del Rio, going to the capital, the road winds towards the north, in a long circuit, through and along lofty ridges, forming one boundary of this defile, along which runs the Rio del Plan; after a mile or two it inclines from the northwest to the south-west, and along this route, the spurs, or points of lofty ridges, spreading out like the fingers on a man's hand, are seen from the road; between these ridges, deep valleys, or gorges run down towards the river, which, from about a mile above the site of the American camp, runs through a deep precipitous ravine, which continues like an impassable gulf along the whole range of the road eastwardly; on the other, or south side of the river, rises the other wall of this defile or basin, along which there is no regular road.

After passing some three miles along the road, the traveller, who is now brought by the southern direction of it close to the river again, sees on his right a towering eminence crowned with a fortress and military works, apparently inaccessible if defended, a spot, from its position, like a giant guarding the portal of this rugged defile, commanding all the subordinate strongholds of the ridges and salient points of this naturally strong place of defence, and the key to the whole position; on his left, to the south, the deep impassable ravine of the river. This is Cerro Gordo. The road, winding close under the shadow of the lofty Cerro Gordo, in another mile comes to another, but less lofty hill, under which the Mexican camp was pitched, more than four miles, by the road, from Plan del Rio.

The reader, even without a plan before him, may form some idea of this scene of one of the most gallant battles ever fought or to speak more correctly, of a series of battles, comprising all the different duties of an army acting in the offensive, under every conceivable disadvantage. The perilous reconnaissance the night march the clearing away of such obstacles as must be encountered among the mountain fastnesses the driving in of outposts and skirmishers the manoeuvre to be done with the precision of a parade, on a field day, under the plunging shot of batteries commanding their positions the charge the rush up the steep mountain-side the storm the bayonet thrust the close conflict ending in victory. For the defence of this pass,

1. The Mexicans had thus, two or three batteries, having in all seventeen guns, on their extreme right nearest to Plan del Rio, protected on their right by the river ravine.

2. Farther west, on the road, where it is nearest the river, a six gun battery.

3. Farther up on the great commanding hill, stood the fortress of Cerro Gordo, fenced round with a double line of advanced entrenchments, with six guns commanding the ravines around it, the circumjacent heights, and road at its foot.

4. On their extreme left was their camp, defended by a battery of five cannon, and having a direct communication with the main work on the steep hill, which was the *point d'appui* of their position. General Scott's plan of action, afterwards so gallantly seconded and carried out by his brave army of less than nine thousand men, was worthy of the science and generalship of this great captain of the age.

He had an army of more than twelve thousand men opposed to him in these mountain passes, who had chosen their positions,— planted their cannon on the commanding heights built up their advanced entrenchments, some of them being strong stone walls their line occupied two miles defended altogether by some fifty pieces of artillery their bronze mouths pointing (as the Mexicans supposed) upon every exposed point which our little army would be forced to pass. The deep ravine and river with its impracticable ground on the south, forbidding the possibility of turning them on that side; with a dense chaparral and another ravine bounding the pass on the north.

That Santa Anna regarded his position as impregnable, may be inferred from the proclamation found in his carriage after the defeat. It is manifest that he eyed the entry of Scott with his gallant little army into this defile, with the same grim satisfaction that Leonidas, at Thermopylæ, regarded the detachments from the Persian hosts advance upon his devoted Greeks; or as Hofer, the brave Tyrolese, watched from his mountain post the trained troops of the French emperor enter the silent gorge of the Innthall, for he says:

Mexicans, the momentous crisis has at length arrived to the Mexican Republic. If our country is to be defended, it will be you who will stop the triumphant march of the enemy who occupies Vera Cruz. Vera Cruz calls for vengeance follow me, and wash out the stain of her dishonour! My duty is to sacrifice myself, and I well know how to fulfil it! Perhaps the American hosts may proudly tread the imperial capital of the Aztecs I will never witness such an opprobrium, for I am decided first to die fighting. If the enemy advance one step more, the national independence will be buried in the abyss of the past.

The sententious humour of General Scott's commentary on this grandiloquent effusion is very characteristic; all that he says about it is in five words: "We have taken that step." He leaves to all admirers and imitators of military bulletins of the "Ercles vein" to fancy how Santa Anna would finish the syllogism.

General Scott having arranged his plans, and selected his officers and their respective corps for the proper duties of each, with that sound military judgement which marks the judicious commander, published his memorable orders on the 17th of April, (General Orders, No. 3.) The second division of regulars under General Twiggs had already been ordered in the advance, and on that same 17th, had already intimated to the enemy, through such gallant messengers as Colonel Harney and Lieutenant Gardner, that the work was begun, and in a way that they least expected. General Twiggs, it must be observed, had arrived at Plan del Rio on the 11th of April, the gallant Harney (the American Murat), with his dragoons in the advance, driving off a body of Mexican lancers who occupied that place.

On the 12th, Twiggs felt his way among the hills, reconnoitering the position, intending on the 13th to commence hostile operations, but Generals Pillow and Shields coming up with their volunteers, on, the 12th, their troops fagged by the unusual march through the sandy road from Vera Cruz, but like gallant men as they were burning to take a share in the coming fight, begged of Twiggs to defer the attack one day; he, appreciating the feelings of young generals anxious to signalize themselves, assented; and during the 13th, Twiggs' movement was still longer deferred by orders from General Patterson (whose sickness placed the volunteer troops under General Twiggs' command).

By these orders he was directed to await the arrival of the commander-in-chief. On the evening of the 16th, Twiggs received his verbal orders from General Scott himself; how they were carried out, the glorious results of the 17th and 18th amply show, but on the 17th are dated the General Orders for the battle of Cerro Gordo; and the highest compliment that could be paid to a commander-in-chief, was paid by the military men of France, when they received with them the published accounts of the battle. It was the common remark among them, "That his orders before the battle were so exactly carried out, that they might have served for his despatches after the action." This merited praise was from men who had a right to express their opinions from men who had been marshalled in the field by Napoleon, Soult, Bugeaud, Gerard, and Lamoriciere; men who had seen fighting under Napoleon's lieutenants on the snowy steppes of Russia, among the Alps, and the burning sands of Africa.

The summary of General Scott's orders were, that General Twiggs should turn the enemy's left, to cut off his retreat to Jalapa, while his batteries and entrenchments should be attacked in front; General Scott, not choosing to run the gauntlet through the fire of the Mexican batteries, decided to make a detour, and throw this advanced corps of his army across his road to Jalapa, and to effect this object, to make a way through the rugged country on the north of the National Road. To effect this with success, the science and enterprise of that useful arm of the service, the engineer corps, was required; those patient and fearless pioneers of our army, that during the whole of this gallant campaign did such signal service.

The official reports of our generals of all grades, and in all the engagements from Vera Cruz to the city of Mexico, are filled with acknowledgements of the incalculable value of these useful officers. Here, upon the fields of conflict, in arduous and actual service, did they bring to the aid of our cause, the accurate and valuable know ledge acquired in their military *alma mater,* West Point. Here, in the silent, dark, and inclement night, when the weary hosts reposed around them, in advance even of the picketed sentinel, was the engineer to be found making his way by the light of the dim lanthorn, through thickets of *chaparral,* wandering over the steep hills, groping his way among the lava fields of the Pedregal, to herald the path of the advancing column of infantry or squadron of charging cavalry, or to show to the artillerist where to place his guns; and, after carrying his valuable researches even up to the enemy's outposts, the engineer returns to his quarters, not to repose, or even to take time to prepare elaborate reports, but to head the adventurous detachment, and pilot the way to the place of conflict, and share in the perils of the fight.

It would be almost invidious to single out any one among that valuable corps who distinguished himself above his fellows during that memorable campaign, but the Virginian may be pardoned if he dwells with some feeling of gratulation upon a name which appeared then, not for the first time, in the annals of the old commonwealth. The service here required among the gorges of these mountains, as well as at the siege of Vera Cruz, and afterwards in the swamps of Chalco, and among the lava-fields of Contreras and Churubusco, and under the batteries of the capital, was well rendered by a worthy son of the historian of the southern campaigns of our Revolution, "Light horse Harry Lee" that gallant and indefatigable partisan cavalry officer, who was as the right arm of Greene and Marion.

The same untiring watchfulness, and dashing courage, that distinguished the sire in the Carolinas, here showed itself in his son of the same metal, though in a more scientific arm of the service, among the hills and plains of Mexico. Lieutenant Beauregard had begun the arduous duty of selecting the track and preparing the road to lead over slopes and chasms, leaving the National Road at its most northerly point, and thus directing the course of the division commanded by General Twiggs, westwardly and to the north of the main work Cerro Gordo.

This duty was carried out by Captain R. E. Lee of the engineers, until the nature of the ground brought the reconnaissance within reach of the enemy's batteries, making it necessary to carry by storm (I had almost said by escalade) the lofty works on Cerro Gordo. General Twiggs, moving early on the 17th, with the second division of regulars, took his position by eleven in the morning, the right of his column within seven hundred yards of the enemy's main work. Here the veteran Twiggs saw at once the advantage of occupying the heights on his line of attack, opposite to the castle and within striking distance.

The rest of the 17th and the night was allotted to the work. The events of the next day of strife, and the results of the enterprise would depend upon his seizing and holding these opposing high grounds, not only by bivouac, but by the erection of a rival battery, to return the compliment of grape and cannon-balls, as well as musket and rifle-bullets. It was an arduous and bold undertaking, but it was done, and effectually done.

He detached Lieutenant Gardner, commanding a company of the 7th Infantry, to observe the enemy from the heights he was met by a large force of the Mexicans, greatly outnumbering his party, but his business was to hold his position; and he did it gallantly against heavy odds, until he was relieved, by the artillery under Colonel Childs, and Sumner's mounted riflemen; these gallant officers, under the command of Harney (in the absence of Brevet Brigadier General Smith, who was sick), came to the rescue of Lieutenant Gardner, with the intent to drive the enemy back to his fortress, and this was thoroughly done, but at the expense of a severe wound received by the brave Sumner, whose command devolved upon Major Loring. Childs was in apparently greater peril than Sumner, but he came off unhurt for, supposing that the work was to be completed at once that evening, and, judging from a continuous fire on his left that the game was opened, a part of his regiment advanced within 150 yards of the enemy's batteries) and, without heeding the recall (more than once given by General Twiggs), he held his position, giving the enemy a foretaste of what he meant to give them next day as a part of the storming party.

Finding himself unsupported, he retired, having barely men enough with him to carry off his wounded. This movement of the gallant artillerist, though apparently rash, doubtless had its full effect upon the enemy's vital point, for they were swept into their stronghold, and the whole division under Twiggs, assisted by the volunteers, were engaged in placing on the opposing height a battery of two twenty-four-pound howitzers and a twenty-four-pound cannon within a deadly distance of the formidable Cerro Gordo and here, during the dart hours of the night of the 17th, were the artillerymen under Major Gardner, riflemen and infantry, directed by the indefatigable Captain Lee, assisted by Lieutenant Hagner of the ordnance; engaged in the heavy, toilsome duty, of dragging these heavy guns up the hill (the men harnessing themselves to the ropes), and preparing this battery to cover the operations of the coming day of conflict; but hard work, like hard fighting, was all one to willing hearts, knowing their duties, and bent on performing them. Nor was this all that was done on that eventful day and night, for the reader must bear in mind, that from the very plan of operations, the battle could not be confined to one point or field of conflict.

The veteran Bennet Riley, commanding the 2nd brigade of this second division, co-operated with Harney of the first brigade, and was marching to the assistance of Childs, when he was recalled by General Twiggs. And on another point of this extended scene of action, General Pillow, of the first brigade of volunteers, consisting of the Pennsylvania and Tennessee regiments, a company of Kentucky volunteers, and a squadron of cavalry, had been allotted to the duty of assaulting the enemy's batteries nearest Plan del Rio; these were formidable batteries, of seventeen guns in all, upon three spurs of ridges pointing towards the east and north, from which the enemy had communication with their other works by roads along the ridges, but which, if assailed in front, had to be approached over a route by no means so easy.

General Pillow was, by the general orders, to attack these in front; the one nearest the river if possible; pierce the position, take them in reverse, or pursue the Mexicans holding them, if they were abandoned. In connexion with this demonstration on the enemy's right, was another laborious and bold movement, performed by Lieutenants Ripley of the artillery, Tower of the engineers, and Lieutenant Laidley of the ordnance, for, with the spirit that animated these corps, they succeeded in carrying an eight-inch howitzer across the river to the south side, planted it on the heights there, so as to support by an enfilading fire, the assault of General Pillow's brigade.

The morning of the 18th dawned. The battery on the hill, next to Cerro Gordo, was in position. The rocket and howitzer batteries attached to the division under Major Talcott were divided, but the cannonade from the hill began at seven in the morning. Colonel Riley with his brigade moved off in a circuit to gain the Jalapa road, by going round the main work. This movement was made under a heavy fire of artillery from the Castle and the enemy's infantry on the slope of the hill. Riley detached part of his force to attack these, while the rest of his command moved on in the original direction with Lieutenant Benjamin, under the guidance of Captain Lee of the engineers. Again, a detachment of three companies was ordered from his brigade to join those already detached, and while Colonel Harney, with his indomitable storming party, was pressing up the slope from the east, Riley's companies were moving at the *pas de-charge* up the opposite side, to meet them at the summit.

Shields, at daylight, moved off with his volunteers, the 3rd and 4th Illinois regiments, and the New York troops, under the command of Colonel Foreman, Colonel Burnett, and Major Harris, crossing the ravine on the north, and taking a still wider sweep through the dense thickets, with the purpose of turning the enemy's left. This route brought them some half a mile to the rear of Cerro Gordo; and upon the five-gun battery, near the enemy's camp. Here the gallant Shields, leading his troops, fell desperately wounded with a grape-shot, which passed through his breast, and the command devolved upon Colonel Baker, of Illinois, who bravely carried out the work which Shields had so resolutely begun.

But the most striking movement of the day was made under the command of the distinguished Harney; he led the storming party from the base of the day's operations, Twiggs' position.

Joined by six companies of the 3rd Infantry, under Captain Alexander, four of artillery, commanded by the brave Childs, now about to complete his work began on the evening preceding, Harney formed his little band, sending his rifles under Loring to the left, to keep the enemy in check there; and observing a large reinforcement coming up from the left on the main road, he determined to anticipate the attack by his riflemen; placed the 7th Infantry on the right, the 3rd on the left, the artillery in the rear; and made his swoop, like an eagle from his eerie.

On went the steadfast Americans, under a storm of shot from musket, rifle, escopet, and cannon; our howitzers, rockets, and heavy gun from the redoubt above, vaulted an arch of iron hail still higher than the hurricane of Mexican missiles. The gallant Harney, his commanding figure towering above his host, cheered them on to the steep ascent. They breasted it like heroes; killed and wounded fell thick around them under the plunging fire from above; the survivors have no time to heed them onward, onward! is the word. The spirit outlasts the breath; the soldiers of the 7th halt not to retreat, but to gather wind for another rush. There is but one word of command from the officers, from Plympton, Childs, Alexander, or Harney, "Charge! charge!"

The first entrenchment of mountain stone is reached the enemy are serried behind it; again Harney's word of command, like a bugle-note, seems to be the motive power of the little phalanx it is surmounted; cleared; the bayonets cross for a moment and it is left behind. Then up up up the steep slope press the gallant party to the next entrenchment, close under the lofty citadel. The same result follows; another struggle, the fiercest and the last, and the position is gained! The Mexican colours are down. The stars and stripes float out from the summit of Cerro Gordo. The gallant Quarter master Sergeant Henry, of the 7th Infantry, is the first to bring down the banner of Mexico, which had so long predominated over the rugged hills of this mountain pass, and down the slope of their famed fortress hurry the flying Mexicans.

This bold charge was made under the eye of the commanding General, who witnessed it in person; he was on the spot inspiring his subalterns and soldiers with confidence, by his martial bearing and calm intrepidity. It is related of him, that perceiving a person severely wounded in the very storm of the battle, and being in formed that it was Captain George W. Patten, of Riley's brigade, he stopped to address some words of sympathy, or kind inquiry, to him, but such was the roar of the conflict, that the wounded officer could not hear the words.

Captain Magruder, of the artillery, who had on the day before gone to the aid of Colonel Childs, under a shower of balls, was now directed to turn the cannon upon the enemy below, towards the west; they were attacked in flank also, about the very critical period when their great work was taken. A part of Riley's command, under the conduct of Captain Lee of the engineers, together with the volunteers under Shields, succeeded by Baker, as before related, coming in upon the Mexicans on their extreme left, routed them effectually.

Though the leader of these brave volunteers fell, as it was supposed, mortally wounded, the command devolved upon one suited to the emergency, Colonel Baker, who, like others of his countrymen, showed himself at home in the chaparral of the Mexican mountains, as well as upon the floor of Congress; his New York and Illinois troops moved upon the enemy behind Cerro Gordo, took his guns, baggage, and many prisoners, and, with a large portion of his command, he joined Captain Taylor, of the light artillery, and part of Riley's troops under Lieutenant Lyon first under the direction of Twiggs, then under Major-General Patterson, who had left a sick bed for the post of duty, and conducted these victorious troops in the pursuit, as far as Jalapa. General Worth, who was ordered to march by the right, in support of Twiggs, came up in time to witness the taking of Cerro Gordo, and was with General Scott in the fortress when the white flag was displayed, and the surrender effected at the position carried by the volunteers.

He passed on with his force, and in four days was master

of Perote. The victory was complete, it was a rout. There was no point unassailed, and no position left to the Mexicans; for on the enemy's right, General Pillow, on the 18th, waiting, as he was directed, to assail the formidable batteries opposed to him, but not until he should find the action commenced on the enemy's left, brought up his command to their post of danger, but the fierce shower of shot from the batteries obliged him to retire his troops out of the fire, and prepare for another attack, the flanking howitzer across the river, under the charge of Lieutenant Ripley, pouring in a steady fire in the mean time. Pillow, though wounded in the first assault, and rendered "*hors de combat*," did not intend to give up the contest, but assisted by Colonel Campbell and his brave officers, was ready for another assault upon battery No. 1, when he heard of the surrender of the key of the enemy's position, and the necessary result was, the surrender of the batteries against which he was acting.

This part of the engagement, though not so successful as the attacks about Cerro Gordo, answered the purposes and fulfilled the wishes of the commander-in-chief. The enemy had work to do at every point of his defences, the simultaneous movement upon him at all points, prevented all succouring manoeuvres, and made quick work of it. The reports of the casualties in Pillow's brigade, testify that even more were killed and wounded of his brigade than in the more successful corps of General Shields.

Thus ended the battle of Cerro Gordo, one of the most remarkable in our annals, for the triumphant results of a battle which from its very character seemed to forbid the possibility of entire success in all its details, being a series of separate attacks against various points lying widely apart, and separated by a country rugged to wildness; done, too, in one combined and well-concerted movement, by troops of all grades of experience, volunteers, who fought like veterans, raw levies even among the regulars, who had not received two weeks' drilling, and never before fired a shot in battle (one-half of the 3rd Infantry under Alexander were of this class), against heavy odds numerically, without regarding the advantages or position, and the defence of entrenchments, for General Scott's army, including his reserve, did not exceed 8500, while the enemy were more than 12,000. The enemy had but to await the attack on their lofty perch, and then fire or charge down upon us; while our men had to cut roads for their march through tangled thickets, over hills and deep ravines, drag their cannon up precipices with their own hands, where the sure-footed mule could not work; and when the word "forward" was given, to spend strength and breath up the steep slopes under the pelting storms of bullets from above.

And as to the "morale" in the comparison, our soldier was in a foreign land, impelled by no hope of plunder (for his stern but prudent leader would not allow it), his sole stimulus, his sense of duty, his sole attraction, the waving folds of the "flower flag" of his country; the Mexicans fought for home, and hearth-stone, for country and kindred, for national honour against an invading foe, under a leader who battled on his patrimonial lands, and had sworn to, conquer or die fighting, with his face to the foe, defending at once his country's independence, and his own estate.

And yet were the Mexicans beaten, even to disorganization; more than 1000 killed and wounded, one general officer killed, and five taken prisoners, 3000 prisoners taken and discharged on parole. The self-sacrificing general-in-chief, Santa Anna, flying ahead of his routed troops. The stunning effect of the defeat lasting for months, and, neutralizing all opposition at La Hoya, Perote, and Puebla, strong places for resistance, filled with valuable military stores and munitions, opening the way to the capital of the country to the victorious march of the commanding general of our army, and giving him time to gather and organize the scanty reinforcements sent to him preparatory to the crowning victories, toilsomely but gloriously won, at Contreras, Churubusco, Chapultepec, and the causeway.

In giving this rapid and imperfect sketch of this great and signal battle of Cerro Gordo, the writer has felt very sensibly his own want of military knowledge. One consoling reflection, however, is, that while he could not (without making his account an army list), name every gallant participant in the struggle, or give every detailed movement, yet he has honestly and carefully striven to keep to the record of the various deeds of bold enterprise and gallant bearing of those who bore a part in the fray. The reader who wishes to form a military judgement of the action, and know who fought and fell there, must turn to the masterly letters of Scott, with the able reports of those of his brave lieutenants who carried out so faith fully the prophetic orders of their noble captain.

The following list of officers, though necessarily confined to those who were in the Valley battles, will show to the reader the names of many who, in those memorable fights, only added increased lustre to their honours won at Cerro Gordo.

LIST OF OFFICERS

OF THE U. S. ARMY AND VOLUNTEERS,

WHO WERE ENGAGED IN THE BATTLES OF THE VALLEY OF MEXICO, UNDER COMMAND OF MAJOR-GENERAL WINFIELD SCOTT,

In the months of August and September, 1847.

THE notes of killed, wounded, &c., and the brevet rank of all officers engaged in that service, are believed to be perfectly correct. In some cases, where no brevet is mentioned, the officers either died or left the service before they were conferred; in a few instances they were declined. Brevets are not commonly conferred on volunteer officers, although their services are admitted, by the army and the nation, to have been in the highest degree meritorious and distinguished.

GENERAL-IN-CHIEF AND STAFF.	PRESENT BREVET RANK.	REMARKS.
1. Maj. Gen. Winfield Scott,		Commanding the army.
2. Lt. Col. E. A. Hitchcock,	Colonel.	Acting Inspector-General.
3. Capt. H. L. Scott,	Lt. Col.	A. D. C., and Chief Adj. Gen's Dep.
4. 1st Lt. T. Williams,	Major.	A. D. C.
5. Br. 1st Lt. G. W. Lay,	Captain.	Military Secretary.
6. 2d Lt. Schuyler Hamilton,	"	A. D. C. Badly wounded, Mira Flores, Aug. 18th, 1847.
7. Maj. J. P. Gaines,		Volunteer A. D. C.
ENGINEER CORPS.		
1. Maj. J. L. Smith,	Colonel.	Chief Engineer.
2. Capt. R. E. Lee,	"	Wounded at Chapultepec, Sept. 13.

ENGINEER CORPS.	PRESENT BREVET RANK.	REMARKS.
3. Capt. Jas. L. Mason,	Lt. Col.	Wounded severely, Molino del Rey, Sept. 8.
4. Lt. P. G. T. Beauregard,	Major.	Wounded at Belen Gate, Sept. 13.
5. " Isaac J. Stevens,	"	Wounded at San Cosme, Sept. 13.
6. " Z. B. Tower,	"	Wounded at Chapultepec, Sept. 13.
7. " G. W. Smith,	Captain.	
8. " J. G. Foster,	"	Wounded at Molino del Rey, Sept. 8.
9. " G. B. M'Clellan,	"	
ORDNANCE DEPARTMENT.		
1. Capt. Benj. Huger,	Colonel.	Chief of Ordnance Department.
2. 1st Lt. P. V. Hagner,	Major.	
3. 2d Lt. C. P. Stone,	Captain.	
TOPOGRAPHICAL ENGINEERS.		
1. Maj. Wm. Turnbull,	Colonel.	Chief of Top. Engineers. Served with Gen. in chief.
2. Capt. J. M'Clellan,	Lt. Col.	Served with Twiggs' Division.
3. 2d Lt. Geo. Thom.		
4. Br. 2d Lt. E. L. F. Hardcastle,	Captain.	" " Worth's "
QUARTERMASTER'S DEPARTMENT.		
1. Capt. J. R. Irwin,		Chief of Q. M. D. Served with Gen. in Chief. Died in Mexico.
2. " A. C. Myers,	Major.	Served with Worth's Division.
3. " Robert Allen,	"	" " Twiggs' "
4. " H. C. Wayne,	"	Ass't to Chief Quartermaster.
5. " J. M'Kinstry,	"	Commanded a company of volunteers at Churubusco.
6. " G. W. F. Wood,	"	Served with Harney's Brigade.
7. " Jos. Daniels,	"	Q. M. Quitman's Division.
8. " O'Hara,	"	" Pillow's "
9. " M'Gowan,	"	" " "
SUBSISTENCE DEPARTMENT.		
1. Capt. J. B. Grayson,	Lt. Col.	Chief Subsistence Department. Served with Gen. in chief.
2. " T. P. Randle.		

PAY DEPARTMENT.	PRESENT BREVET RANK.	REMARKS.
1. Maj. E. Kirby,	Colonel.	Chief Pay Department. Served with Gen. in chief.
2. " A. Van Buren,	Lt. Col.	
3. " A. W. Burns.		
4. " A. G. Bennett,	"	

MEDICAL DEPARTMENT.

1. Surg. Gen. Thos. Lawson,	Br. Gen.	Served with Gen. in chief.
2. Surgeon B. F. Harney.		
3. " R. S. Satterlee,		Chief Surgeon, Worth's Div.
4. " C. S. Tripler,		" " Twiggs' "
5. " Burton Randall,		Attached to 7th Infantry.
6. " J. J. B. Wright,		Medical Purveyor.
7. " J. M. Cuyler,		Attached to 4th Artillery.
8. Asst. Surg. A. F. Suter,		" Rifle regiment.
9. " " Jos. Simpson,		" 6th Infantry.
10. " " W. C. De Leon,		" 8th "
11. " " H. H. Steiner,		" 1st Artillery.
12. " " J. Simons,		" 4th Infantry. Wounded Sept. 8.
13. " " J. K. Barnes,		" Cavalry.
14. " " L. H. Holden,		" 3d Artillery.
15. " " C. C. Keemy,		" 3d Infantry.
16. " " J. F. Head,		" Taylor's Battery.
17. " " J. F. Hammond,		" 2d Infantry.
18. " " J. M. Steiner,		" Magruder's Bat'y.
19. " " C. P. Deyerle,		" 2d Artillery.
20. " " E. Swift,		" 1st Dragoons.
21. Surgeon J. M. Tyler,		" Voltigeurs.
22. " M'Millan,		" 2d Pa. Volunteers.
23. Surgeon C. J. Clark,		" S. C. Volunteers.
24. " M. B. Halstead,		" N. Y. Volunteers.
25. Asst. Surg. R. Hagan,		" 14th Infantry.
26. " " H. L. Wheaton,		" Pillow's Division.
27. Surgeon R. Ritchie,		" " "
28. " J. Barry,		" " "
29. " D. S. Edwards, U. S. N.,		Chief Surg. of Quitman's Div.
30. " L. W. Jordan,		Attached to 14th Infantry.

31. Passed Asst. Surg. Richard
    M'Sherry, U. S. N.,   Acting Surgeon of Marines.
32. Surgeon W. Roberts,   Attached to 5th Infantry, mor-
                                         tally wounded, Sept. 8.

CAVALRY BRIGADE.

1. Col. W. S. Harney, 2d D.,   Br. Gen.   Commanding Cavalry.
2. 1st Lt. Wm. Steele,   "   Captain.   A. A. A. G.
3. 2d Lt. Julian May, M. Rifles,   1st Lt.   Aid-de-Camp.

FIRST DRAGOONS.

1. Capt. P. Kearney, Com. 1st D., Major.   Wounded at San Antonio Gate,
                                        August 20.
2. 1st Lt. R. S. Ewell,   Captain.
3. 2d Lt. Orren Chapman,   1st Lt.
4.   "   L. Graham,   Captain.   "   "   "

SECOND DRAGOONS.

1. Maj. E. V. Sumner,   Colonel.   Commanding.
2. Capt. Geo. A. H. Blake,   Major.
3.   "   Croghan Ker,   Wounded severely, Sept. 8.
4.   "   S. B. Thornton,   Killed, San Antonio, Aug. 18.
5.   "   W. J. Hardee,   Lt. Col.
6.   "   H. W. Merrill,   Major.
7.   "   H. H. Sibley,   Major.
8. 2d Lt. R. H. Anderson,   1st Lt.
9.   "   J. Y. Bicknell.
10.   "   J. M. Hawes,   1st Lt.
11.   "   T. F. Castor.
12.   "   Arthur D. Tree,   1st Lt.   Wounded at Molino del Rey,
                                        Sept. 8.
13.   "   James Oakes,   Captain.
14.   "   W. D. Smith.

THIRD DRAGOONS.

1. Lt. Col. Thos. P. Moore,   Commanding Regiment.
2. Capt. E. B. Gaither.
3.   "   A. M. Duperu.

234

THIRD DRAGOONS.	PRESENT BREVET RANK.	REMARKS.
4. Capt. A. T. M'Reynolds.	Major.	Wounded at San Antonio Gate, Aug. 20.
5. 1st Lt. Geo. J. Adde.		
6. " J. A. Divver.		
7. " Geo. E. Maney.		
8. " J. T. Brown.		
9. 2d Lt. J. C. D. Williams,		Wounded at Molino del Rey.
10. " W. C. Wagley.		
11. " Francis Henry.		
12. " W. Merribew.		
13. " Wm. Blood.		
14. " W. G. Mosely.		

MOUNTED RIFLEMEN.

1. Capt. Chs. F. Ruff,	Major.	
2. 1st Lt. And. J. Lindsay,	Captain.	
3. " Jno. G. Walker,	Captain.	Wounded at Molino del Rey.
4. 2d Lt. Geo. H. Gordon,	1st Lt.	

FIRST DIVISION REGULARS.

GARLAND'S AND CLARKE'S BRIGADES.

1. Bt. Maj. Gen. W. J. Worth,		Commanding Division.
2. Bt. Capt. W. W. Mackall,	Major.	A. A. G.
3. " " J. C. Pemberton,	Major.	Aide-de-camp.
4. Bt. 1st Lt. L. B. Wood,	Captain.	Aide-de-camp.
5. Maj. Borland, Ark. Vol.		Vol. Aide-de-camp.
6. Lt. Raphael Semmes, U. S. N.		Vol. Aide-de-camp.

GARLAND'S BRIGADE.

SECOND AND THIRD ARTILLERY AND
FOURTH INFANTRY.

1. Bt. Col. Jno. Garland, 4th I.,	Br. Gen.	Commanding Brigade.
2. Bt. Capt. W. A. Nichols,	Major.	A. A. A. G.
3. 2d Lt. Herman Thorn,	Captain.	Aide-de-camp, wounded at Molino del Rey.

CLARKE'S BRIGADE.

1. Col. N. S. Clarke, 6th Inf.	Br. Gen.	Commanding Brigade.
2. 2d Lt. R. W. Kirkham,	Captain.	A. A. A. G.
3. " W. T. Burwell,		Aide-de-Camp. Killed at Molino del Rey.

SECOND ARTILLERY.	PRESENT BREVET RANK.	REMARKS.
1. Major P. H. Galt,	Lt. Col.	Commanding regiment.
2. Capt. S. M'Kenzie,		Com'd of Stormers, Sept. 13.
3. " and Bt. Lt. Col. C. F. Smith,	Colonel.	Commanded L. Inf. Battalion.
4. Capt. and Bt. Lt. Col. J. Duncan,	Col., Ins. Gen.,	Commanded Battery, &c., Artillery, Sept. 12, 13, 14.
5. Captain H. Brooks,	Lt. Col.	Commanded reg't, Sept. 13.
6. 1st Lt. M. L. Shackelford,		Mortally wounded at Molino del Rey.
7. " C. B. Daniels,		Mortally wounded at Molino del Rey.
8. " L. G. Arnold,	Captain.	Wounded at Churubusco.
9. " F. Woodbridge,	Major.	
10. " J. Sedgwick,	Captain.	
11. " A. Elzey,	"	
12. " Wm. B. Blair.		
13. " Henry J. Hunt,	Major.	
14. " Wm. Hays,	"	
15. " Wm. Armstrong,		Killed at Molino del Rey.
16. " H. A. Allen,	Captain.	
17. " S. S. Anderson,	"	
18. " John J. Peck,	Major.	
19. 2d Lt. H. F. Clarke,	Captain.	
20. " M. D. L. Simpson,	"	With Stormers, 1st Division.

THIRD ARTILLERY.		
1. Colonel F. S. Belton,	Colonel.	
2. Captain Martin Burke,	Lt. Col.	
3. Brevet Major R. D. A. Wade,	"	Wounded at Churubusco.
4. Captain Robert Anderson,	Major.	" " Molino del Rey.
5. " E. J. Steptoe,	Lt. Col.	Commanding Light Battery, Quitman's Division.
6. 1st Lt. and Adjt. Wm. Austine,	Major.	
7. " Henry B. Judd,	Captain.	
8. Brevet Capt. Geo. W. Ayres,		Killed at Molino del Rey
9. 1st Lt. R. W. Johnson.		
10. " H. Brown,	"	
11. " Francis J. Thomas.		

THIRD ARTILLERY.	BREVET RANK.	REMARKS.
12. 2d Lt. Jas. I. Farry,		Killed at Molino del Rey.
13. " Louis D. Welch.		
14. " Geo. P. Andrews,	Captain.	
15. " Hamilton Shields,	"	
16. " Jno. H. Lendrum,	1st Lt.	

FOURTH INFANTRY.

1. Major Francis Lee,	Colonel.	Commanding Regiment.
2. Brev. Maj. R. C. Buchanan,	Lt. Col.	
3. 1st Lt. Henry Prince,	Major.	Severely wounded at Molino del Rey.
4. " Jno. H. Gore,	Captain.	
5. " Sidney Smith,		Mortally wounded in City of Mexico, Sept. 14.
6. " G. O. Haller,	Major.	With Stormers, Sept. 8.
7. " Jenks Beaman,		
8. 2d Lt. U. S. Grant,	1st Lt.	
9. " H. M. Judah,	Captain.	
10. " A. B. Lincoln,	1st Lt.	Wounded at Molino del Rey.
11. " T. J. Montgomery.		
12. " A. P. Rogers,		Killed at Chapultepec.
13. " D. F. Jones,	1st Lt.	
14. " M. Maloney,	Captain.	With Stormers at Mol. del Rey.
15. " T. R. M'Connell,	1st Lt.	" " at Chapultepec.
16. " Edmund Russell,	"	

FIFTH INFANTRY.

1. Brev. Col. I. S. M'Intosh,		Mortally wounded at Molino del Rey.
2. Brev. Lt. Col. Martin Scott,		Killed at Molino del Rey.
3. Captain M. E. Merrill,		" " "
4. " E. K. Smith,		Mortally wounded at Molino del Rey.
5. " Wm. Chapman,	Lt. Col.	Commanding Regiment after death of superior officers.
6. " Daniel Ruggles,	"	
7. " D. H. M'Phail,	Major.	
8. 1st Lt. N. B. Rossell,	"	
9. " S. H. Fowler,	Captain.	

FIFTH INFANTRY.	PRESENT BREVET RANK.	REMARKS.
10. 1st Lt. P. Lugenbeel,	Major.	Slightly wounded.
11. " M. Rosencrants,	Captain.	
12. " C. S. Hamilton,	Captain.	Severely wounded at Molino del Rey.
13. 2d Lt. F. S. Dent,	1st Lt.	Severely wounded at Molino del Rey.
14. " E. B. Strong,		Killed at Molino del Rey.
15. " J. P. Smith,		" Chapultepec.
16. " P. Farrelly,	"	Severely wounded at Churubusco.

SIXTH INFANTRY.

	PRESENT BREVET RANK.	REMARKS.
1. Major B. L. E. Bonneville,	Lt. Col.	Commanding regiment.
2. Captain Wm. Hoffman,	"	
3. " Albemarle Cady,	Major.	Wounded at Molino del Rey.
4. " T. L. Alexander,	"	
5. " J. B. S. Todd.		
6. " W. H. T. Walker,	Lt. Col.	Severely wounded at Molino del Rey.
7. " C. S. Lovell.		
8. 1st Lt. E. Johnson,	Captain.	
9. " T. Hendrickson,	"	Severely wounded at Churubusco.
10. " L. A. Armistead,	Major.	Wounded at Chapultepec.
11. " Leonidas Wetmore,	Captain.	
12. " John D. Bacon,		Mortally wounded at Churubusco.
13. " A. Morrow,	"	
14. 2d Lt. A. D. Nelson.		
15. " R. F. Ernst,		Mortally wounded at Molino del Rey.
16. " R. W. Kirkham,	"	
17. " E. Howe,	1st Lt.	
18. " L. B. Buckner,	"	
19. " W. S. Hancock,	"	

EIGHTH INFANTRY.

	PRESENT BREVET RANK.	REMARKS.
1. Major C. A. Waite,	Colonel.	Wounded at Molino del Rey.
2. Brevet Major George Wright,	"	Wounded commanding stormers, Sept. 8.

EIGHTH INFANTRY.	BREVET RANK.	REMARKS.
3. Captain and Brevet Major W. R. Montgomery,	Lt. Col.	Wounded at Molino del Rey, Sept. 8.
4. Captain R. B. Screven,	"	
5. " J. V. Bomford,	"	
6. " J. V. D. Reeve,	"	
7. " C. R. Gates,	Major.	
8. " Larkin Smith,	"	Wounded at Molino del Rey.
9. 1st Lt. Joseph Selden,	"	" Chapultepec.
10. " J. G. Burbank,		Mortally wounded at Molino del Rey.
11. " Jno. Beardsley,	Captain,	Wounded at Molino del Rey.
12. " C. F. Morris,		Mortally wounded at Molino del Rey.
13. " J. D. Clarke,	"	Wounded at Molino del Rey.
14. " J. Longstreet,	Major,	" Chapultepec.
15. 2d Lt. E. B. Holloway,	1st Lt.	" Churubusco.
16. " C. G. Merchant,	"	
17. " Geo. Wainwright,	"	" Molino del Rey.
18. " J. G. S. Snelling,	"	" " " "
19. " T. G. Pitcher,	"	
20. " G. E. Pickett,	"	

SECOND DIVISION REGULARS.

SMITH'S AND RILEY'S BRIGADES.

1. Brig. Gen. D. E. Twiggs,	Maj. Gen.	
2. 1st Lt. W. H. T. Brooks,	Major.	
3. " P. W. M'Donald,	Captain.	

SMITH'S BRIGADE.

MOUNTED RIFLES, FIRST ARTILLERY,
AND THIRD INFANTRY.

1. Brev. Brig. Gen. P. F. Smith,	Maj. Gen.	Commanding Brigade.
2. 1st Lt. Earl Van Dorn, 7th Infantry,	Major.	A. A. A. G.

FOURTH ARTILLERY, SECOND INFANTRY,
AND SEVENTH INFANTRY.

RILEY'S BRIGADE.

1. Brevet Colonel B. Riley,	Brig. Gen.	Commanding Brigade.
2. Brevet Capt. E. R. S. Canby,	Major.	A. A. G.
3. 1st Lt. Julius Hayden.	Captain.	Aide-de-camp.

REG'T OF MOUNTED RIFLEMEN.	BREVET RANK.	REMARKS.
1. Major W. W. Loring,	Colonel.	Severely wounded at Garita de Belen.
2. Captain W. F. Sanderson,	Major.	
3. " Henry C. Pope.		
4. " Geo. B. Crittenden.		
5. " Jno. B. Simonson,	"	
6. " J. B. Backenstoss,	Lt. Col.	
7. " S. S. Tucker,	Major.	
8. " B. S. Roberts,	Lt. Col.	
9. " Andrew Porter,	"	
10. 1st Lt. M. E. Van Buren,	Captain.	Severely wounded at Contreras.
11. " Llewellyn Jones.		
12. 1st Lt. Noah Newton.		
13. 2d Lt. Geo. M'Lane,	Captain.	
14. " R. M. Morris,	"	
15. " F. S. K. Russell,	1st Lt.	Wounded September 13.
16. " D. M. Frost,	"	
17. " Jno. P. Hatch,	Captain.	
18. " Gordon Granger,	"	
19. " J. N. Palmer,	1st Lt.	Wounded near Chapultepec.
20. " James Stuart,	Captain.	
21. " Alfred Gibbs,	1st Lt.	

FIRST ARTILLERY.

1. Brevet Major J. Dimick,	Colonel.	Commanding Regiment.
2. Captain Geo. Nauman,	Lt. Col.	
3. " Francis Taylor,	"	Commanding Light Battery, Twiggs' Division.
4. " Jno. H. Winder,	Major.	
5. " Jno. B. Magruder,	Lt. Col.	Commanding Light Battery, Pillow's Division.
6. " E. A. Capron,		Killed at Churubusco.
7. " M. J. Burke,	"	"
8. " Jno. S. Hatheway,	Major.	
9. 1st Lt. Wm. H. French,	"	

	PRESENT BREVET RANK.	REMARKS.
10. 1st Lt. J. N. Haskin,	Major.	Wounded at Chapultepec.
11. " H. D. Grafton,	Captain.	
12. " S. K. Dawson,	"	
13. " J. G. Martin,	Major.	Wounded at Churubusco.
14. " J. M. Brannan,	Captain.	Wounded near Chapultepec.
15. 2d Lt. Henry Coffee,	"	
16. " E. C. Boynton,	"	Wounded at Churubusco.
17. " Thos. I. Jackson,	"	
18. " Truman Seymour,	"	
19. " S. Hoffman,		Killed at Churubusco.
20. " Jno. B. Gibson,	1st Lt.	
21. " J. P. Johnston,		Killed at Contreras.

THIRD INFANTRY.

1. Captain E. B. Alexander,	Lt. Col.	Commanding Regiment.
2. " J. Van Horne,	Major.	
3. " Lewis S. Craig,	Lt. Col.	Severely wounded at Churubusco.
4. " J. M. Smith.		
5. " W. H. Gordon.		
6. " Daniel T. Chandler,	Lt. Col.	
7. " Stephen D. Dobbins,		With Stormers at Chapultepec
8. 1st Lt. O. L. Sheppard,	Major.	
9. " W. B. Johns,	Captain.	
10. " D. C. Buell,	Major.	Severely wounded at Churubusco.
11. " J. B. Richardson,	"	
12. " A. W. Bowman,	Captain.	
13. 2d Lt. Henry B. Shroeder,	1st Lt.	
14. " Barnard E. Bee,	Captain.	Stormers at Chapultepec.
15. " Henry B. Clitz,	1st Lt.	
16. " W. H. Wood.		
17. " J. D. Wilkins,	"	
18. " J. N. G. Whistler,	"	
19. " M. O'Sullivan.		
20. " Geo. Sykes,	Captain.	

FOURTH ARTILLERY.

1. Major Jno. L. Gardner,	Colonel.	Commanding Regiment.
2. Brevet Major H. Brown.	Lt. Col.	

FOURTH ARTILLERY.	PRESENT BREVET RANK.	REMARKS.
3. Captain S. H. Drum,		Killed at Garita de Belen.
4. " S. C. Ridgely,	Major.	
5. 1st Lt. Jno. W. Phelps,	Captain.	
6. " J. N. M. Cown,	"	
7. " G. W. Getty,	"	
8. " A. P. Howe,	"	
9. " C. Benjamin,		Killed at Belen Garita.
10. " D. H. Hill,	Major.	
11. " F. J. Porter,	"	Wounded Sept. 13, at Belen.
12. 2d Lt. F. Collins,	1st Lt.	" at Contreras.
13. " A. L. Magilton,	"	
14. " G. A. De Russy,	"	With stormers at Chápultepec.
15. " S. L. Gouverneur,	"	

SECOND INFANTRY.

	PRESENT BREVET RANK.	REMARKS.
1. Captain T. Morris,	Lt. Col.	Commanding 2d Infantry.
2. " J. J. B. Kingsbury,	Major.	
3. " J. R. Smith,	Lt. Col.	
4. " Silas Casey,	"	Severely wounded Sept. 13th, with stormers.
5. " Jas. W. Penrose,	Major.	
6. " H. W. Wessells,	"	Wounded at Contreras.
7. " Jas. W. Anderson,		Mortally wounded at Churubusco.
8. 1st Lt. C. S. Lovell,	Captain.	Wounded at Churubusco.
9. " D. Davidson,	"	
10. " Geo. C. Wescott,	"	Wounded Aug. 19. With stormers Sept. 13.
11. " B. P. Tilden.		
12. " N. Lyon,	Captain.	Wounded in City of Mexico.
13. 2d Lt. J. W. Schureman,	1st Lt.	
14. " C. E. Jarvis,	"	
15. " David R. Jones.		
16. " Frederick Steele,	Captain.	With stormers Sept. 13.
17. " Thos. Early,		Killed at Churubusco.
18. " Nelson H. Davis,	1st Lt.	
19. " Wm. M. Gardner,	"	Severely wounded at Churubusco.

SEVENTH INFANTRY.	PRESENT BREVET RANK.	REMARKS.
1. Lt. Col. I. Plympton,	Colonel.	Commanding Regiment.
2. Maj. A. Bainbridge,	Lt. Col.	
3. Captain R. H. Ross,	"	Severely wounded at Contreras.
4. " G. R. Paul,	Major.	With Stormers.
5. " Charles Hanson,		Mortally wounded at Contreras.
6. " J. G. Henshaw,	"	
7. 1st Lt. Henry Little,	Captain.	
8. " C. H. Humber,	"	Severely wounded at Churubusco.
9. " Levi Gantt,		Killed at Chapultepec.
10. " S. B. Hayman.		
11. 2d Lt. F. Gardner,	Captain.	
12. " W. K. Van Bokkelen,	1st Lt.	
13. " Ed. K. Smith,	Captain.	
14. " W. H. Tyler,	1st Lt.	
15. " S. B. Maxey,	"	
16. " T. Henry,	"	

THIRD DIVISION REGULARS.

PIERCE'S AND CADWALADER'S BRIGADES.

1. Maj. Gen. G. J. Pillow.		Commanding Div. Wounded at Chapultepec.
2. Brevet Captain J. Hooker,	Lt. Col.	A. A. G.
3. 1st Lt. G. W. Rains,	Captain.	Aide-de-camp.
4. " R. S. Ripley,	Major.	Aide-de-camp.
5. P. Mid. R. C. Rogers, U. S. N.		Vol. Aide-de-camp.

PIERCE'S BRIGADE.

NINTH, TWELFTH, AND FIFTEENTH INFANTRY.

1. Brig. Gen. Franklin Pierce,		Commanding Brigade.
2. Captain O. F. Winship,	Major.	A. A. G.
3. 1st Lt. E. H. Fitzgerald,	"	Aide-de-camp.

CADWALADER'S BRIGADE.

1. Brig. Gen. Geo. Cadwalader,	Maj. Gen.	Commanding Brigade.
2. Brevet Capt. Geo. Deas,	Major.	A. A. G.
3. 1st Lt. J. F. Irons.		Mortally wounded at Churubusco.

NINTH INFANTRY.	PRESENT BREVET RANK.	REMARKS.
1. Colonel **T. B. Ransom,**		Killed near Chapultepec.
2. Maj. T. H. Seymour,	Colonel.	
3. Captain J. S. Pitman.		
4. " E. A. Kimball,	Major.	
5. " N. S. Webb,	"	
6. " C. N. Bodfish,	"	
7. " J. W. Thompson.		
8. 1st Lt. Jno. S. Slocum,	Captain.	
9. " and Adj. J. C. Sprague,	"	Wounded at Chapultepec.
10. " Geo. Bowers,	"	
11. " J. H. Jackson,	"	
12. " Albert Tracy,	"	
13. " J. M. Hathaway,	1st Lt.	
14. 2d Lt. A. A. Stoddard,	"	
15. " T. P. Pierce,	"	
16. 2d Lt. T. H. Crosby,	1st. Lt.	
17. " A. T. Palmer,	"	Wounded at Churubusco.
18. " R. C. Drum.		
19. " John Glackin,	"	
20. " Levi Woodhouse,	"	
21. " W. A. Newman,	"	Wounded at Churubusco.
22. " John McNabb.		

TWELFTH INFANTRY.		
1. Lt. Col. M. L. Bonham.		
2. Captain W. B. Holden,	Major.	
3. " Allen Wood,	"	
4. " J. W. Denver.		
5. 1st. Lt. Charles Taplin,	Captain.	
6. " J. H. H. Felch.		
7. " W. B. Giles,	"	
8. " John L. Simpkins,	"	
9. 2d Lt. Henry Almstedt.		
10. " W. A. Linn.		
11. " A. E. Steen,	1st Lt.	
12. " J. M. Bronaugh,	"	

FIFTEENTH INFANTRY.		
1. Colonel G. W. Morgan,	Brig. Gen.,	Wounded at Churubusco.
2. Lt.-Col. Joshua Howard,	Colonel.	

244

FIFTEENTH INFANTRY. BREVET RANK. REMARKS.

3. Major F. D. Miles,   Killed at San Antonio garita,
                                          August 20.
4.   "   Samuel Woods, Major
          6th Infantry,   Lt. Col.
5. Captain E. Vandeventer.
6.   "   Daniel Chase,   Major.
7.   "   James A. Jones,   "
8.   "   E. A. King.
9.   "   Isaac D. Toll.
10. "   Augustus Quarles,   Mortally wounded at Churu-
                                          busco.
11. "   M. Hoagland,   "
12. 1st Lt. G. W. Bowie,   "
13. "   Thomas H. Freelon,   Captain.
14. "   T. F. Broadhead,   "
15. "   D. Upman.
16. "   J. B. Miller.
17. "   E. L. Marshall,   "
18. "   A. G. Sutton,   "
19. "   J. B. Goodman,   Killed at Churubusco.
20. 2d. Lt. Daniel French,   "
21. "   Charles Peternell,   "
22. "   J. W. Wiley,   1st. Lt.
23. "   H. M. Cady.
24. "   L. E. Beach,   "
25. "   F. O. Beckett,   "
26. "   Thomas B. Tilton.
27. "   W. H. H. Goodloe,   Wounded at Churubusco.
28. "   L. P. Titus,   "
29. "   J. R. Bennett,   "

ELEVENTH INFANTRY.

1. Lt. Col. William M. Graham,   Killed at Molino del Rey.
2. Major J. F. Hunter,   Lt. Col.
3. Captain William H. Irwin, Major,   Wounded at Molino del Rey.
4.   "   O. Waddell.
5.   "   P. M. Guthrie,   "   "   "   "
6.   "   Arnold Syberg.
7.   "   Thomas F. M'Coy,   Captain.

ELEVENTH INFANTRY.	BREVET RANK.	REMARKS.
8. 1st Lt. Daniel S. Lee,	Captain.	Wounded, August 20.
9. " John Motz,	Major.	
10. " C. P. Evans,	Captain.	
11. " B. F. Harley,	"	
12. 2d Lt. G. L. M'Clelland.		
13. " A. H. Tippin,	1st. Lt.	
14. " W. H. Scott.		
15. " R. H. L. Johnson,		Killed at Molino del Rey.
16. " M. Stever.		

FOURTEENTH INFANTRY.

1. Colonel Wm. Trousdale,	Brig. Gen.	Wounded at Chapultepec.
2. Lt. Col. P. O. Hebert,	Colonel.	
3. Major John H. Savage,		Wounded at Molino del Rey.
4. " John D. Wood.		
5. Captain R. G. Beale.		
6. " P. B. Anderson.		
7. " E. Bogardus.		
8. " Thomas Glenn,	Major.	
9. " J. M. Scantland,	"	Wounded at Chapultepec.
10. " J. P. Breedlove.		
11. " J. W. Perkins.		
12. " C. T. Huddleston.		
13. 1st Lt. James Blackburn,	Captain.	
14. " Thomas Shields,		Wounded at Molino del Rey.
15. " H. B. Kelly.		
16. " R. Humphreys.		
17. " Thomas Smith.		
18. " N. M'Clannahan.		
19. " A. J. M'Allon.		
20. 2d Lt. Richard Steele,		Wounded at Chapultepec.
21. " B. Davis,	1st Lt.	
22. " W. H. Seawell.		
23. " R. W. Bedford.		
24. " Perrin Watson.		
25. " A. J. Isaacs,	1st Lt.	
26. " A. J. Hudson.		
27. " J. C. C. Hays.		
28. " S. T. Love.		

VOLTIGEURS.	BREVET RANK.	REMARKS.
1. Colonel T. P. Andrews,	Brig. Gen.	Commanding Regiment.
2. Lt. Col. J. E. Johnston, Lt. Col. Top. Engineers,	Colonel.	
3. Major G. A. Caldwell,	Lt. Col.	
4. " G. H. Talcot,	"	Wounded at Molino del Rey.
5. Captain A. P. Churchill.		
6. " O. E. Edwards,	Major.	
7. " James D. Blair.		
8. " Charles J. Biddle,	"	
9. " John E. Howard,	"	
10. " M. J. Barnard,	"	
11. " J. J. Archer,	"	
12. 1st Lt. B. D. Fry.		
13. " James Tilton.		
14. " A. H. Cross.		
15. " H. C. Longnecker.		
16. " W. S. Walker.		
17. 2d Lt. Charles F. Vernon.		
18. " R. C. Forsyth,	1st Lt.	
19. " T. D. Cochran.		
20. " Robert Swan.		
21. " George R. Kiger.		
22. " G. S. Kintzing.		
23. " William J. Martin,	1st Lt.	
24. " J. H. Smythe.		
25. " James R. May.		
26. " Edward C. Marvin.		
27. " Robert H. Archer.		
28. " Washington Terrett.		
29. " T. H. Larned.		
30. " James E. Slaughter.		

MOUNTAIN HOWITZER BATTERY.

1. 1st Lt. F. D. Callender,	Captain.	Wounded at Contreras.
2. 2d Lt. J. L. Reno,	"	" Sept. 13.

DIVISION OF VOLUNTEERS.
SHIELDS' BRIGADE AND SECOND
PENNSYLVANIA VOLUNTEERS.

1. Major-General J. A. Quitman,		Commanding Division.
2. 1st Lt. M. Lovell,	Captain.	A. A. A. G.
3. 2d Lt. C. W. Wilcox,	1st Lt.	Aide-de-Camp.

SHIELDS' BRIGADE.	BREVET RANK.	REMARKS.

MARINES, NEW YORK AND SOUTH
CAROLINA VOLUNTEERS.

1. Brig. Gen. J. Shields,	Maj. Gen.	Comm'g Brigade. Wounded at Chapultepec.
2. Brevet Captain F. N. Page,	Major.	A. A. G.
3. 1st Lt. R. P. Hammond,	"	Aide-de-Camp.
4. " G. T. M. Davis,		Vol. Aide-de-Camp.

MARINE CORPS.*

1. Lt. Col. S. E. Watson,		Died in November.
2. Major Levi Twiggs,		Killed at Chapultepec.
3. " Wm. Dulany,	Lt. Col.	
4. Captain J. G. Reynolds,	Major.	Wounded at Chapultepec.
5. " G. H. Terrett,	"	
6. 1st Lt. D. D. Baker,	Captain.	Wounded, Sept. 13.
7. " Jno. S. Devlin,		Wounded at Chapultepec. Vol. Aide-de-Camp.
8. " R. C. Caldwell.		
9. " W. L. Young,	Captain.	
10. " J. C. Rich.		
11. 2d Lt. Jno. D. Simms,	"	
12. " D. J. Sutherland,	"	
13. " F. Norvell,	1st Lt.	
14. " J. S. Nicholson,	"	
15. " C. G. M'Cauley,	"	
16. " Thomas T. Field,	"	
17. " E. M. D. Reynolds,	"	
18. " Chs. A. Henderson,	"	Wounded at Chapultepec.
19. " A. S. Nicholson,	"	

NEW YORK VOLUNTEERS.

1. Col. Ward B. Burnett,		Severely wounded at Churubusco.
2. Lt. Col. Chs. Baxter,		Mortally wounded at Chapultepec.
3. Major J. C. Burnham.		

* Officers of Marines not brevetted, were disbanded by law at the expiration of the war. They have since been reinstated. Lieutenant E. T. Shubrick, U. S. N., accompanied the Marines on the march, and during the battles acted as volunteer aide-de-camp to General Shields.

4. Captain C. H. S. Shaw.
5.   "   James Barclay.
6.   "   J. P. Taylor.
7.   "   D. P. Hungerford.
8.   "   M. Fairchild.
9.   "   S. S. Gallagher.
10.   "   Chs. H. Pierson,   Mortally wounded at Chapul-
                                      tepec.
11.   "   Van O'Linda,   Killed at Chapultepec.
12.   "   G. Dykeman,   Severely wounded at Churu-
                                      busco.

13.   "   J. F. Hutton.
14. 1st Lt. R. A. Carter.
15.   "   C. H. Sherwood.
16.   "   A. W. Taylor.
17.   "   C. H. Innis,   Wounded at Belen.
18.   "   C. K. Gallagher.
19.   "   Geo. B. Hall.
20.   "   James Miller.
21.   "   J. S. M'Cabe,   Wounded at Chapultepec.
22. 2d Lt. Thos. W. Sweeny,   "   Churubusco.
23.   "   Chs. D. Potter,   "   "
24.   "   Jacob Griffin.
25.   "   Addison Farnsworth.
26.   "   Mayne Reid,   Wounded at Chapultepec.
27.   "   C. B. Brower.
28.   "   Chs. S. Cooper,   Wounded at Churubusco.
29.   "   J. W. Henry.
30.   "   E. Chandler,   Mortally wounded at Churu-
                                      busco.

31.   "   F. G. Boyle.
32.   "   Jno. Rafferty.
33.   "   David Scannel.
34.   "   J. W. Grennel.
35.   "   Malahowsky.
36.   "   Francis Durning.
37.   "   W. H. Browne.
38.   "   F. E. Pinto.

1. Col. P. M. Butler,   Killed at Churubusco.
2. Lt. Col. J. P. Dickinson,   Mortally wounded at Churu-
                                        busco.
3. Major A. H. Gladden,   Wounded at Belen.
4. Captain F. Sumter.
5.   "   R. G. M. Dunovant.
6.   "   K. S. Moffat,   Wounded at Churubusco.
7.   "   J. F. Marshall.
8.   "   W. Blanding.
9.   "   W. D. Desaussure.
10.   "   N. J. Walker.
11.   "   J. F. Williams.
12.   "   Adjutant James Canty,   Wounded at Churubusco.
13. R. Q. M. W. B. Stanley.
14. A. C. S. J. D. Blanding.
15. 1st Lt. C. S. Mellet.
16.   "   J. F. Walker.
17.   "   W. C. Moragne.
18.   "   J. B. Moragne,   Killed at Belen.
19.   "   A. Manegualt.
20.   "   J. R. Clark,   Mortally wounded at Churu-
                                        busco.
21.   "   A. B. O. Bannon.
22.   "   C. P. Pope.
23. 2d Lt. T. M. Baker.
24.   "   S. Sumter,   Wounded at Churubusco.
25.   "   W. B. Lilley.
26.   "   B. W. D. Culp.
27.   "   James W. Cantey,   Killed at Chapultepec.
28.   "   K. G. Billings,   Wounded at Churubusco.
29.   "   Jos. Abney,   "   "   "
30.   "   David Adams,   Killed at Churubusco.
31.   "   L. F. Robertson.
32.   "   Ralph Bell.
33.   "   J. R. Davis.
34.   "   J. N. Moye.
35.   "   J. W. Steen,   Wounded at Belen.
36.   "   M. R. Clark,   "   Chapultepec.

37. 2d Lt. Charles Kirkland.
38. "   W. R. Williams,   Killed at Churubusco, Aug. 20.
39. "   J. W. Stewart.
40. "   F. W. Selleck,   Wounded at garita of Belin,
                                    September 13.

SECOND PENNSYLVANIA VOLUNTEERS.

1. Colonel W. B. Roberts,   Died in City of Mexico, Oct. 3.
2. Lt.-Col. John W. Geary,   Commanding Regiment.
3. Major William Brindle.
4. Captain Thomas S. Loeser.
5.   "   John Humphries.
6.   "   Clarence H. Frick.
7.   "   Charles Naylor.
8.   "   E. C. Williams.
9.   "   Robert Porter.
10.   "   James Murray.
11.   "   James Miller,   Wounded.
12.   "   S. M. Taylor.
13.   "   James Caldwell,   Mortally wounded at Belen,
                                    September 13th.

14. Adjutant J. S. Waterbury.
15. R. Q. M. E. C. L. Clare.
16. A. C. S. John C. Geven.
17. 1st Lt. Hiram Wolf.
18.   "   Alexander M'Kamey.
19.   "   William Wonders.
20.   "   H. A. M. Filbert.
21.   "   Richard M'Michael.
22. 2d Lt. Samuel Black.
23.   "   Charles H. Heyer.
24.   "   Charles M'Dermitt.
25.   "   James Armstrong.
26.   "   James Coulter,   Wounded.
27.   "   Isaac Hare.
28.   "   A. L. Tourison.
29.   "   J. D. Unger.
30.   "   H. A. Hambright.

31. 2d Lt. William Rankin.
32.   "   James Kane.
33.   "   William P. Skelly.
34.   "   L. W. Smith.
35.   "   D. N. Hoffins.
36.   "   J. Keefe,   Wounded.
37.   "   John A. Doyle.
38.   "   Charles Bowers,   Acted as Assistant Surgeon.